A MAN OF SMALL IMPORTANCE

My father Griffin Barry

by Harriet Ward

DORMOUSE BOOKS

Published by Dormouse Books
1 Church Cottages
Cross Green
Debenham
Suffolk IP14 6QF

© Harriet Ward 2003
First published 2003

ISBN 0 9546046 0 1

Harriet Ward asserts the moral right to be identified as the author of this work.

All rights reserved. No part of this publication may be reproduced, stored in a retrieval system, or transmitted in any form or by any means, electronic, mechanical, photocopying, recording or otherwise, without either the prior permission of the Publisher or a licence permitting restricted copying in the United Kingdom issued by the Copyright Licensing Agency Ltd, 90 Tottenham Court Road, London W1P 9HE.

Acknowledgements

The Publisher is grateful to the following for permission to reproduce illustrations.

Walter P Reuther Library, Wayne State University, Detroit (p.19); Freedom Press (pp.25 and 183); Margaret Hepburn and George Hepburn (pp.30 and 76); Courtesy of the Winona County, Minnesota Historical Society (p.50); Chippewa Valley Museum, Eau Claire, Wisconsin (pp.51 and 54); City of Monrovia, California (p.56); The Mariners' Museum, Newport News, Va (p.59); Charlotte Kurzke (pp.177 and 182).

Special thanks to Judy MacDonald, Audrey Coppard, Jennifer Heseltine, Jenny Gould and Barbara Wright for photographs they contributed. All other family and Beacon Hill School photographs are from the Russell–Barry family archive.

Every effort has been made to contact the holders of copyright material, but if any have been inadvertently overlooked, the Publisher will be pleased to make the necessary arrangements at the first opportunity.

Edited by Steve Attmore
Design by Deborah Matthews
Cover design by Jayne Clementson
Dormouse logo by Clifford Harper
Printed and bound by Biddles

CONTENTS

PREFACE		5
INTRODUCTION	PANDORA'S BOX	7
PART I	**GRIFFIN AND DORA**	
CHAPTER 1	'A VERY PLEASING VOICE'	15
CHAPTER 2	SUMMER 1928	33
CHAPTER 3	GRIFFIN'S HOME GROUND	45
CHAPTER 4	TO RUSSIA AGAIN	63
CHAPTER 5	A BABY BORN, A LOVE LOST	69
CHAPTER 6	TWO LOOKS LIKE CARELESSNESS	84
CHAPTER 7	CRUEL SEPARATION	101
CHAPTER 8	HIGH HOPES DISAPPOINTED	115
CHAPTER 9	THE VISIT	130
PART II	**TRANSATLANTIC VOYAGES**	
CHAPTER 10	DORA'S DESPAIR	141
CHAPTER 11	THE DIVORCE AND AFTER	152
CHAPTER 12	WASHINGTON DC, 1934–36	164
CHAPTER 13	GRIFFIN IN SPAIN	173
CHAPTER 14	DORA'S SCHOOL	184
CHAPTER 15	THE SIEGE OF KINGWELL HALL	198
CHAPTER 16	THE YEARS IN BETWEEN	210
PART III	**DAD AND ME**	
CHAPTER 17	FAMILY LIFE IN LONDON – AND DUBLIN	227
CHAPTER 18	ALMOST FULLY FLEDGED	240
CHAPTER 19	FLYING FREE AT LAST	256
CHAPTER 20	STILL TRYING TO GROW UP	270
CHAPTER 21	COPING WITH LIFE – AND DEATH	282
AFTERWORD		293
ACKNOWLEDGEMENTS AND BIBLIOGRAPHICAL NOTES		295

PREFACE

This book began as a family memoir addressed to my sons, to be read whenever (*if* ever) they were curious to know more about their American grandfather Griffin Barry. As the scope of the project expanded, however, I began to think it would be of interest to a number of readers already aware of our family history (but not this version of it); and to others interested in the professional concerns of my parents and the history to which they contributed – including Dora Russell's management of Beacon Hill School, which I could describe from my own experience there.

By the time the work was finished, literary friends who had read it were urging me to seek a publisher. So I did. Then came a dispiriting series of rejections, most not even asking to see the manuscript. Despite the appreciative pats on the back, there seems to be no room in the mainstream publishing world of today for a small-circulation book of this kind.

What should I do with this hybrid product? Too interesting to hide away in a cupboard, not interesting enough to compete with bestsellers that fly off the shelves. And what a shame not to give an airing to those evocative photos of the school and family I'd been gathering...

Fortunately the development of computer technology, and new methods of reaching a selective audience through the internet, make self-publishing a realistic option these days. Having decided on this route, I was lucky to have freelance friends in the book-producing business who offered their professional services at far below union rates. Steve Attmore and Deborah Matthews transformed a pile of typescript into a book; Jayne Clementson designed the handsome cover; and Cliff Harper's dormouse adds the final touch to my publishing venture. Grateful thanks to them all.

Harriet Ward
October 2003

INTRODUCTION

PANDORA'S BOX

It was already six years since my mother had died and I still didn't feel inclined to look through the box. Glancing at one of the loose letters on the top, I knew why. Even 50 years later, my father's words of 1942 could still set my stomach churning.

> It was a very complicated quarrel and even if I should explain it to you, you wouldn't understand it – not yet, you wouldn't – because, brilliant as you are for an 11-year-old, you don't understand the world your mother and I lived in when you were little...

(Of course I didn't understand it, and couldn't, but that didn't save me from two long scrawled pages of pitiful self-justification and jibes at my adored mother.)

Oh dear, I can't face this... Hastily I replaced the letter and the lid of the box. But I agreed at least to take it home to Suffolk and then – when I'd looked at the contents and perhaps sorted them out a little, to help the archivist – to send it on to Amsterdam. Kate was relieved: its departure would give her a little more storage space in the attic, and after all, the contents of this box were certainly my responsibility.

My mother Dora Russell had accumulated an extensive archive during her very long life. She was the second wife of Bertrand Russell, mother of his two elder children John and Kate, and also of two illegitimate children, myself and my brother Roddy, by an American journalist, Griffin Barry. It was our arrival, in 1930 and 1932 respectively, that led to the scandalous Russell divorce of 1934–35. Thereafter John and Kate were batted like shuttlecocks between their parents' separate households, while Roddy and I were brought up by Dora. We spent our early childhood in the progressive school Dora had founded with Bertie in 1927 and continued to run until it closed in 1943. Dora and Griffin Barry never set up house together.

Of course my mother would have realised from the moment she married the already-eminent Bertie in 1921 that every scrap of paper concerning him would be of interest to future researchers; but Dora was a natural-born squirrel on her own account too. Buried in files and boxes – alongside detailed records of the school and the many other projects of her own professional career – were such treasured items as her British Museum Reader's ticket of 1913 and the florist's label she had attached to her wreath for a lover who had died in 1933. Along with her letters from my father, I later discovered, were a few from his mother and friends of his who had become her friends too, and several from him to me and Roddy during our childhood years. She must have gathered them up from the disarray in our bedrooms along with our dirty clothes.

She was lucky to have spent the last 30 years of her life at Carn Voel, the house in Cornwall she and Bertie had bought in 1922, which had become hers alone when they parted. She loved Cornwall and that house more than any other place in the world – a passion Kate and I came to share – and fortunately the house, falling to bits as it was (Dora could never afford to keep it mended), was commodious enough to accommodate all those books and papers and photographs and other memorabilia without greatly inconveniencing its inhabitants. On my frequent visits with my family I was vaguely aware of 'the archive' that had built up in the attic and her back-bedroom office where, with the aid of a part-time secretary, she was busily adding to it almost till the day she died; but it was not until that event occurred that we discovered how various and voluminous it was. Articles and essays, conference agendas and reports, weekly health records of Beacon Hill School pupils, back numbers of radical journals and propaganda sheets, carbons of her letters to newspapers and thick files of correspondence over decades of lobbying and agitation – not to mention other dense files of family and personal papers full of interest to prurient writers of Sunday newspaper articles. Among the ephemera and trivia fit only for bin-bags was a small treasure trove for future researchers.

After Dora's death in 1986 Kate took on the onerous task of sorting out this part-public, part-private collection. When our brother John died suddenly the following year, leaving Carn Voel empty, Kate came to live permanently in the house she had always loved, after more than half a lifetime in the United States. In due course the different sections of Dora's papers were despatched to appropriate places: those relating to her life with Bertie to the Bertrand Russell Archive at McMaster University, Hamilton, Ontario, in Canada, and those concerning her own independent life to the International Institute of Social History in Amsterdam. There they lie fittingly under the same roof as the papers of Marx and Engels, Kropotkin, Bakunin and Emma Goldman, heroic figures of the political Left whose views chimed in with Dora's own anarcho-socialist ideas.

The box Kate had labelled 'Harriet', containing my mother's

correspondence with my father and with me, remained unopened through two more winters. Yet I could not bring myself to despatch it to Amsterdam uninvestigated. Those few letters from my father to me as a child were now the only ones I had, for I had long since thrown away, or lost, all the others from the time I went to boarding school at the age of 14 until the 1950s – a symbolic loss, I'm sure, as I 'accidentally' rid myself of every physical reminder of a father I had come to hate. Some time after his death in 1957 I realised that I possessed almost nothing that had ever belonged to him, and I didn't mind at all. Nor was there any headstone or tablet to record his life and death, since Roddy and I had neither the inclination nor the money to erect one in London, the city of his unhappy exile. Soon we had both moved on into our separate lives from the flat we shared in the 1950s. When I confess that some years later, clearing out our last belongings from that flat at the end of our lease, I knowingly left my father's ashes in their plain metal urn in a high-up cupboard there – where for all I know they remain to this day – you may justly conclude that my lack of filial respect was somewhat out of the ordinary.

Yet *why* had I hated him so? Over the years I had come to see him as the injured party – or rather, the least blameworthy – in the long and bitter quarrel with Dora (she herself acknowledged in her autobiography how unjustly she had treated him). As a teenager and adult I had developed a critical view of my mother very far from the unquestioning loyalty of an 11-year-old, and at times our relationship had been every bit as fraught as that with my father. In later years, predictably, these animosities were overlaid by the admiration and affection she merited – yet even after his death I had continued to think of Griffin, if at all, with cold indifference.

Why? Did he not deserve the understanding and forgiveness all but very wicked parents are entitled to expect from their children in maturity? Dora at least had lived to know her grandchildren and to enjoy a measure of public acclaim in her venerable old age – whereas poor Griffin had spent his last years ill and penniless in a country where he'd never felt at home, forgotten by his old friends and almost ignored by his own children, even beyond the grave. Over all these years my stony heart had registered only occasional twinges of pity for this sad, defeated man.

Ruefully I reflected on this lifelong sin of neglect. That was *my father* I had casually discarded from my life – and from the lives of my children, his grandchildren, whose genetic inheritance came partly from this American they knew nothing about. Surely I owed it to his descendants to glean what I could from these dusty papers before consigning them for ever to a dark shelf in a foreign land. I knew, after all, that Griffin Barry was an interesting man in his own right, acquainted with many of the luminaries of American literary life in the 1920s and 1930s and a witness of crucial events of world history – the Russian revolution, the Paris peace conference of 1919, the Spanish civil war, the Great Depression in his own country. Having wandered by accident into the lives of famous people, should he be remembered only in the margins of books about them? It was his encounter with Dora, and its consequences, so he always claimed, that had prevented him from writing Great Works like those which had brought fame and fortune to the friends of his youth – American writers John Dos Passos, Edmund Wilson and Dawn Powell, for example, in whose published Diaries and Collected Letters he fleetingly appears. Could that be true? Was there a wasted genius to be discovered in the pages of Griffin's own (unpublished) letters?

Well, no. A small talent, certainly, under-used and 'wasted' in the way that all transient journalism is lost to posterity. For Griffin was a skilful journalist, by trade and by nature: the letters themselves are evidence of that. But what they revealed above all, when I steeled myself to read them, was Griffin's personality and the fateful course of the love affair that had dominated his life. Never mind who was to blame for the failure of the relationship; he was its chief victim.

The contents of Pandora's Box fully justified the forgiveness I owed to my grumpy old dad. It could form the basis, I decided, of a modest literary memorial in atonement. The story told in the letters would be supplemented from other sources and my own memory – and as it turned out, with unexpected information that came my way by chance. These contributions led to further enquiries which sometimes proved fruitful, sometimes not. I'm sure there's more information about Griffin Barry in archives and official records across the United States, but this would add little to the personal story that was my chief concern. Throughout the book I've tried to explain the historical context of events he lived through, for the benefit of readers unfamiliar with it. It's remarkable how closely Griffin's life reflected his own times.

So this is a patchy biography, unfair and incomplete in obvious ways. The result relies heavily on Griffin's own letters, which speak so poignantly for the man who wrote them. Through reading them I came to know him properly for the first time, and confronted questions I'd never considered before. Was it flawed character, or lack of talent, that resulted in a life of non-achievement? Or was Dora to blame for his misfortunes, as he had always insisted?

At first it seemed to me I had to start with my own recollections of someone only dimly remembered after 40 years full of people and events unconnected with him. But delving into my teenage diaries changed my mind. To achieve a measure of detachment, I realised it would be wiser to start in 1928 with the letters from a young man I never knew, so that by the time I came to reconstruct my own relationship with Griffin I could approach the father I had so disliked with more compassion than I had shown the living man.

Even so it was difficult to keep cool in the company of this exasperating pair (yes, Dora too), whose never-ending quarrel blighted my childhood and early adult life. The sour grapes they fed each other did indeed set our teeth on edge, as can be seen in the later autobiographical chapters (meeting my youthful self again was not an uplifting experience). But to be fair to Griffin I've tried not to let the sour taste influence my telling of his own story. I owe him that much at least.

Carn Voel in the 1960s

PART I

GRIFFIN AND DORA

CHAPTER 1

'A VERY PLEASING VOICE'

Dora arriving in New York in 1928

Early in 1928 my mother Dora Russell went on a lecture tour in America to promote her new book, *The Right to be Happy*. She had left her husband Bertrand Russell in charge of Beacon Hill School, which they had opened the previous year at Telegraph House in Sussex. Usually it was the other way round: Dora running the school while Bertie lectured in America for funds to keep it going. When they decided to start a school – mainly because there wasn't one to provide the education they wanted for their own children – they had no idea what a drain on their energies and finances it would prove to be. Nor did they foresee that these enforced periods of separation would weaken their own relationship, by providing opportunities for both partners to pursue outside love affairs. Theirs was an 'open marriage', in which lovers for either party were permitted. They had both had previous affairs, and believed – or tried to believe – that their marriage was not threatened by these side interests.

From Bertie's lecture tour the previous autumn, which he had hated, he encouraged Dora to embark on hers, knowing she'd enjoy it. And she did. This is where Griffin Barry enters the story, as the owner of 'a very pleasing Irish-American voice' speaking up in support of her radical ideas at a dinner party in New York. Finding they had much in common (especially a shared interest in the new Soviet Russia, which they had both visited), they began 'a love affair that was to have far-reaching consequences for ourselves and others'. For a few ecstatic weeks – Dora stayed an extra fortnight in New York – they relished each other's company. When the affair was continued later that year in France – with the knowledge and apparently the approval of Bertie – 'for both of us it was a refreshing interlude, and neither of us at that time (and I, it must be said, never) even considered the notion of a settled married life together'.[1]

Dora's autobiography, *The Tamarisk Tree*, is the only published source for an account of her relationship with my father. It's a rather thin story, reflecting her own retrospective view of him as rather unimportant in the context of her whole life and work. It is also not entirely accurate, and not entirely fair, as my later chapters will show. To begin with, however, we need some basic facts. What sort of man was he, this Irish-American with the pleasing voice, and how did he fit into the America of that time?

In the United States, the 1920s was a period of high Republicanism, when conservative values – and especially business values – ruled. Reckless speculation on the stock market would end with the Wall Street Crash of 1929, precipitating the Great Depression of the 1930s. But in 1928 it seemed that prosperity was normal and would last for ever. No one guessed what hard times lay ahead.

Mainstream American society was very puritanical by the standards of today. There's an amusing example of this in Dora's account of her 1928 lecture tour. At the University of Wisconsin, which even had an Experimental College practising some of the progressive educational ideas of Beacon Hill School, the allegedly enlightened President forbade her to speak on 'sex questions' to a mixed audience of students; so the organisers had to hire a hall off campus, where her lecture 'went off peaceably enough'. Thus her affair with Griffin would have been deeply shocking outside the 'artistic and intellectual circle of

---

[1] *Dora Russell*, The Tamarisk Tree, *Vol 1 (Elek/Pemberton Publishing Co. Ltd., London, 1975), pp.205 and 207.*

New York' where they encountered each other – and for that matter in England too, outside the free-thinking circle of which Bertie and Dora were prominent members. Both Dora and Griffin were 'fringe' people in relation to the wider society of their own countries.

Griffin's fringe was that small but influential group of radical writers and activists, Communist/anarchist by persuasion, portrayed in Warren Beatty's 1981 film *Reds*, with its hero the legendary John Reed. (Coincidentally the film included Dora, along with other 'Witnesses', recalling the real events and people on which it was based.) Reed's account of the Bolshevik Revolution, *Ten Days that Shook the World*, based on his experiences in Russia in the summer of 1917, shook the literary world of America and Britain when it was published in 1919. Reed returned to Russia later that year and after further adventures he died there of typhus in October 1920, one of the few Western martyrs to the Soviet cause.

Dora says that Griffin, like Reed, 'had been in trouble with his own Government over his Soviet adventures' and that they had journeyed to Russia together. Exactly what 'trouble', I've been unable to discover. He and Reed would certainly have known each other in the circles they both moved in, and their paths may have crossed in Russia in 1920, though they did not travel there together. My information about Griffin's life before he met Dora is patchy, but from books by or about his famous friends, and other sources, I can sketch in his American background and trace his movements for a few years before and after the First World War.

Griffin was born in 1884, in Wisconsin. When he was 16, the Barrys moved to California, where his father became editor of the town newspaper (more of his family later: see Chapter 3). Griffin may have started his journalistic career on the west coast before migrating to New York City around 1907, where he immersed himself in the bohemian life of Greenwich Village. Many of the friends he made there would later become key figures of American letters or radical politics. Griffin shared their interest in *avant garde* theatre and literature, but presumably made his own living through freelance journalism, following the path of his older brother Richard. By the 1920s Richard Barry was already a successful journalist, in a more conventional world than the one Griffin had found in New York.

The Village crowd spent their summers in Provincetown, Massachusetts, a fishing village at the tip of Cape Cod, where Griffin's close friends Mary Heaton Vorse and Susan Glaspell became full-time residents. With Susan's husband George Cram Cook, they founded the Provincetown Players in 1915. Their influence on American theatre might be compared to that of John Osborne's *Look Back in Anger* in Britain in the 1950s: a blast of realism and social concern outdating the lightweight presentations of the time overnight. Like the Beat Generation of the 1950s, these new voices were at first raucously out of tune with mainstream American culture – but within a few years they were being listened to. Greenwich Village was the breeding ground for rebels of every hue, and the intellectual powerhouse of America in the first three decades of the twentieth century.

The cultural rebellion in this community was many-stranded: artistic, political, personal, sexual... The literary critic Malcolm Cowley, who became its chronicler, described the pre-First World War Village in these terms:

> The Village [before the war]... contained two types of revolt, the individual and the social – or the aesthetic and the political, or the revolt against puritanism and the revolt against capitalism – we might tag the two of them briefly as *bohemianism* and *radicalism*.[2]

This was the world in which Griffin's adult mind matured, taking up ideas from both these streams. Indeed the two currents were hardly separate, for the same people could be found organising a strike or setting up an art show. In Cowley's words: 'Villagers might get their heads broken in Union Square by the police before appearing at the Liberal Club to recite Swinburne in bloody bandages.' A blend of Art and Politics was not unique to America, of course: contemporary figures in England, like Bernard Shaw and most of the Bloomsbury group, had a foot in both camps.

It's easy to see why Dora and Griffin found immediate rapport. A decade or so after Griffin's enlightenment (he was nine years her senior), Dora had absorbed the same mixture of artistic-political 'new thinking' sweeping through English intellectual life. Although she always despised 'Bloomsbury snobs', she was emphatically a child of Bloomsbury/Chelsea culture with its focus on personal and social liberation, just as Griffin was moulded by the Village. They read the same books, they shared the same credo and the same language: Marxist for the political, pseudo-Freudian for the personal ('class wars' and 'complexes' are scattered through their letters).

Several of Griffin's friends who arrived in the Village from 'Hicksville' (Dawn Powell from Ohio, or Susan Glaspell from Iowa) blossomed into flowers of literary society. Alas, Griffin did not. He always aspired to be a writer of significance, and there are hints in his letters of lonely months he had spent in faraway places trying to become one... But he was a gregarious fellow, no doubt easily tempted back to the round of Village parties, or a foreign assignment. He may have been on such a mission in London in the summer of 1915 when he was recruited for an unusual kind of war work.

Before the US Government joined in the First World War in 1917, many idealistic Americans were already involved in non-military ways – notably in

---

2 Malcolm Cowley, Exile's Return: A Literary Odyssey of the 1920s *(Viking Press, New York, 1951), p.66.*

the American Red Cross. This was briefly shown in the film *Reds* and forms the background of Ernest Hemingway's celebrated First World War novel *A Farewell to Arms*. Griffin would join the Red Cross, too, after an earlier adventure working for another American benefactor.

As soon as war broke out in 1914 Herbert Hoover began to organise the Commission for Relief in Belgium (CRB) to feed seven million civilians whose country (officially neutral) was occupied by the German army and blockaded by the British navy.[3] To carry out this task the CRB gathered up a team of adventurous young Americans – among them Griffin Barry. 'I don't yet know much more about the job,' he wrote to a friend while en route from London to Belgium, 'but the little I've gathered makes it seem the best ever'.[4]

He must have proved his worth, for in the following summer of 1916 we find him doing a similar job in war-devastated Russia, now working directly for the (still neutral) US Government. As the war raged on, American officials were busy succouring innocent victims – in this case German and Austrian civilians imprisoned as enemy aliens behind the Russian lines.

Several months of Griffin's life in Russia in 1916–17 are documented by a handful of vivid letters to his close friend Mary Vorse at home in New York. Mary was the most important of his Greenwich Village friends, and the only one of them I ever knew, many years later, when she was old and I was very young. Her second husband Joe O'Brien (to whom Griffin had introduced her) had died of

Mary and her husband Joe O'Brien, 1913

---

[3] *The CRB was the precursor of Hoover's more widely known American Relief Administration, which distributed aid throughout Europe after the Great War, even to famine victims in Soviet Russia. Ironically, in 1929 Hoover was the US President whose inflexible belief in the free market kept him helplessly on the sidelines as his own countrymen plunged into the Great Depression. No relief for them!*

[4] *Letter to Sophie Treadwell, from Rotterdam, 7 August 1915. From the Sophie Treadwell Papers, University of Arizona Library Special Collections, Tucson, Arizona.*

cancer in October 1915 after a short, loving partnership of writing and campaigning. The great textile strike at Lawrence, Massachusetts in 1912 had drawn the O'Briens into trade union journalism and made their house a centre of radical politics. In August 1916, while Griffin was in Russia, Mary went to Minnesota to help publicise a coalminers' strike in which strikers' families were being victimised and organisers imprisoned – including the O'Briens' close friend Carlo Tresca. Tresca and Elizabeth Gurley Flynn, a prominent feminist, were seasoned activists of the radical trade union Industrial Workers of the World (IWW, known as the Wobblies), which had called the strike. With Flynn, Mary learned to dodge the employers' hired thugs and saw the hardship endured by the miners' wives. (Later she became famous for her reporting from the lawless battleground of industrial disputes.)

The tragedy of Joe O'Brien's early death was deeply felt by the whole close-knit group of his friends. This may explain why Griffin left his job with the CRB after only six months, returning to America in December 1915 to join their mourning; and then, a few months later, taking up his new mission for the US government in Russia. From the tone of his letters to Mary I believe he was one of several casual lovers with whom she tried to assuage her grief. If so, sex was only a small part of their friendship, as these letters show. Griffin greatly admired Mary's writing, and was delighted with a magazine she had sent containing one of her short stories, 'a beautiful thing with delicate nuances and bite and veracity...'. Alarmed by her frequent 'bats' (binges, in American slang of the day), he applauded her mission to the Minnesota strikers as a healthy escape from the wasteful debauchery of her bereavement: 'I like to see you getting mad at the system, and the rich and the great; I like it intensely.'

Erratically typed on rickety tables or moving trains, these letters include snatches of Griffin's own writing equal to anything I've read in his 'composed' pieces. He was a connoisseur of character, and conveys the people he met with painterly skill – a Moscow couple 'talking great ideas in low voices'; a young American 'with a soul like a green apple; an appallingly underfed soul'. Yet there is a passage here which suggests another career path he was perhaps considering at that time. Praising Mary's work, he has 'come across bits in the partial lot I've seen that take my breath away... Yes, I ate up that work-letter word by word. It kept me going through some bleak days. Sometimes I wonder if I wasn't born to like other people's work, or not like it, and let my own go.' Could Griffin have made his name in later life as a literary critic?

Alongside his solicitude for Mary, the letters tell a fascinating tale of arduous journeys 'in a bumpety-bump cart with hay for a cushion', in packed-out troop trains and boats down the Volga; of desperate people clamouring for more supplies than he could muster; of struggles to communicate with his phrase-book Russian and the help of unreliable interpreters – all in all, a very modern picture of generous Americans dispensing aid to needy foreigners.

But it wasn't all work. In Moscow he attended a private reading by Gorky, toured the art galleries, visited the ballet, the opera and the Moscow Arts Theatre under the direction of the legendary Stanislavsky. To encourage his theatrical friends in the Village he passed on the wise advice of 'the Stanislawsky people': how they too had struggled for 16 years as amateurs, until 'up from the provinces came Tchekoff, the man of genius...'. 'The Sea Gull, which we did almost unintelligably [sic] in New York, was the play that made the Moscow Theatre.'[5]

And all this in the midst of a world war. I hope Griffin wrote up his Russian adventures for a wider public, as well as privately to Mary. From the first moment, he was awestruck by this vast, 'untellable' country.

> I stood in the greatest cathedral in Russia today and watched a leisurely mass of three hours. It began with a few old beggars kissing icons and ended with apparently half Moscow under the nave, yet small and lost in the shadows. The choir that stood under the huge gold altar screen seemed to have been picked up from the street – the Greek choirs wear no vestments, they're delegates of the audience – yet the boys and old men sang like anointed ones. I suppose they'd been trained even back unto the seventh generation... And the sound wandered around through a couple of thousand yards of incense and air and came back to you fit to break your heart. It's the singing that gets you first here; there's no hour empty of it.

But the privation and loneliness of his work ate into his soul at times: 'Russia is vast and dark and I feel like a homeless atom.' In the depths of winter in Orenburg, in the Islamic region of the old Tsarist empire, he was ready to give up and come home.

> Outside there is snow and a still and piercing cold and very remote stars come out at night in a sky the color of clear ice. Yet it's all Asia; the desert billows out in every direction like the sea. There are usually more Mohammedans in wadded silks on the streets than Russians. There is a cross above the crescent on top of the Russian cathedral, but that's only a manner of speaking. We're pretty well sons of the Prophet down here. The town is a big one, a new layer of brick and stone laid over an ancient caravan station. Through the place runs a thin spur of railroad, down from the Volga valley and on to Tashkend, somewhere near the geographical center of Asia. We all cling to that thin line, like insects to a stick, and otherwise are lost... [O]ut in these wastes it's unholy to slap together bits of paper for pigeon holes in Washington and Berlin. Yet

---

[5] *In this very summer of 1916, there arrived in Provincetown the young unknown whose work would make the Provincetown Players famous: Eugene O'Neill (played by Jack Nicholson in* Reds*). Even as Griffin wrote, they were rehearsing O'Neill's first play,* Bound East for Cardiff, *in their ramshackle playhouse on Mary Vorse's fish wharf.*

one does what one can, first beating out of the people enough food and warmth to keep alive...

The last of these letters that I've seen is dated 'January 9 1917'. Griffin probably stayed on in Russia until April, when America itself joined in the war and could no longer carry on this 'neutral' work. By that time the strain of the war had broken the back of the tottering Tsarist régime. So Griffin witnessed the first revolution of 1917, the fall of the Tsar in February, but missed the Bolshevik takeover in October. His report to the April 1918 issue of the CRB Bulletin recounts that 'after watching the last gasps of the Romanoff Regime' he had returned home via Vladivostock, Japan and San Francisco (taking the long way home to visit his parents in California en route).

Griffin serving with the American Red Cross in Italy, 1918

After a brief stay in New York, he embarked for France in September 1917, now in the service of the American Red Cross. For four months he looked after refugees at St Étienne, near Lyon, and then was posted to Rome 'to write newspaper and magazine articles on our work in Italy'. From a reference in a later article to seeing 'corpses in Berlin streets', it seems he may have been sent on to Germany after the Armistice.

The records of the CRB, including the Bulletin which circulated among its members into the 1920s, provide useful glimpses of Griffin. Its other personnel were all college graduates, and he may have falsely claimed to be a Stanford graduate to get hired. Yet Stanford University has no record of his attendance, wrote a puzzled CRB official to Griffin in April 1918 (care of the Red Cross). Could he please explain? Ah yes, came the reply... Well, 'I was there as a special student from December or so [1905] to April 1906. I never entered regularly and the earthquake shook me out never to return in April, and that's my sole college experience.' A few other details followed, attesting to his brief attendance at the university. 'Doesn't all this constitute me a Stanford man? I've assumed it does.'[6]

His lack of a college degree would prove to be a handicap at times in

---

[6] *This exchange of letters, several issues of the Bulletin and other invaluable documentation about the CRB come from the Hoover Institution Archives at Stanford University, California. There are several unanswered letters to Griffin at different addresses, 1916–18, about a CRB service medal they were trying to bestow on him. I wonder if he ever got it.*

Griffin's future career. Why did he not complete his studies? Can we believe the earthquake excuse? He admits to 'flunking royally' courses he didn't like; and I know his family were people of modest means... But I suspect he dropped out of college not for lack of brains or of finance, but of staying-power. This episode is typical of Griffin's grasshopper gait throughout his working life. Tracking him through three decades of changing jobs and moving from place to place, I am still uncertain how far his zig-zag course was dictated by outside factors or his own restless nature.

The worthy college boys of the CRB were not the type to become Griffin's lasting friends. (One of them later served with the American Expeditionary Force assisting the anti-Bolshevik forces in the Russian civil war – trying to reverse the socialist revolution Griffin applauded – and on his return to the United States, became President of the University of California.) But several of the important American writers Griffin came to know at this time were fellow workers in the American Red Cross. Ernest Hemingway served in Rome, and based his novel *A Farewell to Arms* in the Italian theatre of the war. The poet E E Cummings was another recruit. John Dos Passos had started as a Red Cross volunteer and then joined the US Army.

Sensing that Europe was the place for all aspiring artists and writers (he hadn't yet decided which he wanted to be), Dos Passos arranged to be demobilised in Paris and began to taste the joys of bohemian life there while attending courses at the Sorbonne. His memoir written many years later, *The Best Times*, provides the next sighting of Griffin in 1919 as a news agency reporter at the Paris Peace Conference. As well as writing up the deliberations of the statesmen in Paris, at some time in 1918–19 Griffin also served as Associated Press correspondent in Odessa, on the Black Sea, an important anti-Bolshevik base in the Russian civil war. These were the best of his times, too – the peak of his journalistic career, and probably of his intellectual life too, hob-nobbing with such an array of talented young friends. In retrospect, I see this period of his life as the 'youthful promise' that was never to be fulfilled.

Dos Passos gives us a picture of Griffin at his most charismatic, and a glimpse of the expatriate American community in Europe which would become his milieu for the next few years.

> Paris really was the centre of the world that summer of the Peace Conference [1919]. It looked as if every man or woman in the United States who could read and write had wangled an overseas job. Relief was the great racket. Those who couldn't disguise themselves as relievers came as journalists or got attached to government commissions...
>
> I've forgotten who first brought Griffin Barry around. He was a small rosyfaced man who knew everything and everybody. At that time he worked for the United Press. He was the insider incarnate. There was hardly anybody he hadn't been to bed with. Griffin was a radical, full of

the lingo of Mabel Dodge's salon in New York. Love must be free. Everything must be frank; talk, talk, talk. He was the future Greenwich Village encapsulated...

It was Griffin who introduced Bob Minor, a big opinionated Texan, whose charcoal cartoons we had all admired in the *Masses* [a radical Village newspaper]... With Minor came Mary Heaton Vorse with her charming look of a withered Irish rose. In fact in the course of a month Griffin brought down every three-barreled name out of the mastheads and bylines of the big circulation American magazines...

Griffin Barry was a catalyst. It was Griffin who produced the Ewers. 'Trilby' Ewer was about to become Foreign Editor of *The Daily Herald*, the English independent labor newspaper.[7]

Through Trilby Ewer, Dos Passos got his first book published by Allen and Unwin (who made this 'unknown' pay part of the publication cost). Behind the scenes of the pageant he describes, Griffin had played another link role by introducing Mary Vorse to Bob Minor, who became her third (disastrous) husband. 'Knowing someone who knew someone' was the usual route of professional and personal advancement for everyone in this group. At this stage in his life Griffin was the provider of opportunities for others; in later years he would be the needy one, hopefully looking up his old friends in influential positions.

Trilby Ewer was also the link to Griffin's next assignment, as a special correspondent for the British *Daily Herald*, the voice of Labour in Britain. By November 1919, the Peace Conference over, Griffin was reporting developments in the Russian civil war from the West's spy-hole at Helsingfors (now Helsinki) in Finland. The new Soviet government was not yet recognised by Western states, which had imposed an economic blockade and sent troops to help the various 'White' armies, hoping, in Winston Churchill's phrase, to 'strangle Bolshevism in its cradle'. Russia was officially 'sealed' and the only way in or out was a hazardous route through Finland. John Reed would have passed this way on his second visit to Russia in late 1919.

It was also Griffin's route in February 1920 when he accompanied the *Herald's* editor, George Lansbury (later leader of the Labour Party), on his epic visit to see the new utopia for himself. Lansbury had started his journey in the company of another Greenwich Village American, Lincoln Steffens, 'a downright good pal', whose famous salute to Soviet Russia – 'I have seen the future, and it works!' – would soon be echoed by Lansbury's own ecstatic reports.

Griffin's great scoop in Helsingfors, before Lansbury's arrival, was an

---

[7] *John Dos Passos,* The Best Times: An Informal Memoir *(Andre Deutsch, London, 1970), p.77. He refers to the future* Village, *not being familiar with its pre-war version.*

interview with Emma Goldman, just off the leaky old tub, the *SS Burford* (known in history as the Red Ark), which was deporting her with 240 other 'anarchists' from America to Russia. In the United States, fiercely anti-imperialist in those days, there had been dancing in the streets when the Tsar fell – especially among the thousands of immigrants who had fled there from Tsarist persecution. But the Bolshevik take-over changed the public mood to hysterical fear of revolution spreading to America. In a 'red scare' similar to McCarthyism in the 1950s, hundreds of Russian-born immigrants – Soviet sympathisers or not – were rounded up and deported. Some were seized at their workplace and bundled on board ship without a change of clothes or time to say goodbye. American Consulate clerks in Helsingfors were kept busy all night, Griffin reported, arranging the welfare of their families in America. The irony was not lost on Emma:

Emma Goldman (Moscow, 1921)

> Emma Goldman pointed out that these are the first purely political prisoners deported from the United States – a country partly settled in the eighteenth century by political exiles. When she went there as a political exile 35 years ago she joined an organisation, then fashionable in America, known as the American Friends of Russian Freedom. Now she proposes to start, under Soviet rule, a Society of Russian Friends of American Freedom![8]

In fact the anarchists, those already in Russia and these new arrivals, were the first and sharpest critics from the Left of the Bolshevik régime. Their divergence from the views of Marxist admirers is well illustrated in the film *Reds* in a discussion between John Reed and Emma Goldman. The real life differences of these two old comrades were much as portrayed in the film.

The anarchists' scepticism was not shared by George Lansbury or Griffin Barry, however. As a socialist newspaper, the *Herald* welcomed the Bolshevik revolution and had been calling on the British government to lift the blockade and 'leave Russia free to work out her own salvation'. 'Hands off Russia' rallies all over Britain at this time underlined the point. Arriving in Helsingfors ('to be met by Griffin Barry... who is always a joy to meet'), Lansbury was breathless

---

[8] *Griffin Barry, 'First Exiles from US', in* Daily Herald *of January 20 1920, p.3.*

with anticipation of what lay ahead:

> ...I wish it were possible to convey to comrades in England the downright joy of the movement as I see it in these parts. All eyes are on Russia: there is no hesitancy, no doubting; all are certain the Golden Age is being born.

He was not disappointed. In Moscow he was delighted to find 'the churches all open, and people going in and out', and to feel 'as free and safe alone in the streets as in London'.[9] He too argued with Emma Goldman and her companion Alexander Berkman (who translated for him on his visits to VIPs), and he too, like Reed, was ready to forgive Bolshevik 'excesses' in the hot aftermath of the revolution.

In his six weeks there Lansbury met all the Bolshevik leaders, from Lenin downwards. The Soviet government was eager to make outside contacts and Lansbury was their first important Western visitor. Griffin went along on at least some of these visits,[10] gathering material for three major articles published in the *Herald* on 26, 27 and 28 February 1920. They were proudly introduced as 'a brilliant and authentic sketch of life in the Soviet Republic', by a reporter whose earlier despatches made him 'well known to our readers'. Griffin Barry 'knew the old Russia well', claimed the *Herald*, citing his work in Russia in 1916–17 that I've already described, and a later period as a war reporter in 1918–19. (Such extravagant praise of Griffin's expertise is perhaps excusable at a time of sparse information from a blockaded 'enemy' country.)

Griffin's first article, headed OLD RUSSIAN ARMY AND THE NEW, compares the proletarian spirit and efficiency of the Red Army (officers working with their men, 'no military show', etc.) with 'the Army I had watched roll through Russian cities, to and from the front, tide after grey tide, in 1916'. The second, WHY LENIN CANNOT BE A TYRANT, attempts to answer that question in a lengthy interview with the Food Controller of Petrograd, who first explained the new rules – 'No Work, No Food', the 'socialisation of private wealth', and the elaborate rationing system supposedly ensuring fairness to all – and went on to describe the checks on arbitrary power, 'all in the Soviet Constitution, and...in use perpetually.' The third, HOW PETROGRAD WAS KEPT ALIVE, describes a visit to a 'People's House' and its vast communal

----

[9] *The first extract is from a long account of his journey as far as Helsingfors, printed in the* Herald *on 14 February; the second from 'Lansbury's Message from Moscow', sent 'by wireless' and printed on the 10th. Apart from this short front-page article, Lansbury seems to have left the serious reporting to Griffin while he travelled around visiting VIPs, saving his own detailed impressions for his books written later.*

[10] *In* My Disillusionment in Russia *(C W Daniel, London, 1925), Emma Goldman mentions Griffin accompanying Lansbury on a visit to the anarchist sage Peter Kropotkin. In* My Life *(Constable and Co., London, 1931 edition) Lansbury records his presence at a meeting with Leonid Krasin, later the first Soviet ambassador to Britain. I can't be sure Griffin accompanied Lansbury to meet Lenin on 21 February, but I like to think of him scribbling away in the corner of some gold-encrusted ex-Tsarist salon while the two big-wigs discussed the future of socialism.*

kitchens where TSAR'S CHEF COOKS FOR THE MILLION, the sub-head proclaimed (17,000 daily, Griffin reports).

The general tenor of these articles is not uncritical – difficulties are admitted, and fairly described; but they are overwhelmingly full of hope, in expectation of better times ahead. There is intriguing historical detail – the Petrograd train was late because 'wood for the engine hadn't arrived, and the men were bringing it from the forest' – but also the tell-tale phrases of so many future reports of conducted tours by groups of well-wishers – 'I was shown...', 'the Director told me...' and so forth. As the true nature of the Soviet system unfolded, especially under Lenin's successor Stalin, public figures who visited in the 1920s and 30s (Bernard Shaw and Sidney and Beatrice Webb, for example) would be ridiculed for their naïveté in believing what they were told. Soviet tyranny and arrogance soon repelled liberal democrats the world over, but Griffin – and even Lansbury, a Christian Socialist who should have known better – found it hard to discard the romantic picture of the 'new dawn' they had seen in 1920.

So did Dora. By coincidence, both she and Bertie visited Soviet Russia in the same year as Griffin, though none of them met there. Bertie accompanied an official Labour Party delegation, in May, and Dora, finding herself excluded from this trip, followed alone, illegally, by the informal route taken by other adventurers.[11] Their very different reactions to Bolshevik Russia would be a source of contention between them for years. From the first moment Bertie detested it, while Dora, like Griffin, caught the left-wing disease of Soviet-apologism and, like Griffin, could never quite shake it off for the rest of her life.

Dora records meeting John Reed in Petrograd on her arrival in June. I don't know whether Griffin did. How long did he stay in Russia, and writing for the *Herald*? As so often in my quest for this man of small importance, I lose the scent for a few months until letters between his literary friends locate him. In July he was spotted in New York City, 'just back from Russia', and in September in Provincetown.[12] But he didn't stay long: by 1921 he was back in Europe.

Griffin in the 1920s – a well-travelled young man

---

[11] At this date Bertie was still married to his first wife, though separated, and courting Miss Dora Black. He had long wanted to visit Soviet Russia, and Lansbury's visit, plus the ending of British assistance to the White armies in late 1919, now made this feasible. He and Dora at first planned a private visit together, and when he joined the Labour Party group Dora, in defiance, decided to go alone. Their disagreement about Russia did not prevent them from going to China together later in 1920. There Dora became pregnant with John, and on their return to England – Bertie having obtained a divorce in the nick of time – they were married in September 1921. John was born in November.

[12] The first sighting is recorded in Letters of Sherwood Anderson, edited by Howard Mumford Jones and Walter B Rideout (Little, Brown & Co, Boston, 1953), p.58; the second in a letter from Dos Passos to John Howard Lawson, reproduced in The Fourteenth Chronicle: Letters and Diaries of John Dos Passos, edited by Townsend Ludington (Andre Deutsch, London, 1974), pp.299–300.

Griffin's wanderings between Europe and America in the next few years may have been in pursuit of love, or work, or both. When in New York he would always gravitate to the Village like a homing pigeon. Though Mary Vorse now lived in Provincetown and others had moved away, his close friends Dawn Powell and Coby Gilman lived on there for the rest of their lives. But the post-war Village was different from the one he had known pre-war. As Malcolm Cowley puts it, the strand of *radicalism* had died away, leaving only *bohemianism* (and very cheap rents) to attract a younger generation newly graduated from college, or returning from the war, like himself. The political strand had disintegrated when the anarchists (and the IWW) had been supplanted by the Communists in wartime strikes and confrontations, just as in Russia the Bolsheviks had pushed them aside along with all non-Marxist socialists. For mainstream Americans the 'new left-wing' of Bolshevism/Communism was Enemy Number One at home and abroad, and all kinds of 'reds' were indistinguishable in the public mind.

With its hierarchical structure, Marxism was also disliked by many American radicals. At this political crossroads some of them turned Left to join the Communists while others moved gradually rightwards into mainstream politics. Just a few, like Mary Vorse, stayed true to the tattered flag of old-style radicalism.

Politics aside, in the Village there was still bohemianism to explore – Art and Sex, basically – and no one was more adept at combining the two than the upcoming young poet Edna St Vincent Millay, 'the reigning and promiscuous beauty of the post-war generation'.[13] Her own neat verse summing up her hedonist lifestyle has been quoted ever since as the essence of Village philosophy:

> My candle burns at both ends;
> It will not last the night;
> But ah, my foes, and oh, my friends –
> It gives a lovely light.

The literary critic Edmund Wilson did not mind sharing Edna with his close friend John Peale Bishop – even literally, it seems, in three-way petting sessions: 'Wilson assigned the lower regions of the poet, while Bishop was entrusted with the top half.'[14] Wilson's biographer attributes his fascination with Edna to 'her intriguing bisexuality and her enchanting promiscuity. She loved sex and, in the true style of the bohemian Twenties, seemed willing to sleep with everyone.' As well as Wilson and Bishop, her long list of lovers included 'the revolutionary John Reed, the radical novelist Floyd Dell and

---

[13] *James R Mellow,* Inverted Life*: F Scott and Zelda Fitzgerald (Souvenir Press, London, 1985), p.100.*
[14] *Mellow, ibid.*

several more obscure figures'.[15]

One of those obscure figures was Griffin. His first meeting with Millay may have been in New York, or in Paris in 1921, when she made the customary pilgrimage undertaken by all the American intelligentsia at that time. In March 1922 they were reported by Hemingway to be in Vienna:

> Oh yes. Griffin Barry is still in Vienna and living, they say, with Edna St Vincent etc. The Rotonde [café] is cluttered with the various young things, female, she's led astray. Like Lady Lil, she piles up her victims in heaps.[16]

It's hard to separate truth from gossip in all this tittle-tattle. Millay's youthful reputation has worked its way into every account of the period. Griffin too was certainly promiscuous – mostly with married women, he later told Dora (for comfort without responsibility, I suppose); and he was also, like Millay, bisexual. Many years later, when he arrived at Dawn Powell's door, broken by the events I shall presently relate, her diary entry recalled his sexual exploits of these carefree days:

> *February 16* [1939]: Griffin Barry, sad, dried up, desperately miserable at 54, once a pretty boy, once the lover of all the famous women and even of their lovers – for he took Edna Millay from George Slocombe and at the same time slept with Slocombe.[17]

Griffin's affair with Millay was short-lived, however. She did not much enjoy her exile and returned home in 1923. That year she won a Pulitzer Prize for her work, married a businessman and dropped out of bohemia into conventional life. Her stature as a poet always outweighed any moral disapproval of her lifestyle, and does so today.

Meanwhile Millay's erstwhile friends stayed on in Paris, having the time of their lives. A favourable exchange rate made living blissfully cheap. Racial and sexual tolerance, adventurous new music, painting, literature – Paris in the 1920s was a haven for experiment and eccentricity, attracting artists and writers from everywhere. Some were already famous or became so; others, like Griffin, just basked in their glow. George Slocombe, a *Daily Herald* man, was a key figure in his circle, perhaps a channel for occasional freelance work (though nothing more substantial, as the paper limped from one financial crisis to another).

---

[15] *Jeffrey Meyers,* Edmund Wilson: A Biography *(Houghton Mifflin, Boston & NY, 1995), p.60.*

[16] *Letter to Sherwood Anderson, in* Ernest Hemingway Selected Letters 1917–1961, *edited by Carlos Baker (Granada, London, 1981), p.62.*

[17] The Diaries of Dawn Powell, 1931–1965, *edited by Tim Page (Steerforth Press, South Royalton Vermont, 1995), p.156.*

One of their mutual friends was the English poet Anna Wickham, 'the English Gertrude Stein' in Slocombe's words[18] (though a better poet, in his view), who would play a part in my own life a few years later. Anna came to Paris in 1922, to recover from the tragic death of one of her four sons from scarlet fever. She brought her eldest son, aged 14, for company, allowing him to share in the night-owl café life which occupied so many hours for all these bohemians – in her case

A portrait of Anna Wickham by Berenice Abbott, 1926

productively, for she wrote poems continually, 'on the café tables, on the backs of menus, on the waiter's apron, anywhere...' wrote Edna Millay to a friend.[19] Edna and Anna got on famously, both personally and poetically. So did Anna and Griffin.[20] He warmly admired her work, and urged her on. They lent each other money, and shared their black moods.

In an undated letter to Anna after her return to England, I find a familiar lament:

> I haven't a job yet. I suppose I must get one presently – the kind that will allow me to create another of my own in my off hours. I must go and look for it this p.m.; this very afternoon.

A photo of Griffin in Red Cross uniform, given to Anna Wickham in 1922. (Dora got one too a few years later.)

[18] *George Slocombe*, The Tumult and the Shouting *(William Heinemann, London, 1936), p.227.*
[19] *Millay, Edna St Vincent*, Letters of Edna St Vincent Millay *(Harper, New York, 1952), p.154. Quoted by Jennifer Vaughan Jones in* Anna Wickham: A Poet's Daring Life *(Madison Books, Littlefield Publishing Group Inc., 2003), p.163.*
[20] *They may have been lovers: they were of similar age, and Anna's marriage was not untroubled. Anna's biographer Jennifer Vaughan Jones has found no conclusive proof either way. Nor have I.*

Oh dear. That congenial Parisian café life, as so many accounts remind us, was a fatal trap for the undisciplined. Griffin was always at his best discoursing with other knowledgeable people on art, literature, politics, glass in one hand, cigarette in the other, into the wee small hours. Nursing a hangover next day, while his friends struggled back to their easels and half-written novels, Griffin would gloomily contemplate his own situation – no work in progress, no published book to wave around – *yet*. Oh, if only he could find some not too taxing salaried work to pay the rent, with 'off hours' for the serious Writing he knew was in him! In 1922, I see, this self-deluding refrain of later years was already established.

Presumably Griffin scraped by in these years with freelance commissions. In the May 1923 issue of *Scribner's Magazine* (American, but with a London office) there appeared an article by him, '"Dearest Portia": The Friendship of George Meredith and Alice Meynell – Told From Meredith's Unpublished Letters'. Did Griffin have privileged access to these unpublished letters from one distinguished poet to another? Probably. Alice Meynell's son, Francis Meynell, was another *Daily Herald* man and a friend of Griffin's. Coincidentally, at this time or later, Francis and his first wife Vera were also friends of Bertie and Dora, and would both get entangled in the Bertie–Dora–Griffin saga ten years after this date.

It may have been the commission from *Scribner's* that took Griffin to England in 1923, where he stayed for several months. We learn something of what he did there from his article in the May 1924 issue of the American magazine *The Forum*, based on his visit the previous summer to the country house in Essex of the Countess of Warwick.[21] During the afternoon the picnic spilled over into the garden of her neighbour H G Wells, who enlivened the proceedings by turning a hosepipe on the guests (among whom were Anna Wickham, as well as Griffin). Both Wells and the Countess were prominent supporters of the Labour Party, and the occasion seems to have been a jamboree for the press and well-wishers to introduce, or raise money for, the Party, then on the verge of holding office for the first time. (The first Labour Government took power in January 1924, but was brought down in October by a famous dirty trick implicating the *Daily Mail*, then as now a very right-wing newspaper.) Griffin's article in *The Forum*, entitled 'The British Soviet', is written in a florid style uncharacteristic of his other political journalism. Perhaps intentionally for his American readers, he writes like a political innocent blundering into an unfamiliar world, rather than an experienced journalist well-versed in left-wing politics.

---

[21] *In earlier years Lady Brooke – who became Countess Warwick when her husband succeeded his father as fifth earl in 1893 – had been one of the many, many mistresses of the Prince of Wales before he became King Edward VII. By this date she had become the best kind of socialist do-gooder, founding technical schools for rural children and involved in numerous worthy causes – another eccentric English aristocrat, like Bertrand Russell.*

Consorting with 'H G' and his friends, Griffin again might have met Dora, though he didn't. She had first visited Wells' house in Essex in 1913, and in later years he and his son Gip Wells were close friends of hers. But in the summer of 1923 – the early, happy days of her marriage to Bertie – she was busy creating Kate, and her new garden at Carn Voel, in Cornwall.

Where was Griffin in 1924 and 1925? Paris, London, New York? I don't know. Two entries in Dawn Powell's diary place him in New York in the autumn of 1926. By 1927, I believe, he was working for The Open Road, an organisation concerned with student exchanges, which in that summer ventured to take a party of Americans to Soviet Russia.[22] The USSR was still not diplomatically recognised by the American Government, so this would have required an 'experienced' courier like Griffin. He was still working for The Open Road when Dora met him in the spring of 1928.

Dora expecting Kate, Cornwall, 1923

So that charming Irish-American, we can see, was well-travelled, politically sophisticated, practised in the art of love – just what Dora wanted for a light-hearted extra-marital fling. But however casual the affair may have seemed to her, in 1928 or 50 years later, it was something very different for Griffin. His love and yearning for her – and later for their two children, Harriet and Roddy – was the dominating force in his life from the moment they first met.

---

[22] *A letter to Dora some years later mentions 'going to Russia' in 1927; and a letter from Anna Wickham to Natalie Barney, 15 July 1927, refers to Griffin passing through Paris en route to Russia.*

CHAPTER 2

SUMMER 1928

You would have been amused if you could have observed closely my conduct as the days approached on which letters might arrive from you. Three days before I telephoned the White Star Line to see if the Olympic had arrived in England; two days before I began to inspect the mail facilities downstairs; one day before I encountered a mailman in the street and complained that my letters were being lost and was referred to the Complaint Department of the General Post Office, and a few hours later I picked a terrific row with the janitress, swearing that her children were tearing up my letters. All of it nonsense, fantastic; nor was I aware of quite what I was doing until later. At last, on Saturday morning, I got up with the lark, having to motor to Williams College. Thus bright and early, the darlingest little boy (spawn of the careless janitress and the very lad my mind had fastened on as a destroyer!) knocked on my door bearing a heavenly smile and <u>five</u> letters – fat, real, undeniable! And there was a sixth! He brought it up in half an hour, having dropped it on the stairs...

This passage from the first letter Griffin wrote to Dora sets the tone of the series between their first meeting in March 1928 in New York, and their second, in July, in France. It also uncannily recalls the man I came to know some 20 years later: irascible, impatient, casting about for someone – usually some poor menial – to blame for his own misfortune; yet also able to laugh at himself for his unreasonable behaviour; and also, I know, quite capable of charming the pants off that little boy and his mother next time they met. Picking my way through the passion in these faded pages – a passion long dead by the time I knew him – I find many other reminders of the man who became my father, scrawled in his familiar rounded hand. These early letters revealed all the characteristics that would give Dora such trouble later – if only she'd been watching.

The practical constraints on this correspondence are hard to imagine today. There was no transatlantic air mail as yet – Charles Lindbergh had made the first non-stop Atlantic flight only in 1927 – so all the mail went by sea. Sailing dates and arrivals were announced in the press: Griffin's later letters, preserved in their envelopes, always state on the outside which ship will carry them; to assist the postal authorities, I suppose, like postcodes today.

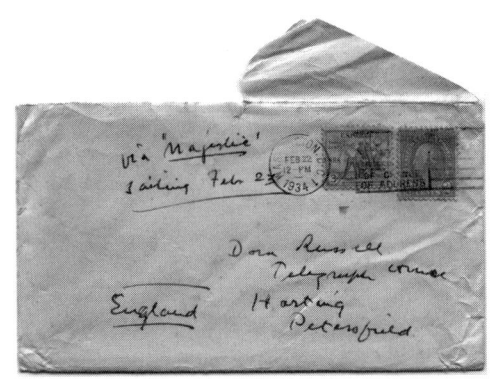

Addresses were delightfully simple in those days

Before the faster liners of the 1930s, voyages took nine or ten days, depending on the speed and route of the ship, and sailings were infrequent. To miss the boat, or receive no letter from one that had docked, meant a long wait for our impatient lovers. Letters written in rapid succession (Griffin often wrote several in a week) would queue up at the dockside and get carried across together.

There was no transatlantic telephone either, of course, at least not for ordinary folk, so the only means for urgent communications were telegrams (processed through Cable and Wireless at Porthcurno). There are many 'wires' preserved in Dora's archive of correspondence – the written confirmation of messages already phoned through – including the one she received in Sussex on the same day he wrote the excited words above: OVERJOYED BY YOUR LETTERS WRITING GRIFFIN. The day was April 3rd, her 34th birthday.

This first sequence of letters is entirely one-sided, for although Griffin was keeping Dora's replies, re-reading them over and over, they must have been subsequently lost in the course of his endless travels. It's clear hers were as intimate and loving as his – she too had worries waiting to be unburdened to a confidant – which may have encouraged Griffin to think he was as important to her as she to him. But already one can see that the obsessional devotion shown in Griffin's letters would have been hard for Dora to accommodate in a life already full of Beacon Hill, her marriage to Bertie, and their own two children John and Kate.

Griffin, by contrast, at once invested his very soul in continuing and developing the relationship:

> This relation of ours <u>must</u> have an outer reality and base; it can't exist in air merely as an idea... The danger of a miscarriage [of it] frightens me a little. If it ends in frustration for either it will, of course, for both; and that would hurt my pride in your intelligence and mine unbearably.

> [This] would go hard with me just now; I have never fully established <u>in myself</u> a belief in my intelligence by any good writing... and (as I seem to be saying over and over) I'm so constituted (despite my reputation as a light lover) that a failure in love becomes a failure in faith in myself and therefore in life.

Yet he fully recognises the imbalance in their situations; he '[does] not dare hope...that you can love me as much as I love you' and knows that 'if our love fails...you still have Bertie, your children and a well begun career'.

Some kind friend should have warned Griffin not to look for his own salvation in such an unbalanced relationship. And the usual prophecies of agony aunts did come to pass. Whether from weakness of resolve, or of character, he allowed the failure of his love affair with Dora – as eventually it did fail – to prevent him from ever achieving a solid piece of 'good writing'; and, it seems, from seeking someone else who might have given him the 'faith in himself' he needed. His letters to Dora over three decades, and those from her that he kept, are a record of this sad story. They also reveal the unconfident personality which made him both culpable and pitiable in the saga of his own downfall.

In 1928, however, Griffin had no thought for the morrow. Brushing aside any underlying doubts, he wanted only to convey to Dora the depth of his feeling and tempt her to further meetings. In language more appropriate to Mills and Boon than the discourse of two mature adults, he looks back longingly to the time they spent together in his little room (at 501 East 54th Street). He could hardly bear his loneliness after she left. At first he had returned to a previous girlfriend, Susan Smith, displaced by Dora's arrival in his life. But –

> Very soon we quarreled – and wordlessly, each knowing that the spirit had gone from our relation and the body should follow and doubtless would... In months I have not seen her, nor Dorothy Harvey nor Caroline nor any of that group. I've buried myself in money making, in fact, wrestled with indigestion – and turned my eyes across the Atlantic. I long for you and am faint for you.

Poor Susan! She was no match for Dora's combination of beauty and brains, seemingly 'Heaven-sent' to stimulate both his sensuality and his intellect. He was simply *dazzled* by her, and flattered by her commitment to him, as far as it went. But now she's back in England, will she forget...? By the end of April he is confident of something solid between them, boosted by letters from her. She asks his advice in dealing with a previous boyfriend she is now trying to shrug off (Griffin advises her to 'find him a wife'). This must have seemed like proof of his own importance to her.

> Yesterday I came staggering to this little room from nervous indigestion and on my way upstairs found two little lovely white letters clinging together in my mailbox. I didn't open 'em but put them on a table beside my bed while I undressed and got into it to lie flat until the pain should pass. Instead of writhing I fell into a beautiful profound sleep! Then I woke and read the letters; the contents confirmed the healing – but it was done long before by the look and touch of your handwriting. I understand why savages are cured by totems.

Griffin's 'nervous indigestion' – a chronic duodenal ulcer – was a lifelong curse from which he almost died a few years later. He lived before the modern wonder drugs and without the blessed National Health Service which later helped me out of the same trouble. In America, he was always too poor to avail himself of whatever remedies were on offer then, just retiring to bed to endure the attack.

The letters were developing their intellectual friendship too. Dora had given him a copy of her book, *The Right to be Happy*, and Trollope's *The Way We Live Now*, the story of a capitalist crook in nineteenth-century England (perhaps as a commentary on the rampant capitalism of 1920s America). It made Griffin realise 'the price you settled, orderly English may pay for the peace that seems to me, wallowing in chaos in NY, so heavenly'.

Comments on her own book show that from the beginning, Griffin instinctively resisted Dora's strident feminism (later he would speak out more boldly on this topic). Although he considered himself a disciple of 'advanced' thinking, including women's rights as well as radical politics, he had been brought up in conventional style. Male chauvinism was ubiquitous at that time, of course. When Dora's first book, *Hypatia*, was published in 1925, the author was designated as 'Mrs Bertrand Russell'. For a woman, who you were still depended on whose Mrs you were.

In Griffin's comments on his reading during 'a tiresome western journey', along with the shared ideas there's also a physical undercurrent, an echo of the thrilling sexual memories sustaining this transatlantic dialogue:

> I've been reading the [Robert] Graves book on Lawrence, fascinated by the little man's temperament not his aims, as who isn't; and, bumping over the western roads, the last Shaw. Mr Shaw helped to bring me up; when I was a kid he was in his prime. Now I find I shield myself from his loquacity. At present there's no room in me to consider social arrangements. And Russia, of course, where I waded neck-deep in the revolution, weakened my belief in revolution by persuasion. By guns? I don't know. I'd be a happier man if I did. But beliefs in us come from below and the gods below in me are not satisfied. Nor do I mean only the phallic gods. You know that. Poor darling dear – you needn't have explained you love me more than sexually. One mustn't subdivide in

these matters anyhow with the puny inaccurate irregular mind. One should have the wit to let oneself be swept through.

But the love stuff in these letters is delicate by today's standards. Only once, a year or two on from here, did I come across the 'f' word, immediately apologised for.

This was the time of frantic speculation on the stock market, leading up to the Wall Street Crash of 1929. Several mentions of 'gambling', and once of 'this absorbing, nerve-racking business tangle on which my freedom depends' suggest that Griffin was also engaged in this reckless capitalist game – surely going against all his (and Dora's) socialist principles. Perhaps he hadn't noticed that. The 'business tangle' may, however, have been a venture connected with the organisation he worked for, The Open Road Inc. Its headed notepaper listed him as one of two Field Secretaries (hence those tiresome journeys, drumming up customers). But The Open Road is failing – in June he reports it is 'bankrupt' – and he is counting the weeks until his job there ends. He had considered taking it over himself ('abandoning writing, and going into business against oncoming middle age'), but he would have needed capital to re-organise it, and anyway he wasn't much interested. A lucky escape: the Griffin Barry I knew would have been the world's worst businessman.

Perhaps, before they parted, they'd discussed the possibility of meeting again in the summer. This is a constant theme of Griffin's letters, begging her to find time to see him ('for a few weeks, not days'), and by early June he is delighted to hear –

> You are definite about the summer! Yes, I'm for the South of France too. I've never been on that coast but I know France well and the accounts people gave me in Paris last autumn of remote lovely towns in the hills made me long for them. And the blessed low French exchange will keep us feeling rich – an important matter, since... I shall have only 100 pounds or so plus a steamer ticket. I hoped to have enough for you too but the relative failure of this Russian project [not explained] will make me poorer than I hoped. But I may have luck before I sail with certain journalistic projects...

Here's another familiar feature of Griffin's insecure, wandering life: a constant shortage of money, always bravely borne in anticipation of 'journalistic projects' in the offing. In 1928 he felt it as a handicap in his courtship of Dora, though it didn't bother her at that time (later, it did).

The last few letters include an amusing picture of Griffin trying to learn to drive the 'antique car' of a friend in readiness for the Austin 7 Dora was planning to take to France. Since she could not yet drive, he would have to chauffeur his 'precious cargo' around. He was relishing the challenge: it appealed to his manly instincts. In the end the car stayed in England, where

Dora eventually learned to drive it. Griffin never did: another lucky escape, this time for road-users in England and America.

With mounting excitement Griffin set sail for Europe on 14 July, having arranged to meet Dora in Paris on the 25th.

Why did Dora agree to that holiday in France? Well, she was a young woman who enjoyed sex, her husband was much older, and Griffin was a real charmer – these are the obvious reasons. In fact it went deeper than that. Bertie had been more or less impotent with her after Kate's birth, a source of anxiety which she confided to Griffin in these letters. For Dora it was doubly sad because she badly wanted more children, and the years were slipping by...

In 1927 both she and Bertie had started outside affairs, Dora with an admirer called Roy Randall (the one she was now trying to shrug off), Bertie with a young Swiss governess, Alice Stücki. In *The Tamarisk Tree*, Dora gives her version of an incident quite comical to outsiders: while she was rushing around in London and Sussex, setting up Telegraph House for the opening of the school there in September, she was summoned to Carn Voel by Hannah, the

Bertie with Alice Stücki and John and Kate, 1926

cook. She arrived to find the outraged Hannah 'mounting guard' over John and Kate to protect them from the moral turpitude of their father, who was spending his nights with Alice. Dora's solution to this domestic crisis was to let Hannah go, regretfully, explaining to her that she and Mr Russell 'did not feel quite the same way about these things' – while Alice, 'a charming girl', was allowed to stay, moving to Telegraph House with the family at the end of the summer. Almost immediately, Bertie left for a lecture tour in America while Dora opened Beacon Hill School for its first term.

The confrontation over Alice was a key event in Dora's relations with Bertie, as we shall see later. Meanwhile both partners in the marriage continued their affairs, Roy replaced by Griffin in the following year – and why not, in Dora's view, for this was what they'd always agreed, hadn't they?

In *The Tamarisk Tree* Dora suggests that Griffin arrived in Europe in July 1928 out of the blue, wanting to see her. In fact we know their holiday had been well-planned beforehand. As to how they spent it – well, one difficulty of basing this story on surviving letters is the lack of documentation for the periods they spent together. Dora recounts their meetings with two pairs of friends: Francis and Vera Meynell and George and Mary Slocombe, whose connection with Griffin we already know about. More poignant for me is her mention of a visit to 'that exquisite place Les Andelys, [staying] in the lovely old hotel Chaîne d'Or,[1] on the bank of the Seine, at a curve of the river, overlooked by Coeur de Lion's castle.'

'The lovely old hotel Chaîne d'Or, overlooked by Coeur de Lion's castle'

In 1986, just a few weeks before Dora died, my husband Colin and I chanced to stay in the same hotel. Only later did we hear from her, all excited by my postcard, that she and Griffin had stayed at the Chaîne d'Or in 1928. I have a beautiful photograph showing the view looking out on the Seine from our bedroom window. Could it have been the very same room, rather modest compared to others the hotel offered, that they slept in?

---
[1] *Dora Russell, op.cit., p.207.*

Griffin lived off the memory of that holiday the following winter, reminding Dora of incidents and places they'd visited, and also apologising for his quarrelsomeness. Quarrels were normal with Griffin, as Dora must have discovered on that trip and learned to forgive. Her account shows them having a whale of a good time, getting to know each other and enjoying 'intelligent conversation and argument' with their friends, 'the kind of party that Griffin greatly enjoyed'. And he couldn't resist looking up old friends in Paris when Dora returned to England.

> I drank strong waters for a couple of nights after you left, once talking and drinking all night, lazily and erotically, in a cafe with amusing people. Now I've given that up as being too expensive in money time and energy... When I meet my ribald friends I perch on the outside of the group, drink beer and note the absence of the little waves of lust that were the only contact, aside from the tenuous chatter, that I had with them.

Dora ended that summer in Cornwall with Bertie and the children, before the school term began in September. Meanwhile, Griffin spent several weeks hopping between London and Paris before returning home in mid-October. In London he stayed in a small flat off Russell Square that Dora had acquired 'to be used by any of us when in London'. I don't know if Bertie ever stayed there, but 38 Bernard Street became a trysting-place for Dora and Griffin, and my birthplace in 1930 (no blue plaque I'm afraid – the whole terrace was redeveloped after the war).

Wanting to stay close to Dora, Griffin tried hard to find work in Europe. Two job chances in Paris came to nothing. Meanwhile, The Open Road in New York had not folded, and had 'better prospects than ever for the coming year'. Its director was urging him to return. He held out as long as he could, but in the end opted for the regular wage that would enable him to pay off his debts (including an unspecified sum borrowed from Dora). As always, he is fretting about jobs and money –

> But don't let this perplexity worry you... You are care-laden already. And let me know how your worries come out. I have more room in my life and mind for your troubles than you have for mine... And, by the way, I discuss your affairs with no one.

I should hope not! The 'worries' Dora was confiding to Griffin concerned her relations with Bertie, hardly fit to be bruited about in Parisian cafés.

Despite their advocacy of 'free love', Bertie and Dora were both deeply jealous of each other's amours. After the showdown over Alice the previous summer, there had been a chance – the last chance, as things turned out – of repairing the damage these outside affairs were doing to their marriage. In the autumn of 1927, from his lecture tour in America, Bertie wrote conciliatory letters. One of these diffidently hoped they might both be ready to give up their lovers the following summer, leaving them free to 'go away somewhere quietly together, and begin again, and live for each other for a time...'. He realised '[t]here is of course no hope unless I can satisfy you sexually', and proposed to seek medical advice about that when he returned home. 'So we must both be frank,' the letter ends, 'and try to find a way of life that would make us both happy... The chief thing, for me, is that you should be kind and gentle, not fierce and fault-finding.'[2] Clearly these two should have sought a marriage guidance counsellor – but instead, they fell to quarrelling again over Hannah (whom Dora had tactlessly re-hired while Bertie was away); and then she went away to America... and there she met Griffin.

If Dora could not give up Roy in 1927, still less would she give up Griffin now. In Paris he had finally decided, with heavy heart, he must return to America, and she knew there were plenty of warm beds for him in New York, despite his protestations of undying love:

> I <u>can't</u> shake off the sadness with which I turn back. I've always been able to get women out of my heart before when I really tried to. I've put real effort into this and can't. I've even lain awake two nights hating you. No good. Can't. I knew as soon as I woke up it was only wanting you. It's all against my principles, this wanting and not having... I'm clear headed enough to know that our love may attenuate by a year's separation.

However, he looks forward to seeing her at Bernard Street before his boat sails. He'll have part of the money he owes her, 'and a pretty dress I found for you here'.

Some kind of pledge must have been made when they said their farewells in London, to explain the euphoric mood of Griffin's next letter. Written over several days, on board ship, it is buoyed up by a new confidence in their relationship:

> I've parted from you for God knows how long, I've been alone for days and shall be for an eternity ahead, I've been seasick restless bored and querulous as before, I behave as aimlessly as usual and look not unlike my old self in the glass (I often look to see) – yet I'm <u>DIFFERENT</u> wholly. Underneath I'm as happy as a king. I could shout for joy sometimes. This is new – new since I was a child, a young boy. Going away from you has had nothing tragic in it... the break has not seemed final for a moment. So much remains that I never had from any other

---

[2] *Letter of 20 October 1927, in* The Selected Letters of Bertrand Russell: The Public Years, 1914–1970, *edited by Nicholas Griffin assisted by Alison Roberts Miculan (Routledge, 2001), p.269.*

being that my soul bobs around amply in what you've left and <u>chuckles</u>. You've made me <u>happy</u>, darlingest.

But oh how he misses her, and laments that 'we are not in physical touch, can't be for a long time. Ah, now it comes over me with pain. I wish we had had a child. I wish we had had a child. Maybe the next lunar month...'.

In *The Tamarisk Tree* Dora implies that her pregnancy by Griffin (a year after this date) was an accident, which she only allowed to continue with Bertie's permission. But these letters show she was at least being deliberately careless, shall we say, from the start of their relationship.[3] Griffin, at 43, despite his rootless way of life, longed for children. A suggestion from Dora that she wouldn't mind if it happened would have filled him with joy – never mind the practicalities.

The newly self-confident Griffin was even bold enough in this letter to challenge Dora's feminist ideas. She had given him more books to read, including her own *Hypatia* – a clarion call for women's rights. He has been struggling with it...

> This morning I brought up Hypatia to read, tasted its challenge, and sat down to write to the woman behind the gun, whom I prize so much when she's doing her hair and talking nonsense behind the firing line; the reactionary male in me having fallen prone at your first round of grape shot anyhow. I think I got no further than the first page. And now having kissed you (all female writers of such books should be kissed between each paragraph to stop their shrewd tongues) – [WOW!] – I think I'll go and read your God-damned book. Dinner first however. The bell has just sounded...

<u>Next day</u> (Haven't yet read Hypatia).

Any feminist today would curl up at such insufferable condescension; but Dora would have been accustomed to routine male chauvinism of that time. She had her share of feminine vanity, moreover, and might not have resented a put-down wrapped up in personal flattery. She certainly *would* have objected, however, to his professed 'dislike of her as a politician', in contrast to what he regards as her real métier as mother and educator.

> So if you go political, as you well may, with its million subtle dilations of the ego (hardly feeble in you already) I lose your inner essence... The school on the other hand is up my street...

---

[3] *After their first meeting in New York, Griffin was worried that 'they had risked a baby', and was disappointed when word came that Dora was not pregnant. She was certainly not ignorant of contraception, as she was in the forefront of the contemporary campaign, led by Marie Stopes, to make birth control generally accepted and disseminated.*

As an example of why he abhors 'political women' he cites a friend who is coming to England, whom Dora will meet when she gets there:

> Talk with her and see if some of the woman isn't lost in the politician. She talks well and freely about herself – or used to – and puts up a pretty good case... But I think she's a mess... There's undoubtedly something I don't get about feminists and feminism. I don't know whether it's a flaw in my sympathy or a flaw in their case... There, I'll go and attentively read Hypatia. I haven't yet. It requires courage for me to listen to that tone from you.

Politics was life-blood to Dora, and quite rightly she would have bridled at the familiar male jibe that women were not 'suited' to that world.

Griffin continued to oppose her aggressive feminism, though later he learned to choose his words more carefully. No doubt that's what Dora meant by her complaint in *The Tamarisk Tree* of his 'masculine anti-female instinct'. But it would be wrong to dismiss Griffin's attitude as mere sexism. Aside from his personal battle with Dora, he was a supporter of feminism in general, as other right-thinking men were learning to be at that time. He writes ecstatically here about another book Dora had given him – 'a lovely document' – 'a work of art on the man-woman theme' – about the eighteenth-century feminist Mary Wollstonecraft, a heroine of the movement to this day. Mary's husband William Godwin, a philosopher of anarchism, was more famous in his day and ours than Mary, yet Griffin scorns the 'shabby inferiority' of this 'tremulous, infatuated, insecure male' in comparison to Mary. That's hardly fair to William Godwin! – but Griffin was reacting as he thought Dora wanted.

In fact his 'anti-feminism' is just Griffin standing up to Dora as best he could. He resented being bossed about (unlike the doormat-men who succeeded him in her life), and having leisure on board ship, without Dora to answer back, he took the chance to 'say his piece'. This letter and others are suffused with his awe of Dora, and envy of her self-confidence. Up to now she had succeeded in every phase of her life – school, university, her marriage to a famous man – in contrast to Griffin's patchy education and working life. Even in later years, after events which brought her failure and unhappiness, Dora always had an air of superiority which ordinary mortals found hard to take. Griffin recognised that much of his antagonism was jealousy – she did *everything* better than he could (even politics, which he might have gone into, but chose not to) – and later, he admitted as much.

This very long letter of October 1928 is useful in giving a picture of Griffin while he was still 'his own man', unbeholden to Dora as yet, and uncowed by her. In the limbo of an ocean voyage, without friends or work to distract him, he writes more expansively than at other times. But I'm still left wondering why his tone is so optimistic: there's no mention of plans to meet again, and the references to 'B' show Griffin's continued acceptance that her marriage was the centrepoint of Dora's life. Yet –

> Today before breakfast, looking back over the Atlantic at the rear of the boat, I found myself worrying that you are coming into a bad time with B. Coming out, I hope it is, rather. Perhaps my going away will make a difference.

But it didn't make much difference. Dora's relations with Bertie remained troubled.

CHAPTER 3

GRIFFIN'S HOME GROUND

Griffin and Dora would not meet again until July 1929, when Dora joined a group Griffin was taking to Russia for The Open Road. This was a suitable jaunt for the two of them, considering their shared admiration for the socialist utopia, but they would have met somewhere in any case. Griffin's letters during the winter make it clear he was determined to get back to Europe (and Dora) after another spell with The Open Road. As I suggested earlier, it's likely they had already discussed having a child together, and they'd have to meet again to make it happen.

What interests me most in the next set of letters are the glimpses of Griffin's American life, his friends and his own parents, revealing more about the younger man I never knew. He writes first from Provincetown, staying with Mary Vorse. Before leaving New York he had found a small apartment, now at 328 East 15th Street, and installed in it a second-hand bed:

> I deloused the damn thing with my own hand the day before I came to the country. Strong, blinding chemicals, and the feeling of being a householder.

'A householder' is one thing Griffin never was, by instinct or in practice, and I cannot imagine him doing anything so practical as fumigating a bed. Yet there it is: he did, at least once in his life. The new flat is –

> not unlike the one you saw save that there is no river. A view of a slice of Stuyvesant Square, across from a hospital where women have babies. Once I brought a basket of strawberries from my brother's garden in the country to a friend having a baby there.

So my Uncle Richard was a gardener, and living somewhere near New York. Until recently I knew almost nothing about Griffin's older brother Richard except that Griffin disliked him, and that he'd written a book called *Father and his Town* about their father and the small town in California where he edited the local newspaper. This book, published in 1941, should tell me a lot about my American forebears, but it's hard to tease out factual information from Richard Barry's whimsical prose. The book is not solely about my grandfather: he's a peg on which to hang a celebration of what its author calls 'the average small town in the generation just gone'. This alone would explain why he and Griffin were not friends, for there was nothing Griffin despised more in his own country than the 'small town values' his brother so admired.

Griffin's attitude, as you'd expect, was in tune with progressive thinking of the time. In the American literary renaissance of the 1920s, books like F Scott Fitzgerald's *The Great Gatsby* derided and satirised money-mad America. Less well known today, but very influential then, were the novels of Sinclair Lewis. His hero-figure Babbitt, in a book of the same name, became a lasting symbol of narrow-minded Mid-west small town life. In Griffin's letters, 'Babbit' (always misspelled, with one 't') was shorthand for everything he despised.

The writers and artists of the so-called 'lost generation' turned their back on materialistic America, often literally by going to live in Paris, where the arts were valued as they thought they should be. Griffin's café life in Paris interlinked with the more famous (and better funded) café life of the Scott Fitzgeralds and Hemingways. Sinclair Lewis was another of his circle, and also an acquaintance of Bertie and Dora (she records a visit by him and his wife to Telegraph House about this time).

I've already indicated the importance of Mary Vorse and Provincetown in Griffin's life. Mary was a much-respected and versatile writer, a reporter of labour disputes and foreign affairs who could also dash off magazine short stories and novels to pay the bills, as Griffin wrote to Dora in November 1928:

> This place has memories for me. And friends. I am in the house of Mary Vorse, my poor old friend whom I have seen through a long series of husbands, lovers, difficult children and bad books and stories (some good) written to support all three. I always turn to her first when I return from anywhere... She has just finished the best book she has ever done, a gay, lecherous little tale of Americans returning from the war, wallowing in the chaos that came to us when our manners and morals, our poor Puritan provincial manners and morals, were suddenly asked to serve a people who had become overnight, all but unconsciously, masters of the world.

This book would have been Mary's novel *Second Cabin*, published that year. Griffin's comment (and the book's theme, apparently) again reflects the times. The First World War had brought America out of provincial isolationism to become a world player, but by this date, to the disgust of people with a world view like Griffin and Mary, it had retreated into its shell again with slogans like President Coolidge's remark, 'the business of America is business'. He spoke for most of the population, however: mass tourism and mass communications had not yet arrived to give at least a few million Americans an awareness of the outside world.

Back in New York, Griffin returned to his pre-Dora social circle – but not, so he claimed, to his philandering sex life. His love for her helps him to bear his 'barren personal life', and 'I turn aside, so far, tacit offers from women to make it less so'. He's very busy at work, often on the road for his employers, or –

> trudging back and forth to our new offices overlooking 5th Avenue from the 23rd storey, in a ridiculous Russian fur coat that I recently rescued from the pawn shop that I won't give up because it's Russian.

By mid-January 1929 he was writing from Madison, Wisconsin ('the town where the president of the university called you "that woman"' – see page 16). Did Dora have a good Christmas? His own holiday shows the typical Griffin, sociable and quarrelsome by turns:

> Caroline Dudley gave a big luncheon with many amusing people and oceans of bootleg liquor [this was the Prohibition era], and I came home and slept away Xmas afternoon... New Year's Dorothy Harvey and Susan Smith and Dos Passos, just back from Russia, and I spent in a remote house in the country heated with stoves for the occasion. Something I said angered Susan who bade me go home or something of the sort; however I didn't... The next morning I got up a little shaken, because all of us had been too emotional the night before and tiresome apologies and reconciliations were in order.

I remember Mary Vorse telling me, years later, that she'd once received a postcard from Griffin: 'After last night I never want to see you again. My next address is Oslo.' That's probably apocryphal, but it fits the picture of the younger, roustabout Griffin Mary was trying to convey to me, who only knew the weather-beaten old man.

His stop in Madison was part of a two-month, cross-continental journey, 'talking about Russia' to entice recruits for an Open Road expedition there. Letters from this journey are full of yearning for Dora, whose love for him 'has made me a more serious man'. If he succeeds in doing anything in future 'save sleep in women's beds', it will be thanks to her. On notepaper of the Rock Island Line, 'en route to Denver', he is eager to acquaint her with his homeland and his own origins:

A lot of our trouble comes from these damned awful plains I'm crossing now. I remember the wrinkles in my grandfather's face, who trekked west twice, once around the Horn in a sailing ship in 1850 and once later in a cart to Wisconsin. They weren't wrinkles of goodness or of thought, either, but of pain. His diary, which I have, shows he only loved God. He has long conversations with him about the iniquity of man – doubtless where I get my flair for pointing out other people's faults. And then my poor grandfather didn't make any money; probably he wasn't very intelligent, though his daughters say he was too honest and good. So he had an inferiority complex. Add that to a talent for other people's faults, and you have my inheritance... We're just getting into Denver, over a plain strewn with cattle bones that look human. Uggh – it's awful.

You can feel Griffin's shudder, out there in Colorado, hundreds of miles from the sophisticated city life of New York that was *his* America. He was born and raised 'out there', and was thankful to have left it. All he ever told me of his youth was to name the town of his birth: Eau Claire, Wisconsin. Now I know a little more, thanks to Uncle Richard and my own researches.

The Eau Claire chapter of Richard Barry's book is merely a prelude to his main theme: a song of praise for the semi-fictional 'Santa Ybel' (in reality Monrovia, now a suburb of Los Angeles), where his semi-fictional Father came to live in 1903 and became editor of the town newspaper. So we can probably rely on Richard for a picture of the Barry family in Eau Claire (remembering that it was written 40 years after they left), while taking 'Santa Ybel', and George Barry's importance there, with a large spoonful of salt. The Barry family certainly lived in both places, and George did *some* of the things recounted in *Father and his Town*, though perhaps not so splendidly and uniquely as his son implies. With these reservations, Richard and I can put together a sketchy family history.

Wisconsin

The Godfearing grandfather Griffin describes was Washington Hayes, their mother's father. After rounding Cape Horn in 'a windjammer', he jumped ship to join the California gold rush already under way. Two years later, having failed to make his fortune, he returned to his home state of Massachusetts. His second journey west would have been in the mid-1850s, I would guess, to join the 'log rush' of the Chippewa Valley on which the fortunes of Eau Claire and several other logging towns were built.

Despite what Griffin later told Dora, according to Richard he did well. By the time his daughter Harriet married George A Barry in 1881, Grandfather Hayes owned a sawmill, a blacksmith's shop, a 160-acre farm and a cheese factory in the village of Durand, some 30 miles from Eau Claire. More than that, 'he held 17 patents on sawmill machinery' – a pot of gold in a town by then known as Sawdust City. He brought up his family of seven children in some style, and not surprisingly was somewhat displeased when Harriet married a printer earning six dollars a week instead of the 'timber prince' he'd been hoping for. George took his wife to live in town, perhaps to escape the scrutiny of his in-laws.

Grandfather Hayes no doubt worked hard, but he was also lucky. Eau Claire and other towns of the area boomed from nothing to substantial cities in just 30 years in the classic pattern of nineteenth-century America – by ruthlessly exploiting the natural environment, with no thought for thereafter. In the mid-1850s the vast amounts of timber needed to settle the West couldn't be hauled economically from the East. To tap the 'inexhaustible' pine forest of northern Wisconsin (which became a state in 1848), Indian tribes were elbowed out with strategic treaties and the log rush began in earnest. The buoyancy of pine allowed it to be cut and stored on the frozen river in the winter and floated downstream on the spring thaw. Huge rafts of sawn planks and other wood products were then constructed in the 'holding ponds' of Eau Claire and other Sawdust Cities, to be floated down the Chippewa River to the upper reaches of the Mississippi and sold in the riverside towns.

It was dangerous, ill-paid work for the thousands of loggers (including many immigrants, mainly from Germany and Norway), and chancy for their employers. Some 30% of timber 'banked' upstream in winter was lost – stranded on the riverbank if there was too little water, or cascading uncontrollably past the sawmills in spring floods. It was costly and sometimes impossible to free 'marked' timber from gigantic log-jams, the epic seize-up of 1869 being only the most remarkable: tree-trunks 20 to 50 tiers deep, a jam 200 yards wide and 2 miles long. In 1884, the year of Griffin's birth, floods swept away all six bridges in Eau Claire.

Despite all these difficulties, timber fortunes were made (though many more lost). But 1884 was the all-time peak year of production. The accessible timber was almost all felled, and by 1888, reported the Eau Claire *Daily Free Press*, 'Valley lumbermen were turning their faces towards the forests of Washington Territory'[1]. The town which had grown ten-fold in 15 years, to 22,000 inhabitants in 1885, then began to lose population, along with its sawmills. By 1900 the 26 mills of 1870 had been reduced to three. Slowly and painfully, but in the long run successfully, Eau Claire reinvented itself as a thriving small city with a mixed economy of farming and manufacturing. And that's how it looked to me when I made my investigative pilgrimage with Jennifer Jones in 2001.[2]

---

[1] *Tim Pfaff,* Settlement and Survival: Building Towns in the Chippewa Valley, 1850–1925 *(Chippewa Valley Museum Press, 1994), p.72.*

[2] *Jennifer is the biographer of Griffin's friend Anna Wickham – see Notes on p.30, and my Bibliographical Notes. She lives in Madison, Wisconsin, from where we made our trip to Eau Claire.*

CHIPPEWA BASIN

Map of the Chippewa River basin

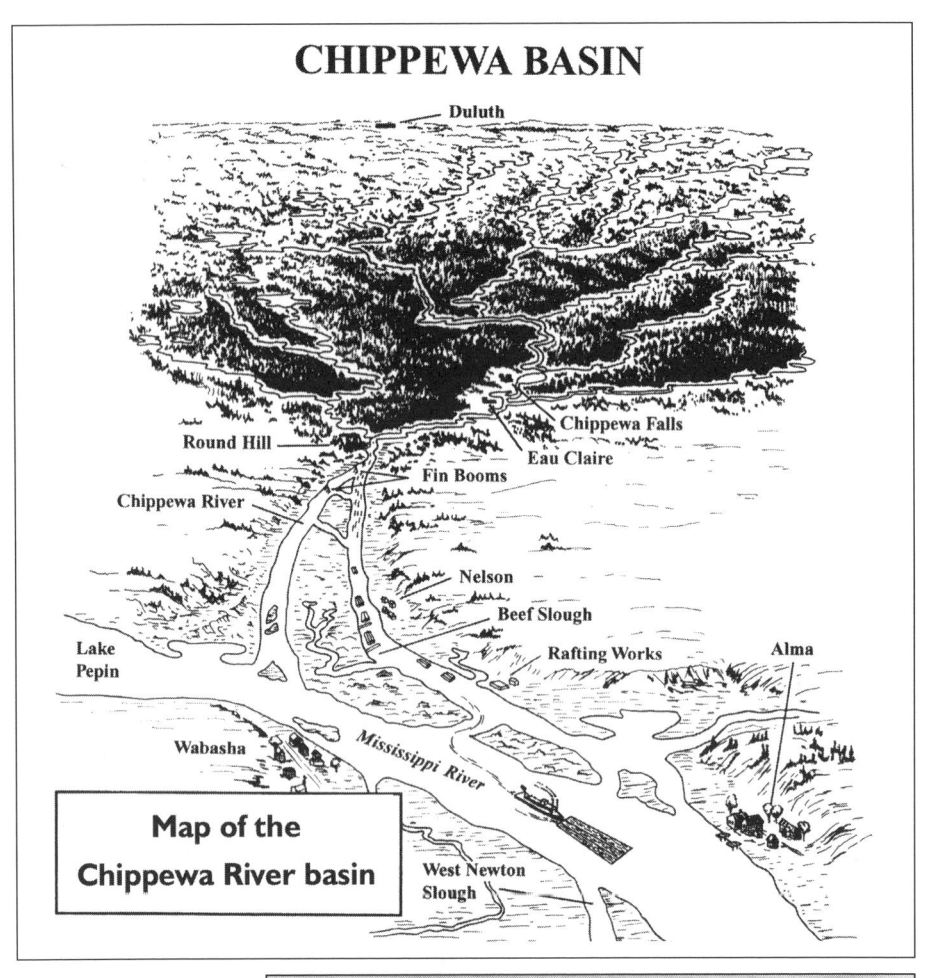

Sorting works at Beef Slough, c. 1870s–90s. As many as 1,500 men were employed there at times.

Flooding in Eau Claire in 1884

Great log jam on the Chippewa River, 1869

George Barry may have been editor of the *Free Press* in the mid-1880s, when far-sighted citizens began to foresee the impending decline of Eau Claire. Richard claims he enjoyed 'sassing' his proprietor, whose fortune rested on logging – 'You old timber thief,' he would say, 'the time will come when you will have to whack up.'[3] But the son may have been too kind in ascribing to his father the sentiments of a later time, when Americans had developed a conscience about the natural environment.

It is often difficult to match up what Richard says with other evidence. He implies, for example, that George was editor of the *Free Press* for most of his '40 years' in Eau Claire, but a more official document gives his arrival in Wisconsin as 1878 (making his sojourn there only 23 years in total), and lists

---

[3] *Richard Barry,* Father and his Town *(Houghton Mifflin Company, Boston, 1941), p.15.*

only five years' connection with the *Free Press*, plus three with the *Leader*, among several other occupations.[4]

This information would have come from George himself, and most usefully traces the Barry origins right back to Ireland. George's grandfather Timothy was the first immigrant, to Boston, and of his eight children, Augustus (Gus?) in time became the father of George. As a young man he volunteered to fight the Seminole Indians in Florida in an ignoble little war of the 1830s, and later migrated to Pittsburgh, Pennsylvania, where George and two other children were born. Augustus 'was a natural musician and this led him eventually to be interested in the manufacture of pianos as a member of the firm of Goodall and Barry', recorded his son George.[5]

George also confirms in this document the most glamorous part of his own history, central to the character portrayed in Richard's book – his service on the winning side in the American civil war. No doubt romancing the tales he was told as a lad, this time forgiveably, Richard recounts how in 1862 George ran away from home at 16 (15, George says) to become a cannoneer with Knapp's Pennsylvania Battery of Light Artillery. He rode over the right wheel of the gun carriage while his partner rode on the left. In battle his job was to clean the barrel of the gun with a ramrod after each firing, then stand back to wait for the next. He also cared for his horse – two horses, when his partner was killed. In three-and-a-half years, he went through all the major battles of the civil war.

Like many old soldiers, George traded off his war experiences ever afterwards. He was known as 'the wheel horse from Eau Claire' in Wisconsin, Richard tells us, and was a big wheel in the Grand Army of the Republic (GAR), too, both there and later in California. Among the many Eau Claire affiliations he proudly recorded himself was his service as adjutant-general of the Wisconsin GAR in 1887.[6]

Perhaps more reliable than his shaky dates is Richard Barry's picture of Eau Claire family life in the *Free Press* years. The editor was paid only a minimal wage and expected to make the rest of his living by other means, his proprietor requiring only that the newspaper broke even. To maintain his family, George operated an almost cashless barter system very like a LETS scheme today.[7]

---

[4] *Entry for George A Barry in the* Historical and Biographical Album of the Chippewa Valley, Wisconsin, 1891–92 *(Chicago, Illinois – reprint), p.789.*

[5] *Augustus died young, at 50, in 1848. In 2001 his great-great-grandson, my son Barney Unwin, by coincidence – or genetic inheritance? – also 'a natural musican interested in the manufacture of pianos', confirmed that Herbert Goodall was still making pianos in Pittsburgh in 1850. This information came from Barney's 1990 edition of* Pierce's Piano Atlas, *a handbook of the piano trade published by its compiler, Bob Pierce, in Long Beach, California.*

[6] *Historical and Biographical Album, op cit, p.789. The GAR was an association of Union veterans of the civil war, something like the British Legion in Britain, and just as conservative in politics.*

[7] *Local Exchange Trading System – a local association in which its members exchange goods or services with each other without using normal currency.*

Eggs and vegetables arrived on the doorstep, travel and theatre tickets were 'free' in return for advertisements or subscriptions to the newspaper. Barry household essentials were procured from certain shops on the same basis. By the same token, they could buy nothing from a store that would not negotiate this exchange (the butcher they dealt with was inconveniently far for Richard, collecting the Sunday joint).

The crunch came when Hannah, the maid, wanted to get married and requested payment of her back wages as a dowry. At $3 per week, the accumulated sum was $500. Hannah could not be persuaded to take it in wares from Elman's Drygoods or the Eagle Haberdashers. So George Barry raised a loan against his library, which Hannah used to fund her family and a successful dairy farm. It took him ten years to pay it off.

In Richard's account, the family fortunes improved – and Harriet was much happier – when George was appointed, in addition to his editorship, to other positions carrying a salary. The family moved to a larger house, and kept two horses. 'Father... never found time to drive, but a boy at the livery stable was always available to take mother out wherever she wished.' I cannot check up on the horses, but the family lived at several addresses

421 Third Avenue as it is today (on the right, adjoining No. 423)

before moving in 1897 to 421 Third Avenue, on the corner of Broadway (a house I saw and photographed in June 2001). Both Richard and Griffin attended Eau Claire High School, whose student magazine *The Kodak*[8] Jennifer and I rummaged through during our visit. They both contributed to this journal, Richard becoming its Business Manager and then Editor – following in Father's footsteps, we see, as both he and Griffin would in later life. But it was Griffin who won first prize in a short story competition in 1898, perhaps one of his few triumphs over big brother Dick. 'A Tale of Two Friends' is a sentimental story of two young newspaper sellers, Tim and Gus, whose notable enterprise and heart-warming loyalty to each other is observed by a customer who befriends

---

[8] *The magazine took its name from the first camera to use a roll of film instead of plates, the Eastman Kodak. For a while the word was loosely used to mean also a snapshot. A few early (incomplete) issues of* The Kodak *are housed along with later ones at the new High School in Eau Claire, the old one having been demolished in the 1950s.*

them. The first-person author is a writer, the setting is New York, with street names Griffin must have looked up on a map. Was this 13-year-old provincial boy dreaming up his own future?

Eau Claire High School in 1900. One of those boys is Griffin Barry, aged 15.

The curriculum of the High School was similar to that of an English grammar school of the period. In 1900 it included Latin, Higher Latin and Rhetoric along with a wide range of academic subjects. Most of its graduates would be destined for the professions. Richard was a member of the Class of 1898, which would make Griffin, three years younger, in the Class of 1901. Mysteriously, neither of them graduated. Without explanation, *The Kodak* reports that Richard left the school during 1897. Another source shows he started as a reporter with the *Milwaukee Sentinel* in 1898.[9] A piece by Griffin in *The Kodak* is dated March 1901, but he must have left school during that year when his family moved to California. The 1890s was a time of sharp decline for

---

[9] Who's Who in America, 1922–23, *Vol.12. Other information from this source will be relevant later.*

the city, and I can only assume that economic misfortune cost both boys their high school diplomas, and forced the move west. Some time during that decade another – perhaps connected – misfortune struck the Barry family, when two younger children, Charles and Abigail, died of diptheria.

Medical bills? George out of work? Richard's version of the Barrys' departure from Eau Claire is rather fanciful, not worth retelling. In fact they were part of a general economic migration from Mid-west to West around this time. The Hayes family seems to have followed in the Barrys' tracks a few years later.

California

It was a depleted family unit that moved west: just Griffin and his parents. Curiously, while Richard continued to list Monrovia, California as his home into the 1920s, Griffin was giving a New York address to official bodies by 1916. From the lack of any later references to his life in California, I guess it was not a valued part of his past.

Exactly when and how Griffin left home, we'll never know. Already 16 when they left Eau Claire, he probably avoided any further schooling and, apart from a taste of Stanford in 1906 (see page 22), any further education would have been self-education. The young adult he became, with his radical-left politics, would have been a rebel with a very loud cause against the Father portrayed in Richard's book.

The 'Santa Ybel' of that book is a composite of several small towns the Barrys lived in, the author tells us. He places their arrival there in 1901, but in real life that was in 1903. They came from Ventura, a coastal town north of Los

An old postcard view of Monrovia

Angeles, and perhaps had lived briefly elsewhere after leaving Wisconsin. However, so many features and events in 'Santa Ybel' are paralleled in Monrovia's history that we can safely deduce it is Richard's main model. In 1903, the opening of a rapid electric railway to the city made it virtually a suburb of Los Angeles, as it is today, about 20 miles north-east of the central downtown area. But Monrovia had, and has, its own identity as one of the 'foothill towns' in the San Gabriel Valley, at the base of the Sierra Madre mountains.

The origins of the town are another case history of nineteenth-century American development, just as typical as that of Eau Claire. This time it was a land rush, set off by the Southern Pacific railroad connecting up with the Santa Fe at Deming, New Mexico, in 1881. As Hollywood has taught us, settlement of the West followed the railroad, and the welcoming climate of California ensured a land boom like no other. The population of Los Angeles grew from 15,000 in 1882 to 25,000 in 1883. Among the energetic prospectors buying up acres in the San Gabriel Valley was one W N Monroe, a railroad contractor from Texas. In 1885 he and three other large landowners 'decided to start a town'.

Railroad contractor Monroe was just the man to clear the new townsite. In a short time he had dozens of mule teams pulling scrapers, scores of white laborers and Chinese cutting brush, preparing the ground for cultivation.

"Clear the land," were his orders, "but leave the oaks!"

Monrovia's founder is commemorated in the town's tourist literature

The four set up a townsite company, started laying out lots, and on 17 May 1886 began selling them. On 8 December 1887, the new city of Monrovia was incorporated. Monroe was its first mayor, and his 'elegant and commodious' home, "The Oaks", became the center of social life for miles around'. That's the folklore of the town. And it must be true, because it's not very long ago and the records have been well kept.[10] Today 'The Oaks' is a tourist attraction, and

---

[10] *By Charles F Davis, Editor,* Monrovia-Duarte Community Book, *published by Arthur H Cawston, Monrovia, California, 1957. The longer quotation, and other phrases in the above paragraph, are from this source. Charles Davis started his writing career as George Barry's apprentice – see next page.*

17 May is celebrated as Monrovia Day.

In fact the over-hyped land boom crashed spectacularly in 1888, sending Monroe and his son off to other construction projects in Chile, Mexico, Alaska... But 'W N' always kept one foot in the town named after him, and eventually settled and lived there until his death at 94 in 1935. Unlike some others in the region, the town weathered the slump of the 1890s and by 1900 was prospering on citrus groves, with a population of 1,500. Ten years later that figure had doubled. Quite early on, Monrovia became known for a TB sanatorium of international reputation, opened in 1895, and for a racetrack founded nearby in 1909. Both events are described with suitable small-town pride and pomposity in *Father and his Town*.

Monrovia's archives record George and Harriet's residence there from 1903 until 1928. Richard's *Independent* was in reality the *Monrovia News*, launched by a local entrepreneur in 1903, with – surprise! – Mrs Harriet Barry as assistant to its founder-editor. In 1906 the fledgling weekly changed hands and George then became its editor and manager. Headed by 'a newspaperman of unusual ability', the paper flourished and became the *Monrovia Daily News* in 1911. George's editorials 'had state-wide readership..., [setting] examples for later comers to follow,' wrote an appreciative successor.[11] Though not the first nor the only newspaper of Monrovia, the *Daily News* was the most important, combined with a print shop and located in the centre of town. When the paper moved into purpose-built premises George persuaded the owner to include an apartment 'over the shop', and that's where he and Harriet lived, at $15\frac{1}{2}$ East Lime Avenue, until 1928. The descendant of his newspaper, the *Daily News-Post*, continued to circulate in Monrovia until 1992.

Richard's picture of Father's office as a lynch-pin of civic life, with George as general advisor to all comers, may be only somewhat exaggerated, at least for the early years. Yet it doesn't quite match a description from another authoritative source:

> The Daily News at that time was a simple and economical newspaper operation. Sole occupant of the front office was Editor Barry, when he was in residence. In those days railroads were generous with passes and the editor took many a free jaunt to distant points.
>
> Next in line to the editor and manager was the general reporter, the paper's work-horse... [later] promoted to city editor... Then there was a girl who wrote social notes, took subscriptions and classified ads, and another girl who kept books, made out the bills, took charge of the carrier boys and counted out the papers.
>
> As the paper went to press, all hands, front and back, helped fold

---

[11] *Ibid, p.34*

the sheets as they came off the press. Bone folders were used and the job was done rather quickly. Circulation was about 600.

It was in that period, the pre-World War I era, that a young man from Iowa, just out of college, presented himself to take the place of the current city editor... The newcomer gave his name as Charles F Davis. Publisher Barry found him without newspaper experience, hired him anyway, gave him a week's sketchy training, then left for an extended visit with his son, Richard Barry, a well known short story writer in New York City. The paper managed to survive, Davis later stated, thanks largely to the good sense of the girl who kept the books.[12]

Those words were written many years later by the 'young man from Iowa'. Charles F Davis went on to become a key figure in newspapers and printing in Monrovia. In retirement, in the 1950s, he and his wife Ellavera – who had also begun her working life under Editor Barry on the *Daily News* – devoted their energies to compiling the history of their home town.

When George visited him in New York City, Richard was launched on a most impressive career. He had already worked on three newspapers, including the *Los Angeles Times*, when in 1904 he went to China for two years to cover the Russo-Japanese war, reporting for three magazines. In 1908 he cruised round the world as correspondent with the Atlantic Fleet, showing off American naval might in the year when Germany and Britain were boosting up their navies in preparation for the war ahead. By the time that war broke out, when he was 33, Richard had added three works of fiction to several political publications. In 1922–23, *Who's Who in America* recorded his marriage to Elizabeth Oden d'Hal, a descendant of two Revolutionary war heroes and related to Robert E Lee.[13] Ten years later he had several more novels and plays to his name, and in 1927 the Barrys had founded the Native Theatre in Mamaroneck, New York, where they now lived. Match that, Griffin. If he had felt overshadowed in High School – and what younger sibling doesn't? – he had a lot of catching up still to do.

All this goes a long way to explain Griffin's adult insecurities and lack of self-confidence. He was of course a product of his family environment. Richard was his father's favourite – his reverent biography shows that clearly – while Griffin was his mother's. Richard came to share George's staunch Republicanism (in 1918 he even worked for the party's National Committee),

[12] *Ibid, pp.30–32.* In Father and his Town *there's quite a bit about 'the girl who kept the books', called Carrie. On page 156 Father proudly points out to her that his management has increased the paper's subscription list from 73 to 2018, and without 'a crate of oranges or a bag of turnips or a brace of rabbits' in payment for them. He was keen to avoid the humiliation of the barter system in Eau Claire.*

[13] *Lee was a Confederate general in the American civil war – a hero in the South to this day.*

The return of the 'Great White Fleet' in 1909. Richard Barry was on board one of these ships.

while Harriet, at least in later years, as we shall see, was a firm Democrat. She was always more than a homebody, but George ruled the roost, and was a bit of a martinet. Perhaps Griffin as a boy had tried to win his approval and was rebuffed: from the only evidence we have (see below), in later years he had little affection for his father. But he remained very fond of his mother and tried to keep connected with her throughout his wandering life.

With such similar interests and talents, the boyhood rivalry of Richard and Griffin inevitably continued into adult life. Griffin may have come to dislike Richard's personal philosophy, but it must have been galling, while he was still trying to get started, to watch his brother's meteoric arc through the very field of work where *he* hoped to make his name. Then imagine, a few years later, Griffin visiting for Sunday lunch from raffish Greenwich Village to suburban Mamaroneck, perhaps with his latest amour on his arm... Could he hold his own in their discussion of work in progress? Could his girlfriend withstand the cool appraisal of his well-connected sister in law? It's not surprising that by the time Griffin met Dora, Richard was no longer part of his world – filed away with a label all his friends (and Dora) would understand: 'my Babbit brother'.

Before we too part from Uncle Richard, we can glean a little more of our Barry heritage from *Father and his Town*. I was interested to learn that George had a long torso and short legs: a characteristic of his Barry descendants too. A few quotations from his writings show wit and skill with words; it's no surprise that his brother Will was also a small-town editor, in Pennsylvania, and that both his sons became writers. He was evidently a good manager of the newspaper, and something of a diplomat, maintaining good relations with the influential people of the town and all the 17 church denominations.

I also see in these pages a self-important bore, a stalwart of the patriotic societies that epitomise American small-town life, known throughout town (Richard says unwillingly) as 'Colonel Barry', from his service with the GAR in Wisconsin rather than his humble rank in the civil war. Yet he hated militaristic bombast, Richard insists, opposing American entry into the First World War in anticipation of the suffering he remembered from 'his' war. He could never forget his soldiering days. When he died, aged 86, he was buried to a bugle call from an old soldier who had been a drummer boy in the Union army.

Richard scarcely mentions his mother, except as the passive foil to George's rather vainglorious activities. He shows the Hayes family as better providers than the Barrys: in Wisconsin, while they were still neighbours, Harriet kept trying to nudge her family up the economic ladder to look them in the eye. For a more rounded picture of the grandmother whose name was bestowed on me I have only the glimpses in Griffin's correspondence. Alas, only glimpses.

* * *

When Griffin made his 1929 continental journey, in much grander style than Grandfather Hayes 80 years earlier, his parents had recently moved away from Monrovia. In June 1923 ill health had forced George, by then 77, to retire from the *Daily News*. In fact for the previous year Harriet had been manager of the paper, while he was still editor. She had been a school-teacher before her marriage, and evidently picked up some editorial skills at George's elbow which she used to supplement the family income once she was free of mothering. She worked on the News when they first came to Monrovia, as we have seen, and in 1913–14 she is separately listed as the editor of Pacific *Poultrycraft* and *The Women's Bulletin* (I doubt if she kept chickens in the flat over the shop, but editing a journal doesn't necessarily require expertise in its contents). In 1928 *California Knitting Mills* was listed at the Barrys' address – another sideline of Harriet's, no doubt, though whether this was a journal or some other business is unclear.

In a farewell message to his readers in June 1923, 'at the end of more than 50 years of newspaper activity', George had added 'I dearly love Monrovia and expect to pass the remainder of my life here.'[14] But he wasn't able to, quite. After the News was sold, the Barrys stayed on for a few years at $15\frac{1}{2}$ East Lime Avenue, perhaps while the fate of the vacated building was being decided. But in 1928 or early 1929 they moved to the coast (back to Ventura, perhaps?), probably to be near Harriet's siblings. That's where Griffin would have visited them in 1929, taking a few days off from his mission for The Open Road.

---

[14] Monrovia Daily News *of Saturday, 30 June 1923, p.1.*

GRIFFIN'S HOME GROUND

Living by One's Wits is More Precarious Than Making a Living by One's Brains.

MONROVIA DAILY NEWS

READ OUR WANT ADS — **The HOME NEWSPAPER**

THE WEATHER: Fair and Warmer.

VOL. XIII No. 256 MONROVIA, CALIFORNIA, SATURDAY, JUNE 30, 1923 $5.00 PER YEAR

By early March Griffin was on his way back eastwards, stopping off –

> ...in a vast infinitely standardized extremely comfortable and dreary Chicago hotel – a hell of a place with padded carpets and swarms of negro servants and thousands of hurrying, tense-faced Babbit patrons.

From the comfort of this hotel he wrote a long letter to Dora, which included a graphic picture of his parents. It is worth quoting at length, as the only full view of them through his eyes:

> In California I saw my parents who are old and poor and proud; they tried to conceal from me how little money they have and how depressed. It was a sad visit. I brought my mother a bolt of smoke-blue Chinese brocade and ivory beads to wear; she accepted them with scarcely a smile on her tired old pioneer's face that always sees a fabulous country at the end of each day's trek and never finds it and never gives up. She feels so disgraced poor dear because she isn't rich like everyone else. She is protected from want but in spirited Americans to be poor is to have failed. Of course it's never mentioned by the culprits. One day we drove in Mother's rattling little Ford 120 miles into the high mountains to a fruit farm into which my mother had just put blindly nearly the last of my father's little property – a farm that proves to be no good and is now lost. My mother at 70 drove and I her husky son sat beside her and pointed out defects in the driving, in a manner you'll remember.
>
> We're a shiftless proud quarrelsome rather good-looking Irish-American family that I deplore and am very like. I came away with the stench of mortality in my nostrils, my heart running with pity and something like fear inside and outside very stern and nervous. My father at 83 is over the battle at last, his earlier explosions of rage drained into gentleness now: he damns the evil-doing politicians quite aimiably,

---

C. C. HOWARD PURCHASER OF DAILY NEWS

Practical Newspaper Man of Kirksville, Mo., Takes Over the Paper; George A. Barry Retires After Fifty Years in Harness

C. C. Howard, until recently the editor and owner of the Kirksville Daily News, of Kirksville, Mo., a practical newspaperman of sixteen years experience in the daily field, has purchased the Monrovia Daily News and the Weekly Monrovian and will assume charge at once.

follows the new scientific spirit intuitively and exactly and sang me the saga of his ancestors – people of substance in Pennsylvania whom he ran away from when he was 16 to the wars.

We'll meet Harriet again later in this story, but his father gets no further mention in Griffin's letters. Not even his death is recorded there.

CHAPTER 4

TO RUSSIA AGAIN

Back in the New York office, Griffin soon wrote to Dora with an exciting proposition. The Open Road would be sending a group to Russia in July with him as courier; would Dora like to come? The two-week trip would cost her 'about £75', and 'if you haven't any ready money I can supply all or part of that'. The monetary offer was typical Griffin bravado (in fact the trip cost considerably more, and before it was over *he* would be borrowing from *her*) – but evidently the cost was no barrier for Dora. She accepted with alacrity, keen to see what progress had been made since her last visit in 1920; and, of course, 'we would have great pleasure in each other's company'.[1]

Busy with preparations, Griffin was eagerly looking forward to 'prowling about' in Russia for 'a book about Americans in Russia I want to do', he wrote. Afterwards he planned to spend about two months in Europe working on this, but after that – ?

> I'm now debating whether to come back here for the same job next year... I don't know if I'm wise to put up with the terrific drains on my energy this job is taking increasingly; at the same time I don't dare give up the prospect of the substantial savings another year of this infernal jig-dance would mean.

This time, however, the dilemma was resolved before he left for Europe.

> I've had a row with the Open Road – a long story, that has kept me oppressed and insecure all spring – and I shan't go back to them next year. That means I must wangle a profitable series of Russian articles to do, for which there's an opening; but it means I'm giving up my fairly fat salary a year earlier than expected; and it leaves me anxious.

---

[1] *Dora Russell, op. cit., p.210*

On 19 July Griffin arrived at the Port of London on the Cunard liner *Tuscania*. After a few days in London with Dora, on the 24th, with the rest of the Open Road party, they embarked at Hull for Helsingfors (Helsinki), still the usual route into Russia for western visitors. Dora recalled some fuss and bother when the *Oberon*, a French ship crewed by Finns, had too few single cabins for the elderly Americans Griffin was escorting. She admired the adventurousness of such old tourists.

For Dora, being in Griffin's company was the least memorable aspect of that trip to Russia. One sentence in *The Tamarisk Tree* sums it up: 'Both Griffin and I were pretty tired and quarrelled endlessly about our relationship.'[2] The rest of her account concerns the places they visited and people they saw who fitted into her lifelong interests and causes. Soviet Russia in 1929 was still in its 'Leninist' phase – before the much worse tyranny of Stalin was fully established – with experiments in education, rights for women, and child welfare. Dora was 'immensely impressed' by an explicit film about abortion (legal in the new USSR; still a back-street affair in Britain) which she arranged to show, secretly and only in censored form, to an international congress on Sex Reform held in London that September, which she helped to organise. To prepare for this congress – and fit in a holiday in Cornwall first – she returned to England in mid-August, leaving Griffin bereft and lonely in Moscow to do some important writing.

The projected piece about Americans in Russia (now 'a story', no longer a book – and in any case never written) was set aside for two major articles about Russia for the American magazine *Fortune*. His struggle with these articles is a regular theme of his letters until he finally got them finished and sent off in London several weeks later. He seems to have stayed in Moscow until late in September and then made his way, via Paris, to a reunion with Dora in London in early October. The exact chronology is hard to establish – most of the letters are only dated 'Monday', 'Thursday', and so on. Letters between them took only a few days, even at a time when Russia was still largely isolated.

Their recent quarrels echo through the letters. Without Dora's side of the correspondence, except for a few quoted phrases flung back at her, it's hard to know what the conflict was about. There seems to be a battle of wills going on: Dora accusing him of trying to 'control' her, Griffin denying it. She was also feeling 'put upon' by Bertie. This is the Dora we all knew: fiercely independent, battling with any man trying to exert proprietary rights over her. So long as she felt secure, she was fearless and domineering; later, when she felt alone and vulnerable, she would cast about in vain for 'someone to look after her'.

Without Dora to share his experiences, Griffin moped. Added to his mental

---

[2] *Ibid, p.211.*

torment over his writing, he had caught the 'dysentery' she had suffered while there:

> Only now I've reached the kasha and toast stage but I'll be fit in a day or two. I've been draped over an iron pallet in a small room rented from Americans...but yesterday I tottered into a swaying droshky, curled my legs over a mound of bags and smiling rather foolishly into the mellow autumn sun (the weather's beautiful darling!) reached this haven... which is speckless and quiet and large and has a patient peasant cook that I've rented with the place until Sept. 30... where trees rustle always out the window and the air's filled alternately with calls to prayer from the dying Russian church (there are several of the great white-washed peeling objects in this quarter, pathetic as stranded elephants) and the crisp, regular songs of young Pioneers marching over the dusty cobblestones to Sunday demonstrations.

This is one of very few references to the Russian environment outside his window. It makes an interesting contrast to another description he wrote of religious life in Russia – remember that Orthodox mass in 1916 with 'half Moscow under the nave'? (See page 21.) If Griffin noticed the contrast, he doesn't remark upon it. His heart was with the marching Pioneers now.

Considering that Washington had not yet recognised the USSR, there were a surprising number of Americans around – friends 'keep turning up at the Grand Hotel', and tomorrow he's going to see 'a new town the Americans are laying out on the Volga'. We get another glimpse of Soviet economic life from some kind of official jaunt to Nizhni Novgorod –

> ...to witness the end of the [trade] Fair which has become a stern Communist-controlled commerce. We ate an endless banquet, laughed to watch the Commissar of Trade assure the Persian merchants he wasn't making a colony of them which is exactly what he's doing as far as possible with cheap goods. But the Bolshies need outside credits and it's all for the good of the cause – that cause you trip over every hour of the day here. Never was a cause so adhered to, I think.

Confining his researches to Moscow, except for the trip to Nizhni, Griffin caught no whiff of the crimes being committed in the name of 'that cause' in the Russian countryside at that time. In 1928 Stalin had ordered the 'liquidation of the kulaks' (the richer peasants), who were seen as a threat to the new egalitarian society. As their farms were collectivised into large state-run units, some five million peasants were killed or deported to Siberia. The result was a terrible famine. Soviet agriculture never recovered from these events, rightly seen today as a crime against humanity to match the Holocaust.

Griffin's ignorance of all this is not surprising: foreign correspondents saw only what the authorities wanted them to see. 'Exact information is incredibly hard to get', he complained, and he was feeling very out of place in a world 'half on Mars and half in the stable' (a phrase which could equally apply to Russia today). Nevertheless by mid-September he was making progress with his writing, and began to cheer up.

> So there's a serene spot in me, as there always is when I work. I go skulking about with no self-respect at all when I don't work, ready to quarrel with anyone, miserable inside and suspicious even of you, my beloved. Knowing there are sheets of paper behind me filled with blocs of words pumped up from anywhere near the innards of me, makes a change like magic – I always know the change is coming, and can feel it now coming after the long camel-trot of daily application... Russia gets more complex and more <u>different</u> as I penetrate it further. I feel out of it the longer I stay. But I know what I'm kept out of is warm, smelling of the stable and dung and rich human flesh, peasanty, peasanty. I'd have to climb back centuries to enter there and feel at home, and so would you...

Griffin may have felt 'out of it' in Russia, but news from America came regularly. First the bad news: his mother is in hospital with a broken leg, caused, he feels sure, by an accident in the 'amazingly infirm Ford car' in which she 'charges about Southern California'. He's not too worried about her immediate welfare, however; her rich sister living nearby and 'my prosperous Babbit brother whom I never see' will attend to it. Later he realised she must have been badly hurt, when he received a long letter from her, 'lying for 12 weeks in a plaster cast in a California hospital, able to move only above the armpits'. His affection for her shines through a long reminiscence here of this 'valiant little body' who has 'a kind of savage, go-it-alone independence' that he likens to Dora's character.

His mother's incapacity creates financial problems for Griffin, however: she won't be able to send him the $100 he had loaned her temporarily, which he now needs, so he may have to borrow £10 from Dora to get himself to Paris... No, he won't after all! (and here comes the good news from America) –

> I hear my American stock has made money and will make more and an American here has insisted on advancing me 100 roubles to be deposited in dollars in America when I get there – whenever that may be. I have $100 and no expenses but food and incidentals until Sept. 30 therefore!

This was the time when stock market speculation in America reached fever pitch: the frenzy that would end with the epic Wall Street Crash only six weeks later. A friend of Griffin's in New York was 'investing' money for them both. Griffin learned that he had made $800, 'so I feel solvent though I can't touch the money while it's increasing by bounds'. Oh you fools, you fools, take the money and run! – someone should have warned him and his deluded friend. But no one did. Like millions of others, these two were hoping to make thousands, not hundreds, so they waited... and lost it all. Griffin's later letters don't reveal all the details of the denouement. When the market crashed his friend was able to rescue some of their investment, but instead of putting it in a sock under the bed he bought more shares, assuming they would rise in value when the market 'bottomed out'. But the Wall Street index went on down, as America slid into the worst depression of its history...

None of this had yet occurred, to cloud Griffin's horizon. But unfortunately the American woman changed her mind about the other deal and wanted her roubles back. So Griffin had to borrow from other sources – including £10 cabled by Dora – to pay his way to Paris. He set off cheerfully, 'knowing I have writing worth money in my kit and a little grove of dollars growing other dollars in the American stock market'. His last commentary on his Russian adventures comes from Paris:

> I'm still sleepy from the 3 nights I sat up in the 3rd class carriage I took from Moscow to Paris from motives of economy – also curiosity about what my fellow travellers would be like. Some of 'em were Polish communists fleeing from what they said is a White Terror in Poland – a motherly middle class woman and her four young children who were jammed with me in a dirty car full of illiterate peasants going to work for the British in the Transvaal and sundry diseased-looking Jews from the Pale. I got a hacking cough and no sleep from them, and a vision of what the seething pot of central Europe is like under the tidy surface. We sang the International through the car windows at prosperous-looking Germany – forlornly, when I considered afterwards the realities.

Except for those peasants en route to South Africa (I wonder what they were going to do, in a country not lacking cheap labour), this motley group fits neatly into European history of the time. Poland, reborn as a nation in the peace settlement of 1919, had then fought a war with the USSR, winning so much territory that it became the largest state in eastern Europe (it was cut down to size again after the Second World War). At this time it was a right-wing dictatorship: hence those communist refugees. The Pale (of Settlement) was the area of Poland/western Russia where the Jews of the Tsarist empire were required to live until the Soviet government allowed them to assimilate into the Soviet Union. For generations they had been emigrating westwards, mainly to America, as perhaps Griffin's fellow-passengers were. Most of those who didn't leave would later perish at the hands of Nazi invaders. Germany, just at that moment, was both democratic *and* prosperous, but it was all about to fall apart when the effects of the Wall Street Crash hit Europe, paving the way for

Hitler. These were the last weeks of calm before more stormy weather to come.

In 1929 Griffin, like Dora, still placed some hope in the 'new world' of Soviet Russia. That's what the half-finished articles in his bag would try to convey, I guess. Crossing the Channel to England, he was wondering 'how to put the facts so they'll be understood or tolerated in an American bourgeois magazine...'. It wouldn't be easy.

In August 1929 the Russell family went on holiday to Porthcurno as usual.

Porthcurno Valley, 1929

From 1870, when the first transatlantic cable connecting mainland Britain with North America came ashore at Porthcurno, the valley was dominated by the Cable and Wireless Company. In this postcard view, almost all the buildings, except the beach café in the foreground and Sea View boarding house (upper left, with dormer windows), are part of the Cable and Wireless operation. Carn Voel is about half a mile up the hill from the café. In front of the café a path leads down to Porthcurno beach.

Porthcurno, 1929

In 1940 tunnels were blasted into the hillside behind the white building on the right, to house the vital communications work of Cable and Wireless. Otherwise, the valley remained almost unchanged until modern development began in the 1960s. Cable and Wireless continued to dominate the scene until the company closed down its Porthcurno operations in the 1990s, leaving a museum in the wartime tunnels to commemorate their pioneering work.

CHAPTER 5

A BABY BORN, A LOVE LOST

Their quarrels in Russia forgotten, Griffin and Dora had a happy reunion in London. The times they spent together were always a heady mixture of arguments and warm companionship. Quarrelsomeness was part of Griffin's nature, and at this stage it was no barrier to Dora's affection for him. Perhaps the cut-and-thrust of their discourse fulfilled a need in her that Bertie did not: in *The Tamarisk Tree* she remarks how 'amazed' she was to read years later in his autobiography that 'he had thought I did not love him because I argued with him heatedly about Russia! What sort of love is it that does not allow the lovers to disagree?'[1]

For these two, disputation was the very stuff of their relationship. So long as they debated abstract questions of politics or literature it was the pungent spice of being together, leaving no aftertaste. But arguments about their own relationship governed Griffin's life. If they had parted on bad terms he broods miserably until he knows she still loves him. An angry letter brings despair; a loving one elation. It's hard to imagine Dora losing sleep over a letter or getting up in the night to re-read one, as he did. Working away on his articles for *Fortune* – writing all night to get them on the boat train next morning – he knew he was only one element in Dora's busy and engrossing life. Their relationship was still as lop-sided as when it had begun, and perhaps had reached the point when Griffin would begin to withdraw – but for what happened next.

In September Bertie had again gone to lecture in America, leaving Dora single-handed at the school – and free to visit Griffin at Bernard Street. Before long she suspected she was pregnant. She wrote at once to Bertie in America, 'to know what he wished me to do'. To her relief and delight he advised her, by cable and follow-up letter, to do nothing. 'Since I cannot do my part, it is better

---

[1] *Dora Russell, op cit, p.233*

someone else should, as you ought to have more children'.[2]

That letter is printed in full in *The Tamarisk Tree*, proof positive that whatever recriminations followed later, Bertie had given her permission to go ahead. By her own account, they had often discussed having another baby, and 'he would not object if I were to have one by another father'. She is deliberately vague about *who* wanted another child: 'For myself, with my many activities, I was not specially anxious to embark on pregnancy, but above all I would have been glad to fulfil his need. He may, I think, have interpreted my mood at this time as a desire in general for another child, which he seemed unable to give me'.

All this is disingenuous. Surely Dora was trying to become pregnant, if only by doing nothing to prevent it. Griffin had been introduced to the idea after their holiday in France in 1928, though he had given little thought to the matter since. Comforting remarks in his letters show Dora's continuing distress at Bertie's impotence, and her jealousy of rivals with whom he could succeed. Her thoughts must often have turned to Griffin, who could give her sexual satisfaction *and* – with luck – another child. Bertie's generosity when a pregnancy did occur seemed to show her gamble had paid off.

Griffin's first response looked like the classic reaction of the philanderer: he skipped off to Paris. Dora was furious. There she was in Sussex, anxiously awaiting word from Bertie, coping with multiple crises at the school – sick children, a burst boiler, staff tantrums – while Griffin was swanning around in Paris with his pals! Hastily he assured her she was not 'deserted' – how could she think so! – what a brute he was to leave – 'If you need me <u>actually</u>, let me know and I'll come to you instantly, finding the money somehow'. No, he insists, it's just the better work prospects that brought him to Paris, and which now make it difficult to leave. He is waiting, waiting for news – from *Fortune* magazine, from *Harper's*, from a man due back from New York about a possible job in Berlin... His best hopes lie with *Fortune*, he feels, of which he's just seen a copy:

> It's a pretentious rich-looking volume of advertising for the excellence of American methods of money-making, out of which I may be able to make some money, I think quite a lot, during the next few months, without doing anything more dishonorable than reporting facts in a certain idiom. But I shan't know whether my connection is good until I get a reaction from my Russian article in about a fortnight...

Alas, when *Fortune* finally sent his $125 pay-check it came with a letter 'raising hell about the character of the Russian stuff I wrote'. That's hardly surprising: *Fortune* was a glossy journal for businessmen, who would not share

---

[2] *Ibid, p.222. Other sentences quoted here appear on the same page or p.223.*

Griffin's view of Russia no matter how hard he tried to fit their 'idiom'.

Though anxious to deny his 'café personality, which seems to dwarf anything else in me with you', he was clearly enjoying Paris, as he always did. There were plenty of his friends around: one young woman who is renting him a cheap and comfortable room, 'a spoiled astray girl about your own age from a rich American arriviste family'; another he likes better, 'a very old friend who's watching over a handsome young lover of hers at the American Hospital'; and the Slocombes, who took him on a four-day trip to Switzerland to find a suitable school for their daughter. Returning to Paris after a brief visit to London, he was disappointed to learn that 'my old friend Dos Passos with a new wife disappeared to Switzerland with Hemingway the day before I came'. But the Dudleys are there, ready to entertain him at Christmas, as they had done the previous year in America.

Weaving through the social chatter is Griffin's gnawing worry about how he's going to live up to his coming responsibilities as a father. 'This indigence of mine must end, and you can imagine the nervous strain of waiting to see if a way is opening up to make it do so.' At least he's had 'good news from Bill' which means 'the money for your confinement is safe' (hopes soon dashed, I fear: this was the money Bill had saved from the stock market crash, and then foolishly spent on more shares). But the tone of this correspondence changed once Dora had received Bertie's reassuring letter from America. Griffin made a brief sortie to London to talk things over with her – 'especially the matter of a name' – before Bertie's return. He was still worried about how she will feel 'when he comes back and you find your relation to him hurt because of this child'. But all went well. A meeting was arranged between him and Griffin, and as Dora records, 'they did not dislike each other'.

With Bertie's agreement to accept her baby into the family, Dora thought her marriage was safe, and her pregnancy could go ahead without worry. In their circle such arrangements were not unheard of – secure marriages which accommodated outside affairs, even including children; and she had Bertie's written consent to this one, hadn't she? It seems there was no discussion of a pact they had made in 1919, before they were married, agreeing to tolerate each other's lovers but also stipulating, on Bertie's side at least, that this did *not* include having children by other partners. Dora may have conveniently forgotten the arrangement, and Bertie apparently was ready to disregard it. True to his word, in due course the new baby was registered as Harriet Ruth Barry *Russell*.

Nevertheless there were warning signs at this time that Dora overlooked. As well as the brief 'instant response' letter displayed in her autobiography, Bertie wrote others from America on the subject of her pregnancy. They were all loving and supportive, and firm on two points: she should not have an abortion, and he would take full responsibility for the child. In one of them, however, written at four a.m. after sleepless hours, he reveals in the politest way the jealousy and hurt aroused by her news. 'I do not feel the slightest anger... [but] it increases the feeling that you do not belong to me; I feel aloof, though friendly. It causes a diminution of love, though not of goodwill... It is only that the instinctive tie of common parenthood is loosened.' In the morning he would decide whether to send this letter... And he did send it.[3] These misgivings, so tentatively expressed that Dora may perhaps be forgiven for discounting them, would become more insistent as the months ticked by.

After the tricky negotiation with Bertie, Griffin returned to Paris to continue his search for work. But prospects were few, he was restless again, and pining for Dora...

> So I shall return by the end of the week. Thank God. It's hell being away from you. I don't think I could stand being as far away as Paris just now, even for a short time – unless the job were <u>very</u> glittering, and would pay in money for a deadweight of misery and worry.

A later paragraph, dated 24 December, shows that all the 'misery and worry' was telling on Griffin's health:

> But do let's see each other soon and long enough to <u>get through</u>. The quarrels we always have at the beginning bow me down; I'm at this moment bending over with indigestion that hasn't left me since the last one.

It was lucky he returned to London when he did. Over New Year 1930 he became desperately ill at Bernard Street and was only narrowly rescued from death by Francis Meynell, the Russells' physician Dr Streatfield, and the surgeon who performed an emergency operation for a perforated duodenal ulcer.

Inevitably the first letter of his convalescence concerns how to pay the medical bills. It seems that both doctors agreed to cut their normal fees drastically and to wait for payment, eventually provided by Dora. Griffin would have been in worse trouble without her backing, in those days before the National Health Service.

I don't know what he used for money in the following months – in fact right up to September 1931, when he started a job in Paris. At first he stayed with a series of friends in London and the country to convalesce, and thereafter was based at Bernard Street. Perhaps his Fleet Street friends provided occasional commissions, and Dora, no doubt, regular subsidies. Griffin was an artful cadger all his life, never short of friends to help him out wherever he was.

---

3 *These quotations from Bertie's letter dated 19 November 1929 are taken from Nicholas Griffin, op. cit., pp.289–90. The 'instant response' letter was written on the 14th, others on the 17th and 24th.*

Prominent at this time were 'Trilby' Ewer of the *Daily Herald*, and his wife Monica, and the Meynells, who themselves produced a first baby that spring. Griffin wrote several times from an address in Chelsea with a housemaid and a cook, where he also entertained Dora (with meals provided by the cook). I believe this was the home of Vera Meynell's parents, only intermittently in residence. Other names flit through the pages, including his friend the American journalist Hal Hallinan, a voluntary exile in London with his wife and family. I remember meeting him in 1951, by then working for the *News Chronicle*.

Soon after his operation Griffin was staying near enough to Telegraph House to visit Dora, herself temporarily confined to bed. In between meeting for tea at her bedside they exchanged warm letters.

> It's pretty queer of me not to be able to believe you love me until I read words like these – pretty funny, I know; but not so extraordinary as that you should really think I'm muddled about whether I love you and the baby and not about what to do about that cardinal, ineradicable and fast-growing (this sentence is getting away from me) fact! For I've got to do something about it... and I don't know what to do or where to begin... I'm a fool, of course, but a worried fool. Worried because this operation ether [anaesthetic] doesn't seem to get out of my mind and leave it clear enough to form plans to give that baby as active and useful a father as it's got to have.

In this brief respite from the rat-race Griffin returned to the idea of writing 'a book', by which he meant a novel. He always regarded journalism as a rather ignoble trade, something he could do when he tried hard enough, but essentially just a meal-ticket. To prove himself 'a writer', he must write a book. He and Dora exchanged and discussed books they were reading, and these were not always literary gems, it seems:

> Mind and memories stirred by Three Blind Mice – which smells very familiarly of the bedrooms of young American girls; it stinks of 'em almost menstrually, and is very bad gushy female writing; but it manages to be a good book anyhow. All good fiction writing depends on memory, I've decided that; which means a lot of loneliness and self-plumbing. It's a trick that one may blunder thru' life without learning.

Griffin never learned that trick. By now he was beginning to realise he was not cut out for the 'loneliness and self-plumbing' it required. Nor did he ever achieve a book of non-fiction, to which I think he was better-suited, though in later life he had at least one commission from a publisher friend to do so. That friend and the many editors who employed Griffin must have had faith in his talent, which can be seen in the fluency and imagery of these letters. Why could he never manage the sustained effort to qualify by his own standards as 'a writer'?

I think he lacked the creative imagination for fiction. As a writer he was tied to *facts*; the creative talent of his generation of Barrys seems to have gone to Richard. Griffin was deeply interested in literature and the theatre, and might have made a perceptive critic of the Arts, as he himself mused in his younger days (see page 20). He certainly could have written non-fiction books – extended journalism, let's call it. So why didn't he? Dora thought he was too perfectionist, and too ambitious, citing a remark made to her by Mary Vorse: 'Griffin wants to be a *writer*; I merely *write*.'[4] Griffin's determination to 'get it right' was not reprehensible: surely most thoughtful writers go through that. And like every other writer, he was always longing for a peaceful place and no immediate money worries to do some 'serious work'; yet when he had hidden away in Provincetown one winter, he did none. Social life was a drug for Griffin: if he was living within reach of friends he could not resist their company, and when there were none around, he moped. This addiction was certainly one reason for a life of non-achievement.

His own excuse for meagre accomplishment, as explained in an early letter to Dora, was the 'lack of faith in himself' which he hoped to find through a lasting love. There's something in that, of course: everyone's work benefits from the reassurance of being loved. Looked at from this angle, Griffin's meeting with Dora in 1928 was not, as he thought at the time, the greatest good fortune of his life, but, as we can see now, the greatest tragedy. One thing she did *not* give him was faith in himself. And from that moment on, his obsession with their relationship drained away all the emotional energy he might otherwise have invested in serious writing. The effort to satisfy his yearning for her and their two children became his life's work.

The new dimension of that preoccupation opened up with my birth in the summer of 1930.

✳ ✳ ✳

For the next crucial months of this story none of Griffin's letters have survived to give him a voice. He must have written some, which Dora may have discreetly destroyed at the time, or subsequently lost. For much of the time they were together, or meeting so often that letters were unnecessary. Perhaps it's safe to assume they were affectionate and not too fractious over a period which included the birth and first year of their beloved daughter

---

[4] Dora Russell, op cit, p.240. Mary's remark implies not only lack of perseverence but a longing for the kudos of being 'a writer'. Griffin was rather bumptious in literary company at home, it seems. In her book Provincetown as a Stage *(Parnassus Press, Orleans, Ma, 1994, pp.177–8)* Leona Rust Egan says that Dos Passos 'like most people who knew him, tired of his braggadocio and crassness', while Heaton Vorse, Mary's son, recalled him as someone with 'the egotism of a person of small stature'. Dos Passos's remark is unsourced and probably comes from one of the books of reminiscences by 'Provincetown people' that figure largely in this author's bibliography (see my Bibliographical Notes). True, there was a kind of boastfulness in the old man I knew, who had so little to boast about.

Harriet. At any rate we'll have to rely on Dora's account for the sequence of events, drawing on other sources as need be.

Dora's pregnancy allowed her to be absent from the school for the summer term, so she went to Cornwall. Griffin joined her there for a short holiday before my birth, expected in early July. Their happy anticipation of that event was overshadowed for Dora by the death of her father in June. As a child and young woman, the favourite of his children, she had always had a strong relationship with this very upright man, a senior civil servant in the Admiralty. In 1917 he had taken her as his assistant on a dangerous mission to the United States – dangerous because of U-boat activity – to negotiate oil supplies for the British Navy at war. For this service to the Empire Frederick Black was knighted, and Dora awarded the MBE. A more significant virtue of Frederick Black for our family, however, was his unusual belief that daughters deserved as good an education as boys. All three daughters went to university, Mary and Dora to Cambridge, as did their brother Fred, and the youngest, Bindy, to London University.

Dora was too close to her confinement to attend her father's funeral. I was born at 38 Bernard Street on 8 July, a truly happy event for both my parents. I have a document which eloquently testifies to their delight, presented to me by Dora not long before her death. Until that moment I was unaware she had kept a Baby Book in which she recorded every detail of my arrival in this world, from conception through her pregnancy and each stage of labour to my birth, 'on July 8th 1930 at 5.50 a.m. after a dry, but not difficult labour of four hours and thirty-five minutes'. There follows a daily chronicle of the first nine months of my life – rather preoccupied with bowel movements, of course, but including such endearing details as a list of my first Christmas presents and my outfit for that occasion: 'a pink silk frock and pink silk socks, blue sash, and silk coat, blue silk slippers', and to top it all, 'a round baby's Chinese cap, scarlet, embroidered, with a bell on top'. I've never been so well-dressed since.

Griffin seldom appears in the written record, but many photographs show him as a doting dad, starting with the two of them in a London park just before my birth, through the rest of that summer in Cornwall and on through the next summer, in France. Also crushed between the pages of the book are childhood photographs of him, and a lock of his golden curls shorn at the age of two – still blond and lustrous after more than 100 years in their tissue paper! – and the crumbling fragments of roses sent to 'my rosebud granddaughter' from the California garden of my namesake Harriet Barry. 'Will she accept them this way until she may come herself and gather fresh ones?' (Alas, the two Harriet Barrys were never to meet.)

Another item in the Baby Book, inscribed therein by Dora, is a poem by Griffin's friend Anna Wickham, heralding my arrival:

> Poem for Harriet written by Anna Wickham, who
> visited her at about 2 weeks, &, like a Fairy Godmother,
> brought 3 pairs of socks. 1 white for the woman, 1 red
> for the revolutionary, & 1 variegated in stripes for the artist.
>
> This girl with three good names
> Will be three lovely things.
> The fear and the delight
> Of common men and kings.
> A woman — an artist — a revolutionist
> These exist
> For the first time harmonious
> In one small breast
> Concord shall take the part
> Of Time, to build this heart
> And Justice do the rest.

Anna Wickham, my
Fairy Godmother

This dedication to his daughter, which I have signally failed to live up to, may have been Anna's last appearance in Griffin's life. I have found no further reference to her in his correspondence.

The photographs of Dora and Griffin with me on the steps of 38 Bernard Street, of which she kept many copies, are a familiar image from my childhood. I must have been shown them many times, perhaps to prove I had a real Daddy at times when he wasn't around. I imagine they were just setting out for Cornwall, where Griffin planned to spend a day or two before going to Paris in pursuit of work.

Already installed there were Bertie, John and Kate, and a student from Oxford, Margery Spence (always known as Peter), who had come to look after them as a summer job. Colette O'Niel, a pre-Dora lover of Bertie's, and still his intimate friend and confidant, had recently been there for a visit. In Dora's account, her arrival with Griffin and the baby was the dramatic moment when 'Bertie administered the shock of telling me that he had now transferred his affections to Peter Spence'.[5]

---

[5] Dora Russell, op cit, p.226. The events of that holiday are recounted on pp.226–8.

A BABY BORN, A LOVE LOST

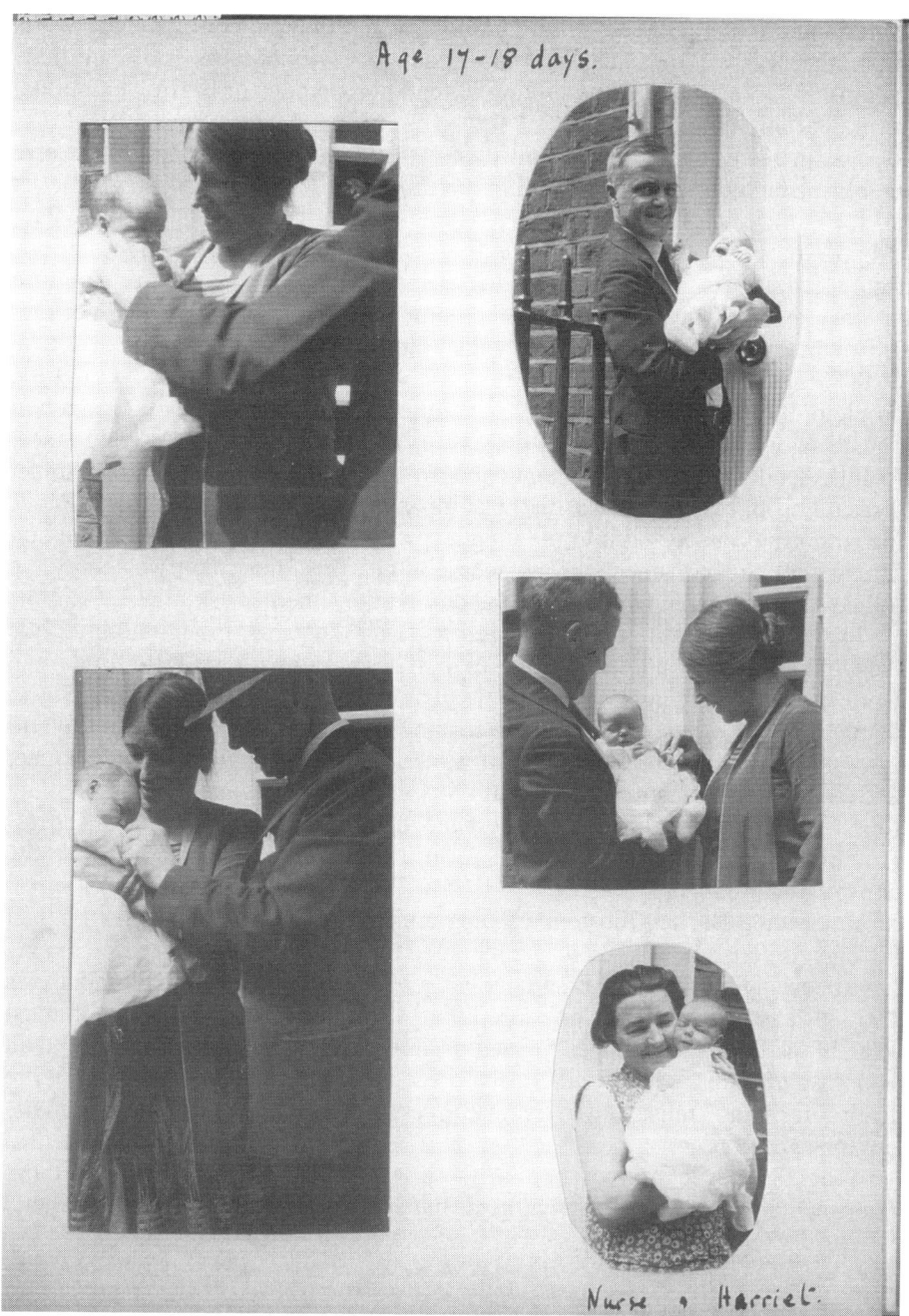

Age 17-18 days.

Nurse & Harriet.

A page from my Baby Book

Other sources suggest a different chronology, but they do confirm that by this time, the Russell marriage was on a slippery slope towards its ultimate collapse.[6] Dora as yet had no inkling of that, nor any idea of Bertie's emotional turmoil at this time.

Griffin's stay in Cornwall, and then in England, was extended by bizarre events recounted in amusing detail in *The Tamarisk Tree*. Early in August he set off for France, via Plymouth, where he intended to look up a new friend, Paul Gillard, whom he and Dora had recently seen in London. Paul was a mysterious figure – mystery of his own making, it seems – who will play a larger part later in this story than he does here, as the companion with whom Griffin got into difficulties in Plymouth. Alerted by telegram that Griffin was under arrest on £1,000 bail, Dora packed me into the family car and rushed off to sort out the problem. It turned out that during his months of illness Griffin had forgotten to register as an alien, which was picked up as he tried to embark for France. Noting that he had been 'popping to and fro' across the Channel, and had Soviet visas on his passport, and was in the company of a 'known Communist' (Paul), the authorities suspected him of being a spy. At least that's Dora's version; and it may well be true, since various people in Griffin's diary, confiscated by the police, were visited and questioned about his movements.

There was a certain amount of 'red fever' at that time, though nothing like the Cold War hysteria later. Writing in the 1970s, and with her taste for drama, Dora probably exaggerated the political implications of the incident. So no doubt did Paul, when she brought him, as well as Griffin, back to Carn Voel to discuss the 'serious consequences' of what had happened. He relished intrigue, and as Dora remembered, 'caused a moment of embarrassment when, looking round the table, he said with a sly glance at Bertie: "I wonder what Inspector Hutchings [of Plymouth police] would think of this meeting of the conspirators."

Ray Monk, Bertie's most recent biographer, after a closer investigation than anyone else has undertaken, has concluded that Paul was a fantasist, who may have been spying for the Communist Party on Fascists he knew in Plymouth (as Dora always believed) – or possibly for British intelligence on his Communist friends (as Monk speculates) – or possibly for no one. Hanging around in Bloomsbury pubs, where Griffin first came across him, he had admired Bertie from afar, and must have enjoyed meeting him in such melodramatic circumstances.

What did Bertie think of all this? Dora says little about his reaction to these unexpected guests in his household, or the events that had brought them there.

---

[6] *Nicholas Griffin (op cit, pp.295–6) points to Bertie's claim that although he became friendly with Peter during that summer, they did not become lovers until six months later. He also notes that Colette O'Niel, in a letter to her mother written from Carn Voel, 'gives no hint that there was anything between [Peter] and Bertie'. But Colette thought Bertie's marriage was finished – see ahead.*

From this time onwards (in fact even earlier), she totally mis-read his behaviour, and did not fully understand it even when she wrote *The Tamarisk Tree*. By then she had read his autobiography, and realised that his offer to accept another man's baby into his family had distressed him much more than he revealed to her. She put this down to his 'courtly behaviour towards his wife which disdained marital bickering'. That's putting it mildly. Bertie's 'courtly behaviour' was in fact a masterly disguise of his seething inner feelings. From the moment he knew about Dora's pregnancy he had been trying to act 'decently' in the light of his own declared philosophy, and had resolved to treat the new child as his own, without favouritism towards John and Kate. But try as he would, he couldn't manage it. As he wrote later, 'the resulting strain of daily and hourly insincerity was intolerable, and made family life a torture'.[7] For him, the holiday at Carn Voel was the beginning of that unendurable strain.

This may explain why Colette O'Niel, writing to her mother from Carn Voel before Dora arrived, had said that Bertie's marriage was 'in shreds, *kaput*', and predicted divorce; a conclusion presumably derived from her own conversations with him.[8] No doubt he managed some courtly behaviour to greet our arrival from London, but a letter he wrote to Colette just after Griffin had left for Plymouth shows his confused emotional state at that moment. And then came that absurd escapade, and two very unwelcome guests for the rest of the holiday.

Bertie instantly loathed Paul Gillard, described as 'a drunken homosexual spy' in his Private Memoirs[9], where he added his own speculations on what kind of espionage he may have been engaged in. His own task in Cornwall, as he recalled, was to keep John and Kate from feeling abandoned by their mother. Usually he and Peter would take them to the beach until tea-time, when Dora would bath the baby, with Griffin looking on. 'But on other days Barry and the spy would disappear for a pub-crawl and come back late for dinner to meet black looks from Dora who was jealous of each on account of the other.'[10]

All this shows how Bertie was *actually* feeling – at least as he later remembered it – at a time when Dora still believed their relations were harmonious. Picture the scene through his eyes – his wife neglecting their own children for her cuckoo baby, the baby's father lounging around with this detestable stranger, and no one to whom he could unburden his own resentful feelings.

---

[7] *From the first draft of Bertie's* Autobiography, *quoted by Ray Monk,* Bertrand Russell (1921–1970): The Ghost of Madness *(Jonathan Cape, London, 2000), p.120.*

[8] *Quoted by Nicholas Griffin, op. cit., p.295*

[9] *Kate has let me see the typescript of this unpublished document, of which she has a copy. It was written in 1953, after Bertie had met and married his fourth wife Edith, 'to explain why my relations with women that I have been fond of were until the last unsatisfactory'.*

[10] *The full significance of this last remark will be apparent later, when Paul re-enters the story.*

A MAN OF SMALL IMPORTANCE

The happy photographs of John and Kate with their new sister on the porch at Carn Voel give no hint of the tension that must have filled the house.

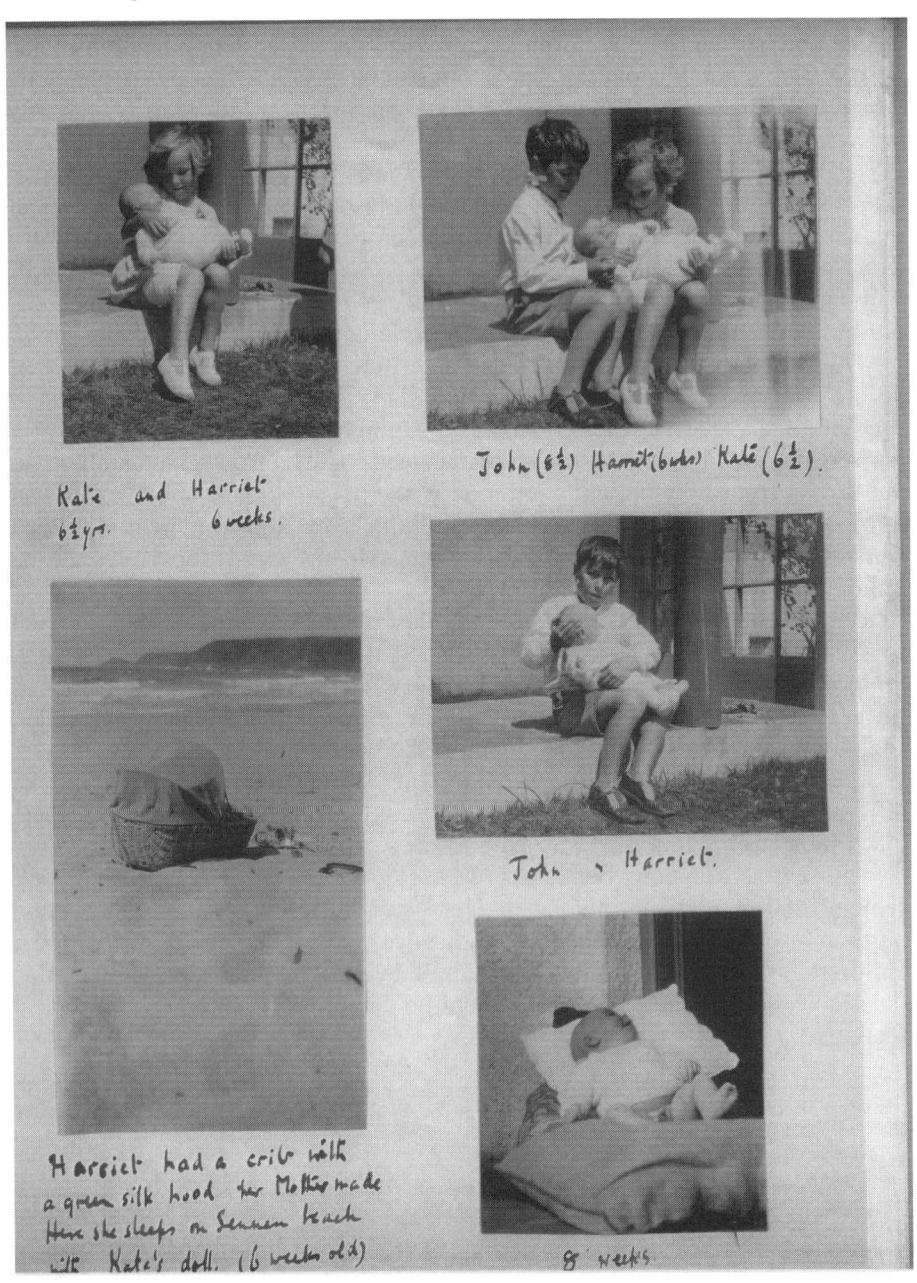

Kate and Harriet
6½ yrs.   6 weeks.

John (8½) Harriet (baby) Kate (6½).

John & Harriet.

Harriet had a crib with a green silk hood that Mother made. Here she sleeps on Sennen beach with Kate's doll. (6 weeks old)

8 weeks.

Griffin and me at Telegraph House, October 1930

Griffin did not dare to leave England just yet. Press reports of his arrest had described him as an 'undesirable alien', which might have made it difficult for him to return. He spent the following winter in London, a year of 'stagnation' for him, according to later letters. I have no idea how he earned enough to live on. The flat at Bernard Street had now been given up, so he rented a room in a friend's flat at 50 Russell Square. This was also a base in town for Dora, kept on for that purpose when Griffin wasn't there. Photographs show he also visited Telegraph House, probably while Bertie was away (he had another lecture tour that autumn). Meanwhile Peter Spence had returned to her studies at Oxford, but she and Bertie continued to meet away from the school.

Dora's reflections on her personal life at this time are entirely concerned with the disintegration of her relationship with Bertie. In retrospect she thought that if they had both severed connections with their respective lovers, their own partnership might have survived. In fact that chance had been lost in 1927, before her relationship with Griffin developed. Since then the marriage had been kept intact by a mask of deception, which Bertie would continue to maintain for some time yet, despite his inner unhappiness. Dora, blissfully unaware of his true feelings, nonchalantly continued her liaison with Griffin. It seemed she could have her cake and eat it too.

Meanwhile she and Bertie continued to run the school together, and were active in political events of the time. Outwardly, the Russell partnership flourished. As the summer holiday of 1931 approached, Bertie suggested to Dora that instead of going to Cornwall as usual they should take a house in France for a 'communal' holiday to include Peter and Griffin. So they rented a villa at Hendaye, a border town adjoining the Basque region of northern Spain, where this odd 'family' of four adults and three children – me with my cot and

The holiday at Hendaye: another page from the Baby Book, lovingly assembled by Dora. Kate recalls that Griffin's striped shorts were considered immodest by the municipal authorities; he was asked to wear a full bathing suit (see next page).

play-pen transported from England – spent two apparently congenial months. Once again there were undercurrents of tension and jealousy during those weeks, but in *The Tamarisk Tree* Dora writes lyrically of this holiday, as she always spoke of it. It must have lingered in her memory as the last peaceful period when, despite the curious set-up, she still felt her partnership with Bertie was secure.

From Dora's account of the holiday it seems the two couples amused themselves separately, apart from meals and joint expeditions to the beach, while John and Kate moved between them. Émilie the housekeeper became so enamoured of 'petite Harriette' that she wrote me a poem in a letter to Dora months later (also preserved in my Baby Book). Despite Émilie's help, however, some tart remarks of Dora's show her irritation when friends of Griffin's turned up, 'as almost invariably happened with him', and he would go off to socialise, leaving her with the baby. I can just imagine it – delightful Dad in the sunny afternoon, bachelor gay after sunset. But Dora's attitude was equally contradictory: she resented Griffin's display of non-commitment, but 'I did not expect anything different. He was not being asked, or even permitted, to establish a family relation with me; [and] I was quite sure that this responsibility was the last thing which he really desired.'[11]

The woman on the left is Edna Millay's younger sister Kathleen

The figure in the centre, to the left of Bertie, is Peter Spence. Griffin is now suitably attired.

✶ ✶ ✶

Griffin left Hendaye ahead of the others, to take up a job in Paris. A week later Dora passed through, taking me back to Sussex, and then returned to spend a few days with him there. It seems she did not tell him at once of her suspicion that she was pregnant again, confirmed early in October when she visited her gynaecologist in London. Once again the first question in her mind was whether or not to go ahead with this baby...

---
[11] *Dora Russell, op. cit., p.237.*

CHAPTER 6

TWO LOOKS LIKE CARELESSNESS

I always understood, as I grew up, that the reason Bertie wanted a divorce was not due to my birth, since he was willing to accept me as a member of the family, but the arrival of Roddy. I saw him as a kind of Lady Bracknell, haughtily admonishing Dora: 'To have *one* illegitimate baby is unfortunate; to have *two* looks like carelessness.' In fact, as we have seen, by the time I was born he was already regretting his generosity, and the seeds of his estrangement from Dora were sown even earlier. As it happens there was an extra objection to Roddy being born a Russell which didn't apply to me. On the recent death of Bertie's older brother Frank, who died childless, Bertie had become the third Earl Russell; and Roddy, as a male heir, would have been in line to inherit the title. Despite his progressive thinking, Bertie's aristocratic lineage was important to him, and he would not have wanted Roddy registered in his name.

Nevertheless his attitude towards Dora's new pregnancy was at first quite accommodating. It's not clear whether this was still a façade of 'courtly behaviour', or due to genuine emotional confusion on his part. Relations between Dora, Peter and himself were very complicated in the months up to Roddy's birth in March 1932. Against Bertie's wishes, Peter had also become pregnant at Hendaye, but later miscarried (or possibly had an abortion at his request). He was unsure how long their relationship would last – or *should* last, since he was 40 years older than Peter – and seems to have made a sincere effort to mend his relations with Dora, judging by several letters pledging fidelity to their marriage. She continued to receive his loving letters – and Bertie remained doubtful about Peter as a new partner – almost to the moment of the breach. The weeks leading up to it are well-documented by their letters as Bertie was away in America until after Christmas, and in January Dora joined Griffin in Majorca for six weeks' holiday before her confinement.

I'm trying to avoid the details of Russell affairs, already thoroughly examined by other writers, but we need to know this much to understand Dora's feeling of betrayal when that breach came. Her account of this painful time is a plaintive and still-regretful dissection of 'what might have been'. If she had aborted her new pregnancy – if she had not gone away with Griffin before the birth – would Bertie have stuck to her? Such speculation was pointless from the moment he left her, in fact, but for a long time Dora could not relinquish her hopes of reversing his decision. This is the backdrop to what emerges from Griffin's many, many letters in the coming months, and the years of separation afterwards. Dora's later bitterness towards him was not only for what he did or didn't do, but because he was entangled in events which destroyed her happiness. A very human reaction.

Griffin's story is now again firmly anchored to his letters, which came thick and fast from the moment he left Hendaye early in September. His new job with Paramount studios was not in the bag until he arrived in Paris. A deal was negotiated through a friend, Howard Young, who also worked there, but the new boss offered less money than Griffin was hoping for, and there was no guarantee of permanence. After a probationary two months the vagaries of the movie business, and the constant wheeler-dealing in this outpost of Hollywood, would decide Griffin's future in his new line of work. Every second letter relays to Dora the latest word on the grapevine as to how long the job may continue...

At first he was very nervous about every aspect of this publicity work, starting with the '3 hours daily from Montparnasse by metro, tram and interminable suburban train' to reach the Paramount lot at Joinville (later he moved out there). After a few days, however, having 'asserted his authority' to grab a desk and a room to work in, things are looking up:

> I'm learning the capacities of my 6 or 7 assistants and was visited yesterday by two of the chiefs, themselves fighting each other for authority and striving each to attach me to his department and follow his plume in the mêlée of jealousies... For some weeks to come it will be like living with a crowd of prima donnas shoved into a packing case together.

You can sense his disgust with the money-grubbing world in which he now found himself ('the spiritual atmosphere here is like the jungle; or rather there isn't any!'); and the disdain of a man of letters for 'people who live in senseless luxury like the Youngs, half out of fear that they may fall into the other class by a wrong turn of the wheel'. It's a pity the letters give only a few glimpses of the 'mêlée' of Paramount studios, for Griffin conveys it well. The correspondence soon became dominated by anguished quarrelling, which I'll come to presently, but when that furore had eased he turned again to contemplate his surroundings. In a letter written just before he left the job we see the odd assortment of people working for Hollywood-in-Europe:

> This is the noon hour and my Turkish secretary, who is a damn bad secretary, an intriguer and stinks of attar of roses, has set going a gramophone in the anteroom playing swooning tangoes. Nobody apparently knows I'm going yet and the Levantine part of the staff, who I think may have had something to do with my sacking for there are spies in every office who connect with an influential Levantine in the high direction, still seek naively to placate my brutal Nordic demand for efficiency by gifts of perfume and sidelong smiles. They're childish and crooked and rather likeable, these Levantines. Fortunately my chief asst. is a very honest and capable Frenchman (who'll now take my place) with whom it's been a pleasure to work. True to my American snobbishness and my American training as to what's a good story I suggested to him the other day that he tell the Paris press how many titles there are hereabouts – there are a good many, camera men, actors and whatnot... Days later I happened to see his birth certificate on which was written his own Breton titles – count, marquis etc. He smiled sheepishly and said that was why he was 'tres democrat' about writing such stories. Agreed with me (and Bertie, as I remember) that a few heads will have to be cut off before a marquis won't write 'em, though. I told him how the Russells had anticipated the English guillotine.

That last sentence may be a reference to the great Reform Act of 1832, steered through Parliament by Bertie's grandfather Lord John Russell (one of the family's notable contributions to English history). And it wasn't Levantine intrigue that lost Griffin his job: it seems there was a general cutting-back at the Paris studios. For a while he hoped for a niche at Paramount's English outpost at Elstree, but nothing came of it.

Back in September he and Dora had had a few days of conjugal life together. Griffin went to work each day while Dora amused herself, as she was well able to do in Paris, a city she loved. Griffin bought her two dresses from the Paramount wardrobe (presumably a perk for employees), and is getting them altered to fit by the seamstress there. When Dora had gone he returned to morose introspection:

> I went to bed early last night and woke up at dawn, each detail of how I have been cheated in life...clearly in my head. Never have I felt so in a trap and consequently with so little love for anybody... I think it is largely my own fault for not having made greater efforts and steered my ship straighter. But it would all have been easier if you had <u>naturally</u> been the friend of the things in myself I most care about. I was the friend of that in you – hence the pleasure of your having a second living husband and hence Harriet, in whom I have so tenuous a share.

This passage is the beginning of a sombre theme of the next few months: his sense of being merely 'useful' to her, not loved for himself, and how shut out of her life – and Harriet's – he feels.

The next day (2 October) he sent a telegram: WRITING ABOUT YOUR NEWS DISREGARD MY LAST LETTER. The 'news' of course was Dora's new pregnancy, and a statement of her dilemma (or a question to him?): should she have an abortion? Many of the next thirty-three letters, until they met again in mid-November, were hasty scrawls written at the office, sometimes followed up with 'considered' replies, typed, written on Sundays, when he had time to think. His first reaction was dashed off in the midst of his 'most hectic day yet' at the job:

> My head is still turning, but mostly with your news and nothing here. I'd <u>love</u> that new infant – gosh, I would! – but I don't see how we can have it, what with lack of money and your family complications. But how I do hate the idea of your having it taken out... How I'd love you to go through with it, if only I were living with you, as I can't. Probably never. It's not so hard on you, our living apart, because you've got your children and are near your racial roots. But it tears <u>me</u>, destroys <u>me</u>. Hence that –

At this point he was interrupted. Resuming later in the day, he completed his apology for 'that fierce letter I wrote you the other day', and returned to his theme:

> Honestly darling I don't believe another child is going to be worth it <u>from my point of view</u> unless we can somehow arrange to live together. I'm going to be an unhappy, drifting middle-aged man pretty soon... I don't mean live together immediately, but next year – yes! After the spring term... I'll have some savings then. Do talk to Bertie about it... I'm only afraid that if I must live this way I shall end by having a grudge against you and be unbearably torn about my children... I suppose Bertie will want to do his best for you and be decent to me but will end by using all his power to keep the framework of his own family together. You – I suppose you'll sacrifice me to B's family and have the child too, for I don't quite see you giving up a 4-months old baby, even though started by mistake...
>
> ...The money question is going to press hard on us if you have the baby; I foresee you not only using up more of your capital but my having to give up the liberty I'd get by my savings from this job if kept till spring or summer – the liberty and hope and happiness without which I can't get out of my forlorn and ignoble way of life.

Some parts of this rambling letter led Dora to accuse him of not wanting the child (which he later denied), but his basic position is clear: if we're going to have this baby, I want us to live together. In the end, however, he had no choice but to accept Dora's terms: she's going to have the baby, and she's staying with Bertie.

It's easy to sympathise with Griffin's feeling that he was just a stud to produce her babies (though he would not have put it so crudely) – but what kind of life did he offer Dora, compared to what she already had? However, she was asking a lot of both her husband and her lover. Was she perhaps following her own agenda, regardless of both their interests?

This pregnancy must have started in early July.[1] Granted it couldn't be confirmed until Dora got home (no easy chemical tests in those days), she must have suspected her condition much earlier. Why did she wait so long before telling Griffin? Presumably Bertie had already been consulted, but not before it was getting late to have an abortion without risk. Abortion was illegal, though everyone knew it could be arranged for people who could pay; but would any doctor have consented to do it at that stage, without good medical reasons? And why on earth did Dora and Griffin use no contraception? All this makes me wonder whether Roddy's birth was truly 'carelessness', or Dora's sly gift of a sibling for me.

In the ensuing cross-Channel quarrel Griffin fought his corner doggedly, sometimes in bitter, despairing letters that are painful to read.

> As I wrote before, I wouldn't have had you stop the child; you would never have forgiven me and I should never have forgiven myself and I shall love it dearly when it comes. My love and ties to you are unbreakable and now very much increased, for a family is different from one little being, and I am the sort of man who wants a family as you must have seen from the beginning. But I can only get at my family by sitting all my life at the Russell gates, metaphorically and actually, and though I have done it for two years I can't do it always... Your reply to all this in your late letters, aside from the expressions of love with which the rest ill accords, is to protest against being bothered at this moment with the 'inconveniences' of my life...and a rather haughty and summary dismissal (very much as if I had begged too long at the Russell gates) of my hope (not put practically for I can see no way to achieve it) that we might make fist to bring up our two children together somehow. Also a letter full of shock at my 'possessiveness' to which the word 'jealousy' will be added now that I have written the above.

This is pitiable stuff, not only for 'sitting at Russell gates' (which is just what happened to Griffin, though it wouldn't be *Russell* gates for much longer) but because he's so painfully aware he has nothing to bargain with. He feels manipulated by Dora in a way that emasculates him:

---

[1] *Roddy was born on 23 March – 'prematurely', Dora always said, but presumably not more than two weeks before term, as she was already in London awaiting the birth, and there were no problems arising from low birthweight etc. If Roddy was born in the 38th week of a normal 40-week pregnancy, he must have been conceived in early July.*

> The core of my bitterness is this: that you will and do and always have attempted to <u>sell</u> me a situation that works to your own ultimate (and present) advantage and to my own ultimate (and present) disadvantage. I had never thought to be bargained with in these matters, nor to bargain, and to be forced to simply kills something profound in me. It takes away something male in me (I suppose it's male) that I always unconsciously had before I met you and worked with in life, and now, being in the way of losing, am far, far the lesser man.

Later in this tortured letter the tone becomes less belligerent, but still despairing:

> I can think of no way out that won't cripple somebody in an unprotected place and of course I feel my own problem keenest because I live with it. I'd trust you instead of curse you if you didn't always oversell your own noble motives and undersell everybody else's... you really do lack almost entirely imagination about other people's interests unless they coincide with your own.

Oh yes, that sounds like the Dora I remember – especially the bit about her noble motives – and also the embittered Griffin I came to know later. These letters remind me why I resisted so long delving into this correspondence. Even 50 years after Griffin's death and 15 since Dora's, I want to run out of the room and slam the door. Recovering my balance, however, I must record that these vituperative paragraphs were balanced by many warm and loving ones; and I'm sure the same was true of Dora's answering letters that I haven't seen. Both of them loved an argument, and they did not hold grudges: they were just the kind of people who could curse each other one minute and hug each other the next. But it was uncomfortable for me, later in this saga, to be physically quarrelled over, especially as by then there were no more hugs.

In other letters Griffin gave vent to his anti-feminism, especially when discussing his future 'rights' over his children. In one instance Dora's 'man-hatred' has been crossed out for a clumsy substitute phrase: her 'hatred of the male in men which women who really *love* men do not have'. No euphemism was needed, in my view. Dora *was* guilty of man-hatred at times; and here Griffin was pleading for a 'father's right' to his children in the same way that separated fathers do today, when the law still favours the prior claim of the mother (for good practical reasons).

It seems Dora was consulting Bertie's lawyer about Griffin's rights of access to these children who would be nominally Russells. No details of what the lawyer said are given, except that Dora thought it was fair to Griffin and he didn't. She did not wish to deny him access (nor did she, in the years to come); but she feared that if his rights were legally enshrined, he might whisk us off to America at some future date. These are the seeds of Dora's anger later when her divorce was in the hands of lawyers and she felt that *her* family of *four* children was being torn apart by Bertie and Griffin both asserting their 'father's rights'.[2]

There is one example here of 'sexism' in Griffin's nature which makes a modern feminist bristle. One of his friends, a pretty and evidently rather promiscuous young woman, he described as a 'female pirate', 'having a good record of seduction'. That's a bit cheeky, considering his own record of seduction. Typical male double standards, of course, but we might have expected better of a bohemian like Griffin.[3] He had come from a conventional background, and often lapsed into the parlance of other WASP[4] Americans, indeed of WASP Europeans too, at that time – for example by categorising friends as 'a Jew' or 'Jewess', or those 'Levantines' he worked with at Paramount – in a way which grates today. Ethnic consciousness had not yet arrived to inhibit such expressions, which sound racist to us.

The letters were not all doom and gloom. Wedged between the arguments, other events of his life are regularly relayed to Dora. He had decided to buy an overcoat with the first surplus from his wage-packet. (I bet that's the one he was wearing in the photograph most familiar from my childhood, taken on board ship on his voyage home in October 1932 – see page 107.) Not only his new coat but Dora's two dresses from the Paramount wardrobe were frequently mentioned – when they'd be ready, and how to get them over to her. To avoid customs duty, they couldn't be sent by post; so one was taken in the luggage of a friend, the second worn across the Channel by another friend. 'You can wear [them] for weeks yet and they'll still be good after our boy comes.' (They were both certain Roddy was going to be a boy.)

As well as these and other friends who trooped down to Sussex to see Dora, Mary Vorse arrived in England to report for *Harper's* magazine on the general election of 1931. This was a pivotal moment in British politics, when Ramsay MacDonald, Prime Minister of the second short-lived Labour government, 'betrayed his party' by forming a National government (a coalition with other parties), which then won the election, sending the rump of the Labour Party into the wilderness until 1945. Dora campaigned vigorously on the losing side, even

---

[2] *Dora discussed her worries about Griffin's paternal rights with Bertie by letter. He quite reasonably pointed out that 'if Griffin is going to have the children legally his, he must meet the financial responsibility'. For himself, he would have been glad 'to let everything go on as it was' (letter dated 29 November 1931, in Nicholas Griffin, op. cit., pp.305–6). It is not clear whether they ever specifically discussed the question of Roddy's registration; but as things turned out, no discussion was needed.*

[3] *Dora met and liked this 'female pirate', and ticked him off for his snide remarks about her. Yes, he admitted, 'I'm more moral about female pirates than male though I don't exactly support either. You've made your point there; it's class solidarity on my part.'*

[4] *The term WASP – White Anglo-Saxon Protestant, the majority population of the United States – denotes their origins in northern, Protestant Europe. Although there was great hostility to Irish Catholic immigrants who began to arrive much earlier, it was the turn-of-the-century 'floods' of Russian Jews fleeing persecution, and Italians fleeing poverty, that led to restrictive laws in the 1920s, ending for ever America's traditional 'open door' immigration policy.*

travelling up to Glasgow, which worried Griffin; but she lived politics as keenly as her personal life, and wouldn't miss the fight for a small thing like pregnancy.

Griffin was keen to engineer a meeting between Dora and his old friend Mary, knowing they'd like each other. But even this caused a spat with Dora: he wanted Mary to sub-let 'their' room at 50 Russell Square, which Dora resented, perhaps because he had written her in 1928 that he'd once been in love with Mary. Eventually they did meet, however, and did like each other. It was probably Mary who arranged Griffin's next assignment of paid work when the job at Paramount ended.

All the recurrent themes of Griffin's relentless pursuit of Dora are in his letters of this period: his desperate loneliness, his longing for a family, his humiliation at having nothing to offer her (and his children) due to his perpetual poverty. With hindsight I could cease my exploration of their relationship with the letters of 1931, knowing as I do that all the events yet to come would not change that basic situation. But at the time he still hoped to win her over in the end – or at least to be granted a part-time share in her life. He felt she did not care about or begin to understand his real character – 'the things I prize in myself' – but she would, oh yes she would, if only they could live together long enough to *know* each other.

By early November such an opportunity was on the horizon. Griffin had heard his job would end on the 15th, but he didn't seem too stricken, not having enjoyed the work very much. However, he'd have only £15 or £20 saved by the time his salary ceased. Dora had promised to spend the last month or two of her pregnancy in Paris with him, but he now has a better (and cheaper) plan – that they should join a group of American friends in Majorca, where they can live on '5 shillings a day or less'.

These wandering Americans in Europe were always looking for the cheapest place to settle down and write or paint or whatever. At that time, it seems, Majorca was the favoured spot. Griffin's spirits soared to think of their being 'quite together for a bit'. In Majorca he'll get on with that Writing that he hopes will 'earn my way out of this necessity for wage slavery'. With Dora at his side, 'my heart welded to your own', he'll be able to work there as he never has before, 'really to establish a connection between this well of talent I've always supposed was in me and the market'.

Mary Vorse would know about prospects in the American market, and Griffin was eager to see her. Finding he could get to Majorca by sea from England just as cheaply as by rail and boat from Paris, and thereby see Mary in London, he booked a cross-Channel passage for the night of his last day at Paramount. His joyful anticipation of pleasures to come was marred only by a last-minute letter from Dora about his children's future. From Griffin's reply it seems she and Bertie had agreed, before he left for America, that Roddy would at least be known as a Russell.

From our children's point of view I'm not sure, either, that it will be good for them to realise presently that the male who seems to be attached to their mother by name and in whose family they are apparently rooted isn't their daddy...

The only other way would be for them to share, with you, my house and Bertie's freely, with of course the clear understanding as to parentage that already exists on all sides; but that can't be done until I'm 'implemented', as they say, economically. Everything hangs on that, including naturally my own spirits.

I wonder how Dora would have enjoyed being a peripatetic wife and mother between two husbands...

Majorcan interlude

Griffin spent three weeks in London before leaving for Majorca early in December. He saw Dora often and they went to parties together in London (he was glad to hear from her later that 'we're an accepted Bloomsbury romance'). He also landed a commission from an American magazine for an article on the British political scene, no doubt through Mary Vorse, engaged on a similar task herself. His progress with this work – or more often, his inability to get on with it – would be dutifully reported to Dora in the coming weeks before their reunion on the island.

The eight-day voyage, calling at Lisbon, Malaga and Gibraltar en route, was stormy and uncomfortable. Griffin described in detail a varied collection of fellow-passengers, 'Mrs Smythe's boarding house afloat', the kind of Britishers he was not used to meeting. Arriving in Majorca, he began prospecting at once for a 'home' to be ready for Dora's arrival a month later. In the meantime, to conserve every peseta, he put up at a basic but cheap hotel. We get a picture of this humble lodging from his later description of Christmas celebrations there:

> How you'd have loved it here last night. The patron gave a Christmas dance evidently a traditional affair, and the comely peasant cook led it with her helper, fat peasant stomachs touching from which had come many babies, and Manuelo the waiter followed and then the chamber maids and the patron and his wife stood everybody some of the queer local cognac and a handsome peasant arrived with his daughter and did some ceremonial dances like those we saw at Hendaye and then I danced in my best night-club manner with Madame la Patronne, a very pretty gold-toothed little being who belongs to one of the established fishing-folk families, is very shrewd and possibly a little crooked about bills but knows how to give a grand, grand party. There's a great deal of bare, wind-swept poverty here, you know, but nobody misses a fiesta. The bar below my room was filled with caterwauling all night; still going on loudly when I went to bed half drunk at three.

Loosely grafted onto the local population lived a number of transient, mostly arty foreigners, 'several score in this one-horse small town'. Among these were his close friend Genevieve Taggard, 'Jed', with her daughter, and an American couple called Neugass. Griffin soon decided they were the only ones fit for Dora's company. Jed was a poet, whose daughter later came to Beacon Hill. She helped Griffin settle in and, like all his women friends the world over, often invited him to meals.

Griffin's soul was stirred by the beauty of the island – the sea, the views, the 'apocalyptic' weather, benign and demonic by turns. He's sure Dora will love it too. With a new confidence in their relationship, he couldn't wait for her to join him in this enchanted place:

> I am so glad when I feel our love is anchored and stable. I go off alone to think about you; avoid people and (which is bad) avoid work to do that. When I am in England dwelling among your non-me interests I am not so happy and punish you accordingly... I think it will vanish presently when I am better established and when we, as <u>we</u>, are better established. I am wild with delight at the prospect of your coming here where we can be alone; in primitive surroundings, too, which suggest what's primitive in us; they're the best things in us, which so many poor devils have lost.

Griffin's visits to Telegraph House had not been unalloyed joy. Although he loved 'the hill' and the Sussex countryside, he had clearly felt ill at ease in Bertie's household, and uncomfortably inferior to Bertie and Dora. He felt he must achieve something worthy of respect before he could face them again on their home ground. As he put it, rather pathetically, '[W]hen Joe grows as big as Rover he doesn't mind visiting Rover, and can be a very nice, sweet, kind dog'. (For Rover read Bertie, of course.)

There's a strand of wild romanticism in these letters from Majorca. Poetic phrases conjure up a vision of himself and Dora curled up by an olive-wood fire, raising their eyes occasionally to survey the magnificent views. 'Stick some poetry books in your bag. Want to read poetry with you', he scrawled at the foot of a page. All the complications of their situation and the wrangling of recent months were forgotten as Griffin contemplated the two-month idyll ahead with his true love. The pages shine with his childish delight in the quest for a cottage or flat to suit her, setting out every detail for her consideration like a 10-year old 'playing house':

> One [flat] had three rooms, the other four, one has two fireplaces and the other one (we must have heat), and there are kitchens and comfortable beds and balconies. No noise except an occasional peasant's cart, and clean washed air between sea and mountains on either side. Excellent meals at the hotel a few steps away, and I'll make your coffee for you over a brazier; if we can find a good maid (unlikely) we can eat in. 100 pesetas a month each; the pound here is at 39 pesetas. Two meals at the hotel 5 pesetas each daily; no other expenses save olive-wood to burn at perhaps 20 pesetas a month more and a char at perhaps another 30.

When Dora was carrying his first child Griffin had not had a chance to be the strong protective male; instead he became ill, adding to her burdens. Now he plays the role in classic style – himself as hunter-gatherer, while Dora reclines on a couch. Everything must be ready before she comes –

> ...so you won't be bothered when you arrive and can lie still and watch the extraordinary scenery and weather and let me fend and forage – and work.

Ah yes, work! – there's the rub. He was supposed to be writing an article, we remember, and at first he mentioned it often: 'I've stuck to my work every day except when seasick' – 'I've done some real work today'. Soon the excuses began for why it's not yet finished: 'article delayed for lack of peace' – 'trying to work in my heatless room' – 'no considerable work done yet'. Meanwhile he'd run out of money and had to apply to Dora for her share of the expenses (£8 would do, £5 for two months' rent in advance and £3 to supplement what he had until she got there). Dora coughed up as usual, but apparently with exasperation, prompting hurt and defensive replies:

> My nightmarish black hour earlier today was because I haven't got this article in sooner, and the fear that I'd always be insolvent and add to your gray hairs. But that's only a nightmare darling that can be added to unnecessarily by undue fears on your part – <u>undue</u> ones. I know some fears are due, but while it's true that I've earned no money yet it is also true that little else has occupied my thoughts, that I forget the necessity never and that I really have, little as I've shown it since we've been together, an earning capacity – quite a big one, perhaps.

As though *thinking about* his need to earn money was half-way there. And next day:

> I went to bed late and woke at five to make bitter replies in my morning-clear head to such things in your letter as the injunction to cease thinking of you so much but to get my article done. I had been trying so hard to do that and been unable partly because I had been saving and planning for our home here together; staying in this unheated room because it's cheaper and waiting cannily until I can get a good place for us...

Excuses, excuses! A few days earlier, however, he had written more calmly and with some insight into his chronic inability to 'get on with it':

> I loved your little lecture...as to how to work. It was quite accurate as to what I should do – though I must really, darling, make false starts and alter and discover the best scheme after I'm half through and then rearrange. But the cardinal thing, daily application, you know so much more about than I.

He attributes Dora's good work habits to her grammar school education, 'what your old father did for you by making you take all those silly school prizes'. His own father, alas, 'appeared to think earlier that just our native brightness was enough, his children's Irish faculty for answering back. Usually it was, in the America of his day, but my wreck of a brother and partly myself reveal how inadequate it is now.'

It's hard to reconcile this self-analysis with what I now know of Griffin's family and education. His high school in Eau Claire, though small and relatively new, had a fairly academic curriculum (and as I learned, Griffin had won at least one school prize himself). It may be that the Barrys' move to California, a more 'frontier society' than Eau Claire, had unsettled him in ways we can never know. Perhaps George Barry grudged his sons 'more education than I ever had', as envious parents sometimes do – in sharp contrast to

Frederick Black, urging on (and able to fund) his prize-winning filly Dora. Maybe father and son quarrelled mightily in those formative years I know little about, from when Griffin was sixteen until he appeared as a young radical in Greenwich Village... I can only speculate.

Equally puzzling is his dismissal of 'my wreck of a brother', who by this date had found a wife and achieved worldly success beyond Griffin's wildest dreams (see Chapter 3). Nevertheless his feeling of being poorly educated compared to the 'college men' in circles he moved in at home – and even more so, in Dora's – is understandable. It undoubtedly contributed to his fretful lack of self-confidence.

Did Griffin ever finish that article? Perhaps so, with Dora at his side, for she 'worked steadily' throughout the holiday, she recorded. She enjoyed the 'small whitewashed cottage' at Fonda del Puerto that Griffin eventually settled on, but little else about her stay. She found Griffin's friends frivolous, while she herself was preoccupied with the political turmoil in Britain and her many personal problems.

Earlier, she had written in distress to Griffin when Bertie invited Peter to spend Christmas at Telegraph House (he couldn't resist pointing out that her feeling 'damped and suffocated' with Peter in the house should remind her 'how I must often have felt in Bertie's house with you'). Clearly the question of a separation was already under discussion. Understandably, Dora's first concern in the shifting sand was her own security – and a terrible fear that Bertie (or Peter) might try to take John and Kate away from her.

Griffin's heart must have been turning somersaults. Each letter from him reflects what Dora has just written. While grimly conceding her right to think first of herself – 'the security for which you fight so shrewdly and with so many defenses' – he blithely dismissed her fears about John and Kate: 'it would be unthinkable for B to be vindictive'. What he *really* wanted to discuss was their own future together: 'Myself I think a divorce and our marriage would probably be a good thing and has been foreordained, in a way, for a good time.' That was not how Dora saw it, but it seems she had not (yet) ruled Griffin out as a future unmarried partner.

Small wonder she could not relax in Majorca, with all this still to be sorted out – not to mention the coming baby. She was touched by a drawing received from 'The Pore Staff' of the school, bewailing her absence, and stowed it away in this archive. Another consolation in her brief exile were Bertie's frequent, loving letters, reporting on British politics, his management of the school, and frankly discussing their marital problems. 'He said in plain words that he did not want our marriage to break up', she wrote in *The Tamarisk Tree* (and that was true). She was expecting that a full discussion of the situation could be postponed until after her confinement.

For Dora the one bright spot in her stay was a visit to Robert Graves at Deya, a bus-ride away. Graves was already well-known, mainly for *Goodbye to All That*, about his experience of the First World War. Later he became more famous, and the chief luminary of the Anglo-American colony at Deya. In *The Tamarisk Tree* Dora records writing to him in 1965, and reprints his reply with its nostalgic postscript: 'Yes, I remember your visit with Barry, how long ago it seems.' [5]

Souvenirs of Majorca

Dora and Griffin returned to England early in March and soon went to their room in Russell Square to await Roddy's birth (this time to take place in a nursing home). Dora deserves the next few lines of the story:

> On 22 March 1932 I received a letter from Bertie in which he implied that he was now in less doubt about his relation with Peter, and wished to live with her altogether as soon as she left Oxford that summer.
> I showed Griffin the letter and said something like 'so much for loyalty'. He said, 'I think it is time that I went back to America.' I threw a teacup at him.[6]

She went into 'premature labour' and Roddy was born early next day. By the

---

[5] *Dora Russell, op. cit., p.242.*
[6] *Dora Russell, op. cit., p.243.*

time she returned to Telegraph House with the baby, Bertie had already gone to Carn Voel with Peter, who did not finish her studies at Oxford.

Dora's dramatic account of her final parting from Bertie wrongly implies that it was completely unexpected. But we can sympathise with her feeling of being deserted by both her menfolk at a moment of extreme vulnerability. It coloured her attitude towards both of them and reinforced her feminist suspicion that men in general were never to be trusted.

* * *

The next phase of the Griffin–Dora relationship (conducted almost entirely through correspondence) is set against the very bitter Russell divorce that ensued. A few facts about the proceedings, and the long-term effect of the divorce on our family, will help to explain the surges of rage and despair on Dora's side. Griffin became her punch-bag as the legal process dragged on and on, made worse for all parties by unwelcome public interest. The Russells were already notorious for their radical views, and Bertie's noble birth added piquancy to the usual prurient curiosity of the British press.

Inevitably the most wounding conflicts were about the children. With his concern about 'the succession' in his family, Bertie now accused Dora of 'false registration' of my birth in the name of Russell. That problem would only be finally sorted out years later.[7] Their wrangling was far worse over John and Kate, aged nine and seven respectively in 1932. They became Wards of Court and spent the rest of their childhood shuttling between Dora's and Bertie's households, unhappy pawns in the continuing war between their parents. The effect on their emotional balance has been graphically described by Kate.[8]

Roddy and I were luckier: we were only bit-players in the divorce, too young to feel Dora's emotional turmoil; and the later war between our own parents was, for the most part, a long-distance affair. For us, the cost of the divorce was to lose our older

On the steps of Telegraph House, 1932. There were not many photos of us all together after this one.

---

[7] *Roddy was registered as Barry from the start, but I remained legally a Russell until I changed my name by Deed Poll in 1945 – see Chapter 18. As Dora continued to use her professional name of Dora Russell, we two, as her children, were also known as Russell until 1945. In due course John and Kate acquired another half-brother, Bertie and Peter's son Conrad. He became Earl Russell on John's death in 1987, and took up his seat in the House of Lords.*

[8] *Kate's book,* My Father Bertrand Russell *(Harcourt Brace Jovanovich, New York and London, 1975), was reissued in a new edition in 1996 by the Thoemmes Press of Bristol, but unfortunately is no longer available.*

brother and sister when, as she had feared, Dora's family of four children became two pairs who met only occasionally. Happily for all of us, Dora was allowed to keep Carn Voel.

During the three-year wrangle of the divorce Griffin was out of the way in America, though not entirely by choice. English divorce law at that time was complicated and hypocritical. To provide the usual grounds of adultery, couples often faked an adulterous situation in a hotel, to be 'accidentally' discovered by a private detective. In the Russell case there was no shortage of adultery on both sides, but for tactical reasons the lawyers decided that Dora should be the petitioner against Bertie, the defendant; and this required her to live 'chastely' for two years. Dora, needing Griffin's moral support, thought this very hard, and moreover there were no restrictions on adulterous Bertie! Nevertheless by her own code of belief she could not keep him locked into a marriage he no longer wanted. Reluctantly, she agreed to the lawyers' plan. Thus on 1st October 1932, faithful chauffeur Hines drove Dora, Griffin and me to Southampton to see Griffin off to America.

Did Griffin want to go? Secretly, I'm sure, he welcomed the divorce, and may also have been glad that the chastity rule gave him an excuse to leave England (though Dora's accusation that he and Bertie had 'conspired' to force her into divorce was absurdly untrue – as she later acknowledged). He was ready to go home for other reasons too. He had always felt out of place in Dora's English life, not only as an outsider in her family but because he had never found any significant work there. Dora, on the other hand, was always busy. In the summer of 1932, with a new baby, the school to run *and* a book to finish,[9] the contrast between overstretched Dora and workless, penniless Griffin couldn't have been greater. By now he was desperate to 'make something of himself' to prove himself worthy of her, and for his own self-respect; and that could best be done in America. He didn't have to go that far away to be seen to be not co-habiting with her, but it's easy to surmise that for his own reasons he persuaded Dora it was time he returned to New York.

It was a fateful parting, however. New York was a long way off, and communication slow in those days. Justifiably or not, Dora did feel deserted, and never forgave Griffin for not being at her side when she needed him most.

---

[9] *This was* In Defence of Children, *published in November 1932.*

A MAN OF SMALL IMPORTANCE

Griffin's last summer with his family, on the lawn of Telegraph House.

Off to Southampton, October 1932

CHAPTER 7

CRUEL SEPARATION

Both sorrowing lovers wrote to each other on the evening the boat sailed, Griffin's letter mailed at Cherbourg, the last call in Europe before the ship headed out across the Atlantic. Both dwelt on the heart-tugging scene of two-year-old Harriet trying desperately to go with Daddy on the boat to ''Merika' instead of home to Telegraph House with Dora. Griffin's later letters show touchingly how much he missed his little daughter. He'd had little chance to establish a relationship with 6-month-old Roddy and enquired far less often about him, to the point where Dora would accuse him of not loving his son as he loved me. Griffin's favouritism towards me throughout our childhood became a cause of many arguments; but paradoxically in our adult life it was only with Roddy, not with me, that Griffin eventually enjoyed the satisfaction of a parenthood that in other respects brought him so much grief.

As he left England, however, despite the pain of parting, Griffin fully expected that his future lay with Dora. Something positive must have passed between them in the summer of 1932 to fill him with hope. Though Dora may have felt differently at a later date about this moment in her life, the thick file of correspondence she kept shows them both yearning to be reunited: it was just a question of how and when that could be arranged.

One stray letter from Dora in late July indicates some options they were debating.

> Harry was very sad. She wants us together some place – & says so. Really I'd rather you didn't take her off to the States... Would be so much better if you could only get fixed in Europe or come back very soon or Harry & I come over on a visit.

My guess is that he'd gone to seek work in Paris, and his lack of success there added weight to his argument that he'd have a better chance in America. He longed to get back to his 'roots' after three years away, a motive for going that

Dora seems never to have recognised. This is one thread in the gradual disintegration of their relationship in the coming months.

The letters on both sides were long and passionate. For Griffin the correspondence was the core of his emotional life, and for Dora at a troubled time, he was her only confidant. He, having the time to do so, wrote long, usually typed and worked-over screeds, while hers were usually scrawled at the end of a long, exhausting day ('Please think before you lash out!' he pleaded). But this exchange is not a calm conversation, a singles tennis match with each ball neatly returned over the net for the next response; it's more like the warm-up session: several balls being lobbed over the Atlantic in both directions at different speeds, depending on whether they caught a fast German boat or a slow British one. Some of these 'balls' would be smashed back furiously to a hurt and surprised recipient, whose angry mood to which it was responding had long since evaporated. Tired of being 'tripped up by indignities I've caused weeks before', Griffin began to identify carefully *which* of her recent letters he was answering.

Even so there was plenty of scope for misunderstanding and injured feelings. In a face-to-face lovers' quarrel the unfair jibes vanish like a puff of smoke, or are forgiven by a follow-up hug. Here they're preserved on paper, to be re-read and brooded over weeks later. So are the passionate declarations, of course. In June 1933, filing away a handful of letters, Griffin came across 'a lovely one...to take away the bitter thoughts that have choked me since the late series... With that between us, even with that having been, all can't be lost.'

But he was wrong. By that date, for a combination of reasons, Dora *had* decided against him as a future partner. Griffin, however, despite what she told him, and however matter-of-factly he wrote to her thereafter, continued to nurse a secret hope that he could win her back. This hope was only finally dispelled on a visit to England in 1935, when he found another man at Dora's side – and later found he shared her bed too.

Griffin kept her letters of these crucial years, the sequence incomplete and some with missing pages, for the rest of his life: a tattered memoir to remind himself, I suppose, in later desolate times, that Dora had once loved him. To this day I do not know how they came into her hands. Did he give them to her in the 1950s, by which time they were on distant but civil terms, or did she collect them with his other few possessions from the Hampstead bed-sit where he died? At some date they joined the archive of Griffin's letters to her, telling a longer, more nuanced story of their falling-apart than Dora's version in her autobiography.

To follow the course of it I have used mainly Griffin's letters. They are in better order than hers, and include other aspects of his life that fit my wider brief. His letters are often taken up with Dora's problems, of course, since his future depended on sorting them out. To understand all that, we need to return briefly to the situation in England, and how it seemed to Dora, when he sailed away in October 1932.

The separation was intended to be only temporary. Griffin was going home to re-establish himself in the world of New York journalism, to earn the money their situation desperately needed; and to provide two years of official 'chastity' to facilitate the divorce. For him the first purpose was the most important – for reasons which will become apparent – but for Dora, the second purpose was the *real* reason he left her to such misery and despair, and with so many problems to face alone. Although they must have agreed before he left that a Russell divorce was the only way out of this four-person tangle (certainly that was what Bertie and Peter wanted), Dora had earlier hoped – and still clung to the hope – that some informal settlement could be agreed between the four of them without resorting to the law.

She later wrote that Griffin's willingness to fall in with the lawyers' plan for the divorce had killed her love for him: 'I had wanted [him] to say that not for all the laws of the Medes and Persians would he part from me and our children, and the others could go whistle for their divorce.'[1] Some months after Griffin left she did begin to accuse him along these lines, but this grievance doesn't appear in her early letters. They are as tender and loving as his to her, occasionally touching on plans for their future together, though she could hardly see beyond the fog of her current troubles. As time went on, however, Griffin became tarred with the same brush as Bertie and Peter, for seeming to favour what *she* saw as a cowardly betrayal of the New Morality they had all professed to believe in.

With every passing week her sense of outrage grew. Underlying everything was her seething resentment that the divorce she emphatically *did not want* was inexorably going ahead. The lawyers' plan was 'abominable', not only for depriving her of Griffin's moral support but as a perfect example of the hypocrisy of the law and the outdated conventions she and other 'modern people' were trying to get away from. Under that plan, she and Bertie were to sign a 'deed of separation' by which they agreed to overlook any previous adultery by either of them, including Dora's two children by Griffin. By this device the lawyers hoped to avoid exposing all that 'misbehaviour' in open court. Dora's revulsion for this legalistic charade kept her from signing the crucial document for many months – to the exasperation of the other side.

There were also endless wrangles with Bertie and Peter over John and Kate, ranging from whether they should stay as pupils at Beacon Hill to buttons missing from their clothes when they went to stay in the new Russell household. But in dealing with that ménage Dora must try not to do or say anything that would prejudice the negotiations ahead over custody of John and

---

[1] *Dora Russell, op. cit., p.261.*

Kate. It was usual for custody to be awarded to the mother, and she expected it; but Bertie expected *joint* custody, and as the divorce approached he took extreme measures to ensure that outcome.

The custody issue affected her relations with Griffin too. Until it was settled she could not risk going to America, as he urged her to do – this would mean 'abandoning' John and Kate to Bertie and the detested Peter. Even a projected summer visit in 1933 might risk her status as the blameless 'injured party' in the divorce proceedings. Her fears on this score were not groundless. There was an official of the divorce court, the King's Proctor, whose job was to ensure the validity of what was presented to the court – that is, no 'collusion', and no 'fault' by the innocent petitioner. The King's Proctor sent his minions to sniff out evidence against petitioners which might invalidate their case (Dora read in the paper, she reported to Griffin, that one of these sniffers had charged cinema tickets for housemaids as part of his expenses). The ignoble purpose of all this sordid activity was 'to preserve the sanctity of marriage' by making divorce as difficult as possible.

Another consuming worry for Dora was the future of the school. She was deeply committed to its ideals, and determined to keep it going, against all the odds. Its finances had always been supplemented by Bertie's outside earnings, which Dora could not hope to match from her occasional journalism and royalties. Now, at the beginning of each term she had to make nail-biting calculations. Which pupils were leaving, what new ones might enrol? Would she be able to pay the staff, and the bills? The fate of Beacon Hill was also tied up with Bertie and the divorce: if John and Kate were removed (as did happen in 1934, when Bertie sent them to Dartington), would-be parents might be put off to see the founder's own children sent elsewhere. Could the school's reputation survive the coming scandal of the divorce?

These were the preoccupations of Dora's letters to Griffin – not to mention her deep-down sadness and regret at the ending of her twelve-year partnership with Bertie. She could not understand how his love for her could be switched off like an electric light and replaced by unrelenting coldness and cruelty. *Why* should he want to 'blot her out of his life' in this way? This trait in Bertie, his ability to detach himself completely from someone he had ceased to love, has struck many outsiders. It is poignant to see its effect on Dora at the time. At first she literally *could not* believe that the nastiness came from him, and assumed it must be Peter 'putting him up to it'. As she wrote plaintively to Griffin: 'I understand anything except love dying & that I don't understand.' Only gradually did she realise – was forced to realise – that it was true: Bertie no longer cared for her at all.

Griffin, struggling to understand the 'barbaric' English divorce law from his American homeland, where divorce was easy to obtain and already commonplace, tried valiantly to support and comfort Dora through all these anxieties. He too could not recognise the civilised and courteous Bertie he had known as the insensitive and cold-blooded Bertie of Dora's letters. Realising that much of her fury and bitter comment came from her own hurt feelings, he tried to soften Dora's anger towards the treacherous pair. He assumed there'd be a calm sea beyond the coming storm when they would all be friends again, urging Dora to 'keep the channels open', not to 'blow her top' about Peter to Bertie – 'he'll only think you're jealous' – and offered himself as a safety valve: 'Go ahead and blow off at me, I shan't mind.' While trying to show himself on her side in every petty dispute, for some time his letters continued in this mollifying vein – otherwise, he feared, 'a disgusting quarrel is starting up that will last years and poison all of us'. (How right he was.) A clumsy attempt to avoid that disaster turned into a serious strategic error in his relations with Dora – and cruelly twisted the knife that Bertie had plunged into her heart.

This and other key developments will be amply illustrated later. Having set out the divorce concerns which dominated this tempestuous correspondence, let's now pursue Griffin's own interests for a while – as he was trying to do himself.

His urgent need for work was not only economic but to prove himself to Dora. Except for his brief spell with Paramount in Paris he had earned no serious money since the trip to Russia in the summer of 1929. He had felt demeaned and helpless being dependent on Dora financially as well as emotionally all that time. Dora was still subsidising him until he found a job; probably she had even paid his passage home. She didn't (yet) make an issue of this: by her feminist code it didn't matter who paid for what in an equal partnership. But Griffin needed no reminder of his indebtedness to feel ashamed of it. He had never minded accepting 'hospitality' from a girlfriend, but every instinct told him that a maybe-husband and a certain father-of-two must become 'a provider'.

This was a new role for him. In his pre-Dora life Griffin had been the proverbial gay bachelor, a rolling stone who spent money freely when he had it and lived like a church-mouse when he hadn't – a church-mouse with better-off friends, fortunately, who could be touched for a loan when he was desperate. This was also the Griffin I knew in later years: so far as I know he never owned a stick of furniture (except that bed he bought in 1928, no doubt passed on to the next tenant) and lived all his adult life in a series of rented apartments and bed-sits. In his early career as a globe-trotting journalist he had needed no anchor and had acquired no savings, confident of landing a new job whenever he needed one. Now, he would discover, jobs were scarce and ill-paid; but he felt sure that with Dora's love to sustain him, he could break the old pattern and become a steady support for her.

Dora later held against him his dogged refusal of one option they'd discussed: that Griffin should stay to help her as Secretary to the school. 'But male pride demanded that he shape his family according to conventional law', she complained, 'and...seek his fortune in a man's world, not hang about a woman and *her* school.'[2] There's an amusing irony here which she seems not to have noticed. In Bertie's courtship of her he had tried to distract her from her own work ambitions by asking her to become his secretary. She indignantly refused, and in a letter agreeing to live with him, 'married or unmarried', she asked to be allowed 'to try to earn my own living in some way that is utterly unconnected with you and your work'.[3] If she had expected that concession from Bertie, didn't Griffin, too, have the right to work of his own utterly unconnected with hers?

His resistance to Dora's idea was perfectly reasonable. Griffin saw himself as a writer, and his own journalistic trade was more easily practised in the world he knew. Added to this was a deep psychological need to get away from England, at least for a while. His letters from Majorca show how humiliated he used to feel as an appendage of the Russell household. Bertie's departure had left him king of the castle at Telegraph House, but he still felt awkwardly out of place in English life. In any case it was the *queen* who counted in Dora's household. She was a powerful personality, as we all remember: anyone in her orbit felt like a leaf in a vortex at times. Now he needed to catch his breath. To earn Dora's respect as well as her love he had first to rebuild his own self-confidence, something he could only do on his home ground.

New York, New York! – 'the city that burns up men', Griffin dubbed it, writing his final paragraphs as the *SS Aquitania* approached the shore. Rising excitement seeps through his shipboard letters (though he mustn't show too much glee) – he'd soon be back where he felt *at home* and was confident of finding a job. America at this time was in the pit of the Great Depression, but lo! at once there were several possibilities – 'it's lovely to be wanted in this shell-shocked country' – and it seemed just a matter of weeks before one would be clinched.

Meanwhile he scurried round to see his old friends: first stop, Mary Vorse in Provincetown. He was touched to find everyone so pleased to see him, coyly relaying to Dora Dos Passos' remark that 'something has made a man of me at last'.

> People I've known for a long time are everywhere; workers mostly, writers. Mary is upstairs in bed now dictating to her typist who is also her daughter-in-law. She is writing a Farmers' Strike story which you will see in the December Harper's. Dos was here last night for dinner,

---

[2] *Dora Russell, op. cit., p.261.*
[3] *Letter dated 1 January 1920, quoted by Ray Monk, op.cit., p.570.*

looking like Henry James already at 37, heavy solid head thickset on his enormous trunk, with his odd croak and his dark wistful Latin eyes – aware of the times as no one else is, too. He is finishing the last book of his trilogy up the street; happy and well-fed [with his new wife] who goes with him on all the erratic, splitting journeys he wants to go... He used to be frantic and searching when I was with him so much. Across the road from him is Susan Glaspell, left alone at fifty by Norman who has taken up with a pretty Jewish girl in N.Y. by whom he is going to have a baby. What he's done is natural; but Susan is tragic and can't work and repeats herself.

Mary and Susan were by now longtime residents of Provincetown, the founders of its *avant garde* society of artists and writers; and Dos Passos a frequent visitor. The trilogy he was writing, collectively titled *USA*, was the American classic of the period that made him famous. Griffin had known him best, as he says, at the earlier, searching period of his career where we first encountered him (in Chapter 1). Was he envious now to see Dos in his stride as a serious writer, while he had not yet set foot on the first rung? Maybe; but in his present optimistic mood anything seemed possible in his own life.

Griffin's cheerfulness was at odds with the terrible plight of his country at that time, a paradox reflected in another passage from this letter. The usual picture of America in 1932 is the endless soup queues and shanty-towns of the millions of unemployed, but this was also the period of the building boom that transformed the New York skyline:

On board the *SS Aquitania*

> N.Y. is magnificent but terrible, starving people mounting in numbers under the amazing growth of new skyscrapers, incredibly beautiful. Bill's office is in the handsomest of all, the Chrysler building; he sits just under a slender silver spire that touches the clouds; the bldg. itself is a spire of offices, with great silver gargoyles arching outwards at intervals down the long flank.

Setting this picture against another – of the apartment at 33 Cornelia Street that Griffin took over from a friend – we get some idea of the contrasts in this city of perpetual change:

> This little flat is minute, but it has two beds and an infinitesimal kitchen and bath. It is an old 3-storey house in the back yard of what must be one of the few remaining horseshoeing shops on the American continent. The black-smith, a young Italian, owns the little house, which is divided into small flats and the tenants go out through the shop between the great rumps of horses waiting to be shod to get their letters and milk and morning papers or to exit.

A modern postcard of the Chrysler building

A few weeks later the ceiling fell in on his bed, but that didn't bother Griffin: 'the landlord is nice and forgave me part of my rent for a while...'. It stayed unrepaired for the rest of his stay and eventually he was glad to move to a better place, but for some time the scruffy pad in Cornelia Street admirably suited his mood:

> I like it here now in this little dump; it seems as England must to the English, secure and cosy and safe and one's own... I'm at home here in this rickety flat because outside is a world I clumsily, like a monkey in a battleship, do <u>know</u>, relatively. In England I was so scared – <u>not</u> scared, shut in – that in all but great moments (perhaps least when we were linked together against something as we were last spring and summer), even you seemed a stranger. Our difference in birth is going to be our greatest problem perhaps.

This is an early intuition of what I believe was always a serious barrier to a permanent union between Griffin and Dora: that he was unchangeably

American and she was unchangeably English. Later in the same letter, arising from a discussion of whether it was the loss of Bertie's *status* rather than his love that hurt Dora so deeply (this jibe caused an explosion!), Griffin sees their difference rather quaintly as a question of 'caste' – that damnable English air of superiority that so irks other people:

> But in some things you say to me in these letters there is as much patronage as anything B. can convey to you... My relation to you, alas, is at present not unlike yours to him in some ways. He must be polite to you, lower caste, for the children you have given him; you must be polite to me, still lower caste, for the children I've been a father to. That's the English caste view; not confined to the island, but nowhere so unconscious and powerful... But darling, the English have been shot at behind hedges in Ireland and India and once by my ancestors in this country for some of the attitudes you have. Have 'em for god's sake if you must (though I wish you neednt) but please be conscious. I shant shoot at you anyhow, my love. I love you, and think there is a queer fittingness in our marriage.

Dora must have winced to read that; but Griffin was partly right. She had undoubtedly enjoyed being Countess Russell, and even more so the intellectual climate of Bertie's world, now lost to her. But she was never a snob.

At first the most likely chance of work for Griffin seemed to be a new political journal aiming 'to make the white collar proletariat revolutionary', in Griffin's words, which Dos Passos had already agreed to write for. In November Griffin had a meeting with its founder, Alfred Bingham, half expecting he would be signed up too. To Dora he wrote rather disparagingly about Bingham ('God, how young he is, in the wrong way') and that he couldn't pay much for contributions. He'd have a go at a trial piece, but he wasn't hopeful of 'getting it through the advisers surrounding Bingham'. Evidently it didn't get through: there are no further references to Bingham's venture.

In fact this new journal, *Common Sense*, became an influential left-wing voice in the coming New Deal era. Mary Vorse was a contributing editor for two years, along with Dos Passos and other friends of Griffin's. Why was he left out? This was the most left-leaning period in American political history; many of the old radicals found themselves listened to at last, and even the American Communist Party, though very small, made a splash. The radical editors of *Common Sense*, however, 'despite their real political differences', were 'united in their rejection of Soviet-style communism, and urged instead the value of a democratic socialist society... In 1933, *Common Sense* served as a center for anti-Stalinist independent radicalism in the United States.'[4]

---

[4] *Dee Garrison,* Mary Heaton Vorse: The Life of an American Insurgent *(Temple Uinversity Press, Philadelphia, 1989), pp.254–5.*

This is probably the clue to Griffin's exclusion from the club (if it was deliberate). In the spectrum of American left-wing opinion he was just a smidgeon *too* far left, too ready to overlook or gloss over the barbarities of the Soviet system that were now becoming known and talked about in the West.

The report of his meeting with Bingham was written on a very important day in American history: 8 November 1932, when Franklin D Roosevelt (FDR) was elected President. (Fittingly, this letter was mailed 'via *SS President Roosevelt*'. That ship was named after President Teddy Roosevelt, of the same clan, who had served from 1901 to 1909.) Griffin was glad the election was over, having earlier complained that election fever had brought the rest of life to a standstill:

> Even the steadiest people seem unsteady just now... with important voices becoming hypocracies [sic] and tomfooleries through radios and with everyone having to pretend something is about to be decided though everyone knows nothing will be. Hardly any work is done or given out. People speak of "after election"...as of the millenium [sic], though everybody knows it is a fake.

Griffin's view of the new incumbent – 'a very shallow, dangerous upper-class American' – was probably shared by all his radical friends on the day he was elected. But their judgement was mistaken: the new president was not what he seemed, and this election did mark a break with America's past. FDR's New Deal introduced a minimal welfare state and went some way to ease (though not cure) the worst depression in US history. Many left-wingers (even Griffin) later found themselves working for government agencies. One of Mary Vorse's old friends, Frances Perkins, became the first American woman cabinet minister, and another of their circle, William Bullitt, was appointed ambassador to the Soviet Union when FDR at last recognised its new government in 1933.

There is some evidence in Dora's archive of the effect of this election on ordinary Americans. Griffin's mother wrote to Dora, also on election day, that she had 'never witnessed anything like it', 'a most exciting and inspirational time', 'a wonderful housecleaning'. She joyfully welcomed FDR's expected landslide, as did her close friend Mary Kinkaid, who had worked throughout the summer for the Roosevelt campaign. 'Doubtless you are far ahead of me in your political philosophy', Mrs Kinkaid wrote to Griffin, 'but it seemed to me wise to aid what promised a step forward.' She did read *The Nation* and other 'courageous periodicals', she assured Griffin, 'but I am still a Democrat'. The views of Griffin and his friends were too extreme for mainstream liberals like her.

The moment he stepped ashore Griffin had mailed a long overdue letter to his mother, now widowed and living in straitened circumstances in California. Its optimistic tone about his future with Dora brought an ecstatic reply which

Griffin sent on to her, with its 'debt of gratitude to Dora' for making Griffin, and her, so happy, and wishing her 'strength to meet the cross-currents into which these things have brought her'. A month later she wrote fulsomely to Dora herself along these lines.

Together with another to Dora, from 1931, and a few to Griffin, these letters convey an impression of my namesake grandmother as a doughty old lady, hard-working and independent, sentimentally free with her God Blesses when writing about me and Roddy, and with a touch of Griffin's temper as she awaited non-arriving letters from him. Her emotional investment in these unknown grandchildren, the only ones she had, was almost as deep as Griffin's. Perhaps she saw us as a replacement for her two youngest children, who had died in infancy in the 1890s. In the last weeks of her life, recovering from her third hip fracture, she still clung to the hope of crossing the Atlantic to meet little Harriet and Roderick. (She didn't make it.)

Mary Holland Kinkaid was a family friend who had worked on George Barry's newspaper in California. She had known Griffin since he was 17, and also 'had the honor of being the only person with whom your Mother could indulge in a talk about her grandchildren'. She wrote to him again in February 1933 about her own affairs and his mother's, a letter also forwarded to Dora in his effort to acquaint the two women he loved with each other. Financial misfortune had left both these old ladies, in their seventies, still having to earn a living. Now a great stroke of luck had befallen Mrs Barry, though it meant moving from California to Portland, Oregon: she was going to keep house for her widowed brother-in-law, nearing retirement from the civil service. This was a relief to Griffin, feeling guilty about his ageing mother.

But the relief was short-lived. A few months later Uncle Martin was made redundant by government cut-backs and went to live with his son; so Mrs Barry too was out of a job. No doubt she ended her days in California, where she had other relatives: there are few further references in Griffin's letters until he reported her death in 1936.

In the closing months of 1932 Griffin's mood veered back and forth, from euphoric fantasies about his future life with Dora to profound gloom when he reflected how far it was from realisation. Looking ahead, he could see 'no hope of personal happiness without living with you, always', while Dora could only promise 'I suppose I'll come to believe in you and me soon...'. In fact she had not yet taken the decisive step towards divorce, still quibbling over the terms of the deed of separation. In despair, after a night 'on a bed of live coals', Griffin voiced his nagging fear –

> ...that you are going to regret to your dying day the kudos of the Russell marriage if you go out of it on any terms, no matter what. If that is so I think it's unsafe for us to go on, since I can't hope to take Bertie's place in your life, nor shall try to.

A MAN OF SMALL IMPORTANCE

Food for Griffin's soul – photos of the children, autumn–winter, 1932.
The curly-haired boy is J J Maberley, a pupil at the school, and the baby is Roddy.

'Perhaps you and Bertie can resume', he went on – but if not, he begs her to analyse exactly *what* she is losing by parting from him, and what she still has. Dora's reply to this letter, densely packed as usual, indicates some of this 'balance sheet' in her life:

> Lately I've discovered how I <u>love teaching</u> in itself & the secretarial work irks me horribly... I didn't really mean it was <u>perks</u> I missed – but I'm used to living as a public person, like my father... And I don't want to be a wife & mother for the rest of my active life – not only.

Griffin naturally hoped the divorce would go ahead, though he tried not to say so too loudly. Dora, still vainly hoping it could be avoided, felt under pressure on all sides. Late in December her lawyer advised that 'satisfactory' terms had been obtained for the separation deed. Griffin cabled her: ONLY HAPPY ABOUT DEED IF YOU ARE OR WILL BE AFTER ALL CANNOT BE HAPPY ALONE AND PROBABLY YOU CANNOT EITHER. On the last day of 1932 Dora signed the hateful document.

By this time Griffin's optimism about finding work was wearing thin. His hopes were now pinned to a playwright friend, Jack Lawson, who was soon off to Hollywood as a scriptwriter and might find an opening there for Griffin too ('at $100 a week!').[5] For economy's sake his friend Red Owen was now sharing the tiny flat, but even so he had to swallow his pride and ask Dora for more money. How this pennilessness ground him down! His close friend Bill Commons was getting 'old maidish' about further loans (he'd try Jack Lawson instead), and even Dora didn't seem to realise how hard he was trying to remedy the situation:

> It's only that when you (affectionately) cast me for the role of butterfly and yourself the ant and I contrast the hard realities of my life here, my struggles to get on and keep buoyant...well I get damned sick and sore.

In a later section of that letter, however, he reported a firm hope of getting the Foreign Affairs editorship of a new magazine to be launched in February as a rival to *Time* – paying only $40 a week, half what such a job used to be worth, but that would soon improve if the journal (and Griffin) were successful. He'd hear his fate next week...

But he didn't – nor the next week, or the next. As though to distract her from this dismal topic he relayed gossipy news about his friends, some evidently

---

[5] *John Howard Lawson, whom Griffin had probably known since 1918 – Lawson was another Red Cross ambulance driver in the First World War – became a prominent victim of McCarthyism in the 1950s, one of the 'Hollywood Ten' convicted of contempt of Congress for refusing to answer questions about their political affiliations before the House Un-American Activities Committee.*

known to Dora: Adelaide Kuntz, 'slimmer and happier than in England, still living with the American lesbian who looks like the late Cal Coolidge[6] ... She drips comfort; daughter juicy and dramatic and cruel, boy much sweeter and put upon... Rosalinde is here too, looking for a job; tells me what a pleasure woman has to do to get jobs in NY in this slack season, which includes sleeping in odd positions with a Jew who wont give her a letter to the head of the radio unless... But she didn't.' Yesterday he'd met Dos and Katy on the street and together they 'tramped about this Italian quarter where I live and dropped into a cellar where we had some of the contraband wine they call red ink and then to a vet. to see if Dos's French poodle, which they have instead of a child, has the mange which he hasn't, and Dos bought some hamburger steak which Toto carried in the parcel at our heels...'. Dos had once met Bertie on a train and liked him very much personally, 'but still thought him a wraith of the 18th century'.

Have I said yet how vividly Griffin writes about people and places? In a letter to Dora around this time he reported a compliment from their good friend Jed Taggard, whose daughter Marcia was then at Beacon Hill:

> ...apropos of a very literary description I'd given of Terry in love with Marcia – or is it the other way round? – 'people who can write a letter like that ought to be ashamed not to write constantly'. Good old Jed.

Yes, good old Jed, you were right.

---

[6] *Calvin Coolidge (1872–1933), 30th President of the USA (1923–9), a Republican.*

CHAPTER 8

HIGH HOPES DISAPPOINTED

17 January 1933: 'Well, my own, I've just got that job.' Griffin could hardly contain his excitement as he retailed the news to Dora – 'do you mind if I see things rosy jes for a minute?'

For several weeks everything he wrote about his new job was positive. The pay was poor, but 'within 9 months the mag. will either succeed or bust and then there'll be a reconsideration [to] about $125...and what's more, a chance to buy stock in the company which...should yield in a few years the sort of private income Bill has from Time.' Griffin's friend Bill Commons – his erstwhile stock market partner of 1929 – was on the staff of Time, with which News Week (later Newsweek) would now be competing. (Before long Griffin was sourly comparing Time's Foreign Editor's annual salary of $16,000 with his own measly $2,080; but he was still hoping for a big rise 'when Newsweek turns the corner'.)

He was immensely proud of being hired 'entirely on my record and three long personal talks', surely proof of his professional standing in the city where he was known. At a party that night – for the opening of a Broadway play by his friend Dawn Powell – for once Griffin, too, was due for congratulations from the assembled company. Jed Taggard was there, enthusing about the possibility of Dora coming over in the summer for a symposium at Bennington College, where she was now teaching; and beyond that, she felt sure Bennington could be persuaded to offer Dora a job if, as seemed likely, Beacon Hill had to close. Griffin's future looked rosy indeed, on all fronts: 'Just today, I strut. But tomorrow I'll have to begin to work, and goodby to the leisure I can spend covering yellow paper with words to my beloved.'

It is heartening to see Griffin at work at last, doing what he felt he did best. He liked his editor, Mr Williamson, formerly of the *New York Times*, 'a hardworking, shy man, not flamboyant', though he was less sure about the 'hardboiled and rather fancy young men' who made up the rest of the 20-or-so staff. 'It's lovely to get my hand in again, reading mounds of newspapers and writing all week articles on the Sino-Japs, the Berlin riots, the London busmen...', while secretly feeling 'I can write figure 8s around anyone else in the office.' His confident mood continued for several weeks – 'up since 7, poring over the foreign news' – until he had to endure that familiar ritual of a newspaper office, when the lowly hack on the newsdesk gets his story re-written by the boss:

> I worked 20 hours at one sitting on Japan 3 days ago and at midnight after the last papers came in handed in my story – pretty good, I thought. The money man on the paper, a twisted war wreck named Capt Martyn, English, once a foreign editor himself but quite plainly with no flair for writing and inadequate background, took it and revamped the whole thing, tossing the pages over for my approval as a matter of form, but since he was my boss he knew I couldn't object to what he was doing. Together we rewrote my beautiful story between midnight and 6 a.m. and I cursed inwardly – but not outwardly, for I must and shall keep this job. Having passed this test with Martyn – I was cheerful and grinned, like a good soldier – I think I am all right now. Bill told me he was sacked from Time because he wasn't a good foreign editor; doubtless one of the things he wants to do with this paper for which he has engineered the capital is to show them he is.

So far Griffin's self-esteem was only slightly dented. 'Luckily it's quite clear to me that I know foreign affairs better and can write better than anyone on the staff – easily; and that inclines me to be patient.'

These glimpses of his working life in the early weeks of 1933 are only fragments of his still-frequent letters. As usual they were dominated by Dora's troubles and fickle moods. She had cabled her congratulations on the *Newsweek* job, but she was so engrossed in her own affairs that Griffin felt he was 'writing to her back'. Hardly had he settled into his new routine when he received another blast of outrage from England, fired off in a black mood. Griffin of course got his share of the blame, but he felt its main target was Bertie, 'for whom, in God's name, I am not responsible'. After some deliberation, and without consulting Dora, he unwisely forwarded her letter to Bertie; because, he explained, 'it seems to me you cannot be aware of how she is feeling'.

This letter of Dora's, written on 20 January, 'a magnificent letter, full of temper and hate and love', in Griffin's words, is missing from his collection. I can only guess its contents from other sources. Phrases included in Ray Monk's biography of Bertie illustrate the theme I mentioned earlier: that calling in 'the law' to sort out their personal problems was a shameful betrayal of their ideals. 'I'd rather do it by love than by law on both sides – & that's my whole case – that the way of love has been discarded.' 'Don't see why we shouldn't sleep & copulate as we damn please without economic and emotional slavery to follow.'[1]

From the moment she signed the deed of separation, Dora had regretted it. This was the Big Lie that made a mockery of the ideals she and Bertie had trumpeted: its very purpose was to deny the years of free love which had allowed him his many affairs and brought her two adored children by a man she loved. Now she was being swept along to a fearful, insecure future by a dastardly route which 'everyone' except her approved. Griffin had no idea what thin ice he was treading whenever he expressed any view of these matters that deviated an inch from hers. Dora expected him to 'defend me against the world in everything'; anything less was disloyalty.

His supreme act of disloyalty was to send that letter on to Bertie; and he was about to make things worse. When Bertie wrote back to him stating what seemed a 'reasonable' case for joint custody of John and Kate, and his proposed financial settlement on Dora, Griffin sent a copy of this letter on to her, expressing sympathy – in guarded words, but sympathy nonetheless – with some of Bertie's points. In later letters he continued trying to damp down the fireworks, even hoping that once the status of John and Kate was settled, 'you could bring yourself to tolerate Peter's existence'.

Thus step by step Griffin moved further into the enemy camp. His nonchalant mention of one or two 'talks' he'd had with Bertie in England seems to have convinced Dora (quite wrongly, as she admitted in *The Tamarisk Tree*), that the two had struck a bargain behind her back. And there was more. The letter from Bertie of which he'd sent her a copy contained an icy sentence that Griffin had scarcely noticed. Justifying his actions, Bertie wrote that Dora had 'destroyed their spiritual relation' in 1927; 'since then I have not liked her, and I stuck to her only for the sake of John and Kate'.

Dora was dumbstruck. So the last five years of their marriage had been a hollow shell! Years including Beacon Hill School, the summer in Hendaye, all those loving letters up to the moment of Roddy's birth – all that time Bertie 'had not liked her'! That 'dislike' cut her to the quick – she refers back to it time and again – and Griffin's unconcern as the carrier of such grief did his own case no good.

Looking back at the tangled mess from afar, it's tempting to say Dora shouldn't have been surprised by this cold message. The hurt on both sides from their affairs of 1927 (hers with Roy Randall, his with the Swiss governess) had never really healed; and in April 1932, just after he left her, Bertie had

---

[1] *Quoted by Ray Monk, op.cit., p.144. Monk found only typed extracts among Bertie's papers, but it is possible Griffin sent the whole letter in 1933, which would explain its absence from the sequence of Dora's letters he preserved.*

written to her in similar terms as he now wrote to Griffin.[2] She did not yet realise, or did not want to face, Bertie's extraordinary duplicity – that he *had* been increasingly unhappy since 1927, but had skilfully hidden his true feelings. And it was doubly humiliating, of course, to have her 'true love' with Bertie exposed to Griffin as a sham.

Griffin came in for his own share of wrath in her tirade of 20 January. His rebuttal indicates the charges against him. Yes, he did live off her for a couple of years, and feels guilty for doing so. Yes, he could understand she felt deserted when he left, but he was in no position to help her 'until I got away from you and on my own feet'. Yes, he did urge her towards divorce after Bertie had left, thinking 'it would be a civilized one', but he had been ready to live with her if she remained married, 'and still will if you drop the divorce'. But 'it is quite unfair to say...that I hung around to watch [your marriage] break and profit by it...' And it was grossly unjust to say the school might fail because he wouldn't stay to help her with it – its difficulties were for quite other reasons. 'I think it is a very bad fault in you to blame on individuals you love the blows of fate, which all have to endure.'

A fair point. (Griffin's reading of Dora's character was usually accurate.) But he was slow to realise how much the school meant to her, seeing it merely as a barrier to the joint life in America he was hoping for. Later he realised that so long as it survived she would never leave England – 'I'll just have to get over there somehow' – but secretly he kept hoping that economic forces would remove this factor from the complicated equation of uniting his life with Dora's.

Dora's outburst in January began a new, angrier phase in her correspondence with Griffin. Her doubts had not yet crystallised into outright rejection: intemperate letters were always followed by loving ones which renewed his hopes. Nevertheless he felt aggrieved that while he understood and sympathised with her predicament, she made little effort to understand his. 'Somehow you haven't got a right picture of how I'm living and acting now at all... I read letters addressed to a man not me.' His work, just as much as hers, was hard to bear while 'I have only a vacant and insecure personal life to support the strain.' These faint protests went unnoticed. Finally, in a long and bitter letter, Griffin blew his top. Their relationship had plenty of room for 'legitimate egoism', he allowed, '[b]ut an egoism that forgets what sort of person the other is, what situation he's in, what his motives and needs are because they are inconvenient to one's own power-scheme; that's killing.'

---

[2] *In a letter dated 15 April 1932, reproduced in Nicholas Griffin, op.cit, p.406: '...I don't think you realize what my feelings about our marriage have been for a long time. My love for you was killed by your behaviour about Hannah...'. They had quarrelled fiercely about Hannah, the Irish cook whose 'loyalty' over the Alice affair Dora had rewarded by re-hiring her while Bertie was away – see p.41.*

Dora deserved the rebuke. If not egotistical, she was... self-centred, shall we say (and she was certainly given to power-games). She could not picture Griffin's New York life, and rarely showed any awareness of his concerns. Of course she had every reason to feel distraught and hard-done-by at that time, but pity poor Griffin too! – at times feeling merely 'a dump for your daily annoyances', he complained, and so often unnerved by her letter-bombs: 'darling I get so <u>rattled</u> at your tigrish pacing back and forth in the cage of our situation'.

I wish he had lived to read her belated apology in *The Tamarisk Tree* for what she put him through in these years. His ordeal was far from over yet.

At least the job was still going well, for the moment, though we can begin to see the political distance between him and the other *Newsweek* staff:

> As usual on Monday nights, last night I worked till 4, the god-damned Greeks having to go Fascist after midnight and I to sit up and write a witty, informed treatise on them afterward, which I damned well did... I live in a welter of news all day and wish I had no revolutionary training, so that I'd be more comfortable near my colleagues who are white-minded about anything outside this country and, mostly, inside. The banking crisis here bores me inexpressibly, any change that will result amounting to nothing at all though there will be a lot of ballyhoo and I'll have to pretend I'm serious about that. Here I am scolding the universe, like you.

Roosevelt's resolution of that boring banking crisis halted the slide into economic chaos – no small thing to millions of Americans who were losing their savings, houses and jobs because of it. Having no such bourgeois encumbrances himself, his eyes trained on the outside world, Griffin felt detached from their problems. After the meddlesome Martyn had imperiously re-written his article, the editor, Williamson, had promised Griffin it wouldn't happen again. This made him cocky. But the editor himself was not always satisfied with what Griffin wrote, and he rashly did not heed the warning signs:

> Poor Williamson, a kindly man naturally I think, has become hollow-eyed and nervous. He snaps when I object to his changing – only a little! – my racy, informed stories to a more conservative way of putting things. Inevitably I shall have to fight for my point of view and, of course, may get sacked in the process.

Besides his work, other topics of interest occasionally interrupt the personal saga in Griffin's letters. Dora's book *In Defence of Children*, finished in haste the previous summer, had arrived in New York bookshops. He sent her reviews, with promises of 'better ones' from people who knew her and her work. In one such titbit he couldn't resist a boastful aside – perhaps to remind Dora of his sexual desirability?

> I've seen [no reviews] but what I sent you. I hear F.P.A. put a rhyme into his Herald-Tribune column about Bringing up children being quite a tussle, According to Dora Russell, or something of the sort; havent seen it. F.P.A. is the wise-cracking columnist, rather influential in N.Y., whose wife has just been delivered of her fourth. I might have been its father, but saw to it I wasn't; anyhow I once lived with her in Paris – before F.P.A., when Esther was a virgin. Naturally F.P.A. has never forgotten <u>that</u> and likes to find things I'm connected with absurd... I suppose the NY. intelligentsia will vote you a learned scold, as a lot. Your real audience will lie "out yonder" in the colleges and educated people whose minds burrow but dont want to be chic.

Griffin was right that Dora's book would be of most interest to a relatively small circle concerned with education and child rearing. That it received any attention at all in major American journals is an indication of the much smaller intellectual community in those days. Such a minor work would today pass unnoticed in the avalanche of print pouring off university presses on both sides of the Atlantic.

As for sexual matters, there seemed to be scarcely a woman in New York Griffin had not bedded in his heyday. In another letter this boast sits rather oddly alongside an accusation that Dora only wants him sexually, not as a husband. He knew other women too who were more keen on lovers than husbands:

> It's curious; it seems to be in the air in this generation of women. Two of my oldest friends here, your age and sort, each having inherited incomes recently, are about to move out from their husbands and pick up lovers as they like, which they've been doing for years anyway. I've been talking to them lately; both are old friends. I had affairs with both years ago. Regretfully and fondly waving farewell to their husbands; nice conscientious women, both. Husbands of course baffled, bewildered, unhappy...

Come now, Griffin. If it was 'natural' for your friend Norman Matson to walk out on his 50-year-old wife Susan Glaspell, leaving her 'tragic and unable to work', why shouldn't these women walk out on their husbands? No wonder he set Dora's feminist antennae quivering at times.

Griffin came close to the truth about her view of him, however, with his rueful reflection in another letter: 'you wanted a Bohemian lover in me who would amuse and excite you and give you a good time, not a "steady" who bases his life and hopes on you and whose paternal and husbandly feelings are aroused.' That was indeed the nub of the problem; and with every passing month Dora's conviction grew that Griffin was not good husband-material.

At the end of March, Griffin was trying to reconcile himself to a future without Dora. After that 'dislike' letter relayed to her by Griffin, she had made what she later called 'my last attempt to preserve some human relations with Bertie', a direct plea to him 'not to distort and destroy the memories of our life together...'. She sent a copy of this letter to Griffin, which convinced *him* that his own case was irretrievably lost. It seemed that nothing now remained of their five-year relationship – except Harriet and Roddy.

For some time they'd been discussing a summer plan for Lily to bring the children over for what I shall henceforth capitalise as The Visit, fully described in the next chapter (where Lily will also be properly introduced). Griffin now turned his attention to the practicalities of this event: where we would stay, how to pay for it and so on.

Suddenly the tone of Dora's letters warmed up again. Was there a grain of hope after all? He begged her to ask her solicitor if she could come over too, without arousing the suspicions of the King's Proctor. Again he ventured onto thin ice:

> It would be too bad to upset the divorce. But I suppose you want to; in fact you say you do. That I cannot comprehend in you for if only in the interest of your love for B. – as you define love and say you feel it – then divorce is both the only honest and practicable thing to do... The only other possible conclusion is that you want to hang on to legal wifehood, which is against your principles.

Before he signed off he knew that such remarks would get him into trouble – 'But it is vital; the issues must be faced.' Later he would suggest Dora was reluctant to release Bertie for jealousy of Peter. This line of attack was a tactical error, of course. Impugning her motives for resisting the divorce only drove Dora to defend more vociferously her 'real' (noble) motives, while also inviting more wrath on himself.

At Easter, Dora took a group of school staff and children to Cornwall. At once her spirits lifted ('this is such a healing place'), bringing a brief sunny interval to her transatlantic letters. The house was looking shabby – she wished she had £50 to spend on it – but the beaches were marvellous and there were bluebells on the cliffs. Harry calls Carn Voel 'her 'Merican house', and at St Levan beach she looked out to sea for Daddy. A crumpled letter written there enclosed some sand, and at the end my scrawled H alongside X – my first-ever letter to Dad! Dora's deep attachment to the house and that patch of the planet is well conveyed:

> Carn Voel is sacred to the children... It cradled Harry as well as the others & now Rod has been there, thank goodness. Some mystic feeling about the place made me want to see him there – as if it would give him the magic of living as it has often done to me. We could all be so happy there & perhaps we will, one day.

Easter 1933 in Cornwall – 'such a healing place'

Ben Glue, the school chauffeur, and Lily carrying Roddy, with 'J J' (left) and Harriet behind.

Despite the joys of outdoor life, Dora was hungry for intellectual company. To that end she sought out her acquaintance Mary Butts, a well-known writer, then living at Sennen, in Cornwall. Finding this encounter disappointing ('Mary Butts & Gabriel came over but behaved rather gentleman and lady like – she thinks of me as Lady Russell'), she remembered Paul Gillard in Plymouth, who had last been at Carn Voel in the weeks after my birth (see Chapter 5). No doubt he welcomed an opportunity to deepen his connection to a household he so much admired.

> Paul Gillard is here & most delightful to the children. He seems very happy to get some intelligent talk – we went over everything under the sun last night – you would have enjoyed it so much. He said you had made a great difference in his life, stirred him out of provincialism & complacency...
>
> I'm not flirting with him, sweetheart. Like all the young intellectuals he says I ought not on any account to divorce, as it will set back the modern point of view incredibly. B's turning mean and possessive doesn't, in his view, invalidate the argument for a new & extra-legal morality – on the contrary it confirms it.

Her letter went on to develop this theme, which must have dampened Griffin's spirits. He was puzzled by her remark that she wasn't flirting with Paul – the thought had not occurred to him – but in the light of later developments, she probably .. More important to Dora at that moment, however, was Paul's support for her view about the divorce. Up to then it had been her against 'everyone'; now she had an ally for the battles to come.

Back at Telegraph House, Dora plunged into the busy summer term. Meanwhile there were developments in Griffin's life. He had a stroke of luck when his friend Edmund ('Bunny') Wilson – already 'a very arrived critic' in Griffin's envious words – invited him to share his rented house at 314 East 53rd Street, as soon as his current guest, T S Eliot, moved out. Griffin's account of his new home shows us another glimpse of the older New York so fast disappearing under skyscrapers. He thought it would be perfect for The Visit, which he was now planning and saving for:

> This house is one of two small, old wooden houses shut into the hurly burly of the upper east side; they're a little bigger than London houses and in the backyard are 6 or 7 young trees of the kind called The Tree of Heaven. Muriel Draper...has the next house and is doing over the garden which is common with Bunny's. There's a grass plot for the children and flower beds and a stone seat and summer shade and a little green table with 3 green seats. There's a door from the garden into my room, next to which is a kitchen, quite big, where Lily could get all the food the kids want. Until Bunny leaves [for Provincetown] I'd sleep out and give Lily and the kids this room, afterward we'll have the two floors above.

Griffin always lived just ahead of the bulldozers, it seems:

> Bunny and I walked to the East River the other night looking for a restaurant and I saw in the next block what was left of the slummy old place where you came in 28, a razed place now waiting for a tall building for the rich to live in. The swift dirty river ran alongside, nothing else left.

Edmund Wilson was, at that time, a widower. His young daughter was being cared for by his mother, only in her father's charge for holidays. These two wife-less men ate out every night until Griffin found 'a frugal and excellent black servant', who reduced their expenses: Hattie's wages for daily cleaning and cooking cost less than eating out. Wilson's own reminiscences of these years complain that Griffin's 'unctuous old woman's voice' and his endless talk of Dora got on his nerves at times.[3] Otherwise they seem to have rubbed along together amicably enough. He does not reveal whether they ever spoke of Edna Millay, the onetime lover of both of them. Perhaps neither of them knew of the connection. By now she was a very arrived poet, much praised by Wilson and other literary critics.

From this time in Wilson's house we also get a picture of T S Eliot on a brief return visit. First Griffin recounted to Dora a talk he'd had with Eliot about Bertie. We can skip that (I'm taking a break from Russell affairs), but it's amusing to note in passing that both men were connected to Russell by a similar route: Bertie had once had an affair with Eliot's wife, and Griffin with Bertie's wife. At the time, it seems, both were ignorant of the other's intimate link with the great philosopher.

> Eliot's a strange being to wander into this scene; do you remember his very beautiful musical voice like a wind instrument? I came into the house at midnight to find Bunny who is a Marxist critical pundit sharpshooting Eliot on Shakespeare's later period. They had been at it since dinner in a cheap speakeasy and Bunny to keep it up had drunk heavily; both were befuddled and at two staggered up to bed zig zag. Eliot defined himself – Wilson fuming but...liking Eliot too but immensely scornful of his incredible snobbery, recognizable as out of Boston in its queer English dress... He is well advised to live in England. The USA would tear him apart.

Meanwhile Griffin's transatlantic quarrel continued, through 'thickets of misunderstanding' and arguments worn thin through repetition. In trying to disabuse Dora of the idea that things could have carried on as they were, he occasionally let slip remarks implying a common 'masculine' cause with Bertie. This increased her suspicion that she was being 'handed on' to Griffin by tacit agreement between them.

The absurdity of this idea should not blind us to her real suffering. Reading her letters of this period, I've been trying to understand the Dora who wrote them. She was still young, not yet 40, yet at times she felt like a 'faded drudge' whose best years were over. (Despite her denials, *of course* she was jealous of

---

[3] *Edmund Wilson,* The Thirties: From Notebooks and Diaries of the Period, *edited by Leon Edel (Macmillan, London, 1980), p.401. There are other passing references to Griffin in the sections of this book covering the short period when they knew each other well.*

young, beautiful Peter.) In those days her passionate hopes of improving the world were invested more in people than in causes: 'Nothing in the world ever *is* real except in the light of personal relationships – not for people like us.' Her heart overflowed with deep loves and deep hates, and in these months a deep *hurt* that completely overwhelmed her. Dora just could not control the anger that welled up, lashing out like a cornered beast at the people she held responsible for her wounds.

The deepest wound was Bertie's 'dislike' in that fateful letter. At first she was ready to shoot the messenger too:

> If any woman had written so to me about you, I would have turned back every accusation with words of fire. But you agreed with him in "disliking" me... I can't in my heart give up my relation to Bertie... I get no further on towards realising that our whole life together, his & mine, is now meaningless... You can't forgive me feeling like this, because you are a man, & men say women must choose between them, though men may love as many women at a time as they choose. Well I can't choose, Griffin – that's all... I want to love you but I can't if neither you nor B nor Peter will let me love him too.

Griffin's consoling letters ameliorated her distress a little, but her plea to Bertie received no answer; thereafter he would only see her in the presence of lawyers.

It's hard to see what Dora could have expected once things had reached this stage. Of course it was unrealistic to think of 'going on as before', and equally so her other notion, that the foursome could have separated amicably into two new households, without a legal divorce. But we must give her credit for honestly believing the Russell 'open marriage' could have worked, since Bertie too had proclaimed and practised it for years; and she was right to feel betrayed when he repudiated their credo (he later told the divorce court it had been her idea, not his). The cardinal fault on his side was his continued loving behaviour towards Dora when, for him, the marriage was already dead; and on Dora's side, to have pursued her love affair beyond reasonable bounds, relying on Bertie's forebearance to preserve their marriage.

I believe she did love both Bertie and Griffin at the same time. Their very different qualities fulfilled different needs in her – Bertie a kind of father figure, a man of awesome intellect and refined wit, outwardly cool and very English; Griffin by contrast the brash, heart-on-sleeve American, guileless, tempestuous, with a raw intelligence she could mould and a wild romantic streak to match her own. Bertie provided the public life she revelled in, while Griffin appealed to the raffish, almost wanton side of her character – perhaps the closest she could get in real life to the 'raggle taggle gipsy' she longed to run away with ('respectability is such a burden to me', she once wrote to Bertie). Her relationship with Griffin was *sensual* in a way her marriage had never been. Consider this, from a letter written only a few weeks before she decided to break from him:

> I know I've been so busy explaining how much I cared for Bertie that you can scarcely have realised how much I loved you too – <u>do</u> love you... There are moments when I love you <u>utterly</u>, Griffin, sweetheart, feel you like the breath in & out of my body, & then I get frightened... Just understand now what I've missed all these years – it seems cruel – I was so vital & beautiful & I loved Bertie, but he only treated me first as a child to lavish affection on, & then as mother & burden bearer – seemed to forget latterly that I had looks & charm. Took a lot from me, darling, gave me my home & two children, but not – I see now – the sexual warmth & understanding that give one ease & grace & peacefulness. You see, after all, sex is the determining factor... [With Bertie] one has a comradeship of the mind – with me it worked because I have one...
>
> ...[O]ne doesn't love people "just for sex" the way people say – all loving is sex – infinite varieties of it. The way I feel for you goes into the very depths of my body – nothing external about it... but there's a rather terrible helplessness about you that makes me fight you wildly with my tongue & my head, because my instincts & my body can never resist you.

Unhappily for Griffin, however, by now the warfare 'with her tongue and head' occupied more of Dora's letters than the passion in her heart. His old ulcer trouble was back, sometimes so bad he had to miss work. This increased his nervousness about the *Newsweek* job. His financial calculations, most urgently for The Visit in the summer, crucially depended on whether it would last. At the end of April he was not sure it would, though he didn't know if this was because, as he sometimes sensed, 'News Week is beginning not to like me', or because the journal's finances were rocky. Already he was looking ahead to other jobs he might try for, 'should News Week die suddenly or, in a fit of economy, get rid of its foreign editor'.

Foreign editors were very busy at that moment in history. In January 1933 Hitler and the Nazis had taken power in Germany and were now embarked on their infamous agenda. In Russia, Stalin was forcing through the Five Year Plans which transformed the USSR into an industrial power (just in time for the Second World War). Even in America, preoccupied with its own economic troubles, there was a ferment of discussion about world events. 'All the belles lettres people have gone political; Dos always was but Bunny Wilson who used to write about Proust now lectures me on Marx continually', Griffin complained to Dora. Mary Vorse would soon be off to Germany 'to do Hitler for Harper's and the New Republic', while he himself had been 'writing all week about the wretched engineers in Russia'. She'd see his report in *Newsweek* – what did she think of it?

Those 'wretched engineers' were British employees of Metro-Vickers, working on contract in the USSR, who were accused of 'wrecking' (sabotaging) the machinery they were installing in Soviet power stations. The Metro-Vickers case was an early example of the notorious show trials of 'internal enemies' by which Stalin tried to cover up his own economic failures. Few people in the West believed the trumped-up charges against these men, but there was just enough evidence, as presented by Soviet propaganda, for defenders of Soviet Russia to believe 'there might be something in it'. Dora found Griffin's report more credible than what she was reading in England:

> I've just been reading over your report of the Russian trial – great it is – so much of the evidence was suppressed in English papers. Looks like they were intelligence people all right...

I too have read Griffin's *Newsweek* report, dated 22 April 1933, and subsequent instalments of the story. It is very competent, in the abrupt, racy *Time/Newsweek* style still favoured today. His reporting is not markedly pro-Soviet, though with hindsight it looks naïve, assuming the rigged proceedings were fair, and giving credence to Soviet hints that the engineers may have been British spies. In fact it reflects a typical, 'open-minded' view of Soviet affairs in the American liberal press in the New Deal era. Except for the right-wing Hearst newspapers, there was less automatic hostility towards Soviet Russia at that time than in the Tory-dominated British press.

It may be that Griffin's personal politics were too far left for *Newsweek*, as he suggested himself, but on the evidence I've seen,[4] he was well able to deliver what was required. Exactly why he lost this job a few weeks later, and many others over the years, remains a mystery. (Griffin told Dora he feared *Newsweek* was going broke, but we know it didn't.)

Until the axe fell, however, his fears were balanced by hopes of the big rise in salary he'd been promised earlier. The uncertainty made it difficult to plan for The Visit (less exciting for him now Dora had said she wouldn't be coming). He hoped the children wouldn't arrive until August, when he'd have banked his July salary... But that didn't suit the other parties, so our passages were booked on the *SS American Banker*, sailing 7 July, due in New York on the 17th.

Just as this news reached Griffin, he was given two weeks' notice. It was an especially bad moment, not only on account of The Visit. His new impecuniousness was the last straw in a long-running argument with Dora about money. This was more than a little spat: it touched on important issues. While working at *Newsweek* he'd sent her an occasional £5, and presents for the

---

[4] *An American friend sent me a selection of* Newsweek's *foreign reporting from the few months when Griffin was its Foreign Editor (see Acknowledgements). No bylines are given, so I can only be certain of his authorship in the case of the Metro-Vickers trial, but no doubt other pieces were also written by him.*

children, but preferred to hang on to the small surplus from his earnings while his own life was so insecure. This infuriated Dora. After subsidising him for months, in fact years, she had expected a regular sum, however small, now he was working – not just occasional 'hand-outs'. Griffin's attitude about 'his' money was another factor that told against him as a future partner. He was not mean, quite the opposite; he simply didn't have the financial instincts of a parent. Children need food and clothes every week, not just occasionally.

Dora had never been emotionally enslaved to Griffin as he was to her, and thus saw more clearly the limitations of their relationship. Her affection for him was never the kind of selfless love that wanted the best for *him*; but the more common variety that grew from what he meant to *her*. Thus she had felt 'deserted' in October 1932, but would never acknowledge his own valid reasons (explained time and again in his letters) for returning to America. Now the long separation, without their physical passion to confuse her mind, had convinced her they could never live together. The problem was, how to convey her decision to him?

Her letters of the next few weeks, though not exactly saying so, looked more and more like the brush-off to Griffin. 'I gather you want me to give up any idea of living with you,' he wrote in mid-June, hoping to be contradicted. After all the loving letters that had passed between them, Dora still hesitated to strike the hurtful blow. So instead of setting out plainly the sound reasons for her decision, she wrapped it in a barrage of unfair accusations and self-pity that made it all seem *his* fault. It was characteristic of her to look for culprits for her misfortunes, and her vanity made her always prone to self-deception. A worse deception at this moment was that, secretly, she now had another man in her sights.

Griffin did not know until later that Paul Gillard had been acting as school secretary during the summer term. By Dora's own account her romance with Paul did not blossom until the term was over, but she already knew he admired her. He also gave her what Griffin had withheld: approval of her continued opposition to the divorce. Paul's support prompted another spate of 'curses and insults' to Griffin on the subject, and made her determined to contest every point in the divorce proceedings. She was not able to stop it, but her endless prevarication, with Bertie's intransigence and counter-ploys on the other side, embittered and prolonged the negotiations beyond all reason. The poison lasted for years, just as Griffin had predicted.

In New York, Griffin's joyful anticipation of The Visit was blighted by the tone of Dora's letters. When he got the sack he'd half-expected she would cancel the plan, and was glad she didn't, or at least pretended to be (Dora must never doubt his long-term reliability as a partner, despite this spot of bad luck). Now *he* was tempted to cancel, to rush over to England to see if she meant what she was saying. Realising she did, his letters became abject and pitiful – while trying hard to remain dignified:

> Your letter about being "through" with me came early yesterday. A lot of cruel replies came to my mind as I stumbled about confused and hurt for a while but I didnt send em and I'm glad I didnt, for they would have been the tiniest and most passing part of what I feel. I really do love you as a person, Dora, beyond my claims on you...
>
> It's hard for me to defend myself from some of your attacks because I can't recognize myself in the creature you are attacking. I didnt plot with B. to deprive you of the security of your marriage and get you for myself... I havent... I didnt... I dont...

...and so on. Slowly it dawned on him that further argument was useless – yet he still couldn't believe she was rejecting him: 'You write to me now like an enemy' – 'You've got the whole thing twisted in your mind somehow...' In a desperate throw, he humbly offered himself as school secretary (not knowing she already had one) – providing he could keep 'at least half my time, and more than half my ego' for Writing. After his valiant defence of his ego against Dora's sustained attack, this is sad to see.

In between the tortured paragraphs, the letters on both sides were busy with practical details of The Visit. The children were fully recovered from chickenpox, but Harry's boils might still need some attention (boils were a plague in those pre-antibiotic days). Griffin had borrowed a cot for Roddy – and, best news of all, had received an invitation from Susan Glaspell to take us all to her house at Truro, near Provincetown. Wilson's house would be fine until then – he'd already gone to the Cape, so we'd have it all to ourselves.

> Hattie the black cook is a love, and will halve her time here for half pay... She'll be a wonderful creature to Harry and Rod – wonderful to look at; and Lily will like her. She talks a queer trailing southern dialect they'll have never heard before.

It is poignant to see all these preparations for an event which symbolised their union just at the moment when Griffin and Dora's relationship should have come to a natural end. Her love had died, and his would have withered away in time, if contact between them had ceased at this point. Perhaps he would have been able to build another, happier life if that had happened, instead of becoming an envious onlooker, from afar, on the family life he could not share.

In July 1933, however, Griffin did not foresee that bleak future. After all the ups and downs of the last few years, and knowing how Dora's moods could change, he had not lost hope of winning her back. Meanwhile he was looking forward to getting in some practice as a flesh-and-blood Dad.

CHAPTER 9

THE VISIT

Our trip to America, when I was just three years old and Roddy 15 months, is where my own memories of Griffin begin. For years as a small child I nursed two or three visual images which came to represent far-off America and My Daddy – walking along the New York quay holding his hand; shelling peas on the wooden steps of the house we stayed in; and a wonderland of toys in a playroom on the ship – whether on the outward voyage or coming home, I don't know. Added to this treasure box were a few things Lily told me – how she was seasick for two days on the way over, leaving us to the care of the ship's crew; how Roddy began casting to the winds a handful of dollar bills Griffin gave him to look at. I was so proud that Roddy did *not* remember this magical episode of our shared childhood, while I could pretend I did – one up to big sister!

All these years later Lily can still contribute to a reconstruction of The Visit through her two letters to Dora, one from the ship going over and the other from Cape Cod, preserved along with Griffin's. Whenever Lily had charge of us while Dora was elsewhere she would write the kind of news bulletins my own family used to get from London in the 1970s on our holidays in Cornwall, 'Just a line to say...'. So here in Dora's archive I learn from that familiar left-leaning script that after a week at sea, we were both 'wonderfully well & full of Vim', and Roddy, especially, a mascot of the crew. The stewardess had taken me to see 'several kittens and 27

Lily setting off with her charges

130

horses' on the lower deck of the *SS American Banker*, and the only thing that worried me on shipboard was the foghorn.

Escorting us to America was the first big responsibility Lily undertook for our family. I believe she first appeared in our lives in the year of my birth, 1930, when she and her husband came to work at the school, Walter as cook and Lily as a general helper with the children. Before that they had spent some years 'in service', that is, as domestics in rich households – standard work for people with little education at that time. Later Lily was promoted to Matron, a job for which she had no professional qualification, but her fund of common sense and general medical know-how – the kind every housewife had in the days when the doctor was only called in for something serious – was quite sufficient to run the Beacon Hill sickroom. Walter's cooking must have been adequate too, but his unpredictable temperament caused mayhem in the kitchen at times. He was a decidedly odd character, as we all knew in later years too; he would not have lasted at the school but for Dora's indulgence and Lily's support. She was his lifelong prop.

Lily soon became a prop for our family too. Close to Dora's own age, she was one of several women in Dora's life who loved and admired her and were unstintingly loyal through thick and thin. She may have been overawed by Dora at first, but these letters already show an easygoing relationship. She was not uncritical of Dora or 'GB' (as she always referred to Griffin), or any of the other adult players in the long-running family quarrels she observed from the sidelines. She came to know their sufferings and their foolishness better than anyone else. But she never saw it as her role to interfere or comment, just to give help and support when it was needed.

The arrival of Harriet and Roddy tied her more closely to the family, as distinct from the school. Lily loved children but had none of her own, so we became her children, and Roddy her special favourite. My childhood memories of her, naturally, are clearer for later years than those wispy recollections of the trip to America in 1933. She was the warm hearth at the centre of Beacon Hill School: all the kids, some of whom were very young, could find comfort with her. But Roddy and I always knew we had a special claim on her affections and special rights of access to Lily's Room, a cosy refuge in the big draughty houses which were 'home' for us, except for holidays in Cornwall. We had privileged access to Dora's Room too, but somehow or other she was always busy...[1]

Lily also had charge of two American pupils on the journey to New York – Joy Corbett,[2] and Marcia, Jed Taggard's daughter, returning home for the

---

[1] *I remember best the years when the school was at Kingwell Hall, in Somerset – see Chapter 14, where Lily's role in the school is further described.*

[2] *Joy was the illegitimate daughter of an American teacher who so admired the Russell educational philosophy that she sent Joy to Beacon Hill from the age of two. She usually spent the shorter holidays with our family as her mother, Una, couldn't have her during the school year. Joy will reappear as an adult in Chapter 19.*

summer holidays. Jed and Griffin between them gave Lily a whirl in New York City in the few days we spent there. On the first night Jed bore her off to 'the handsomest movie she could think of', and the next evening, leaving Hattie (the black cook) to mind the sleeping children, Griffin took her to a show, bought her an ice cream soda, and showed her the skyscrapers.

On board the SS American Banker at Southampton (Joy Corbett on my right)

These treats did not win her over: in later years all she could remember was how sweltering hot it was. 'I don't think I could Have existed long in the City', she wrote to Dora from Cape Cod, 'everything seemed to be dangerous to me the House the garden the Windows the streets I had that feeling all the time I was there & G. was rather nervous about the Children which made things worse for me...'. She was right about Griffin's fears: he couldn't wait to get us to the safety of the countryside.

He had awaited our arrival with mixed feelings. Of course he longed to see his children and show us off to his friends, but he knew our stay would delay his search for new work and use up his meagre savings, leaving him no funds for a visit to England to resolve his tangled relations with Dora. On 29 June he agonised over a long letter, suggesting it might be better to cancel the whole arrangement, find some commissions for articles from Europe and come over to sort things out with her. In the end he didn't send a cable 'Cancel', but he did send the anguished screed.

Further hurtful letters came from Dora during our stay. Most of these are missing from his file, but one that is there, written on 24 July, must have sunk his heart into his boots. Another long list of his alleged crimes ended with a cool dismissal: 'I love to think of you in relation to the children & I hope all the time for your own fulfilment, but somehow it no longer seems to have anything to do with me.'

Despite the cruel barbs still flying across the Atlantic, Griffin was overjoyed to have us with him. His first report to Dora was the usual fond parent's discovery that his own children are something special: 'Yesterday a tableful of New Yorkers in the garden gasped at their health and beauty. There aren't children here like these.' Studying our pudgy faces for traces of his Irish ancestry, he pronounced Harriet a Barry, and Roddy like Dora (an accurate perception). Oh, how he preened before the procession of our admirers! He was especially touched when one old friend, Edna Kenton, arrived with 'a straw bag crammed with ingenious, intelligent gifts that she could ill afford to buy'.

But the small, stony garden and other aspects of life in New York City soon convinced him that this was no fit place for us:

> Yesterday Lily and I toiled up through the hot streets crammed with charging busses and shrieking lorrymen to a bit of a park on the river a mile beyond my old flat – a poor affair filled with anemic incubator babies and slattern Irish nurse maids with bad teeth. Rod swaggered crowing to an old woman on a bench and clasped her knees; she drew away as if she had been stung. Then she began to talk to herself and presently burst into hot tears and looked away fiercely. I drew our children away, appalled... I am glad our children are well born, bits of salvage from the jungle life.

Griffin must have seen such derelicts in city parks all over the world; only now did the instincts of a bourgeois parent make him recoil from them.

A few days later he and Lily were both writing ecstatic reports of Cape Cod and Susan Glaspell's house, 'a pretty shingled affair filled with books inside and surrounded by flower beds'. Griffin described the area as Cornwall without the cliffs (Cape Cod has dunes instead). Lily and I thought so too:

> Harriet has great impressions of this place which she calls Cornwall. I must say I think she is right. It is very much like it the House is situated 10 miles out of Provincetown a most beautiful Run through miles of Country Lanes and White Houses dotted here and there with lovely gardens and flowers. It just reminds me of the Journey from Penzance to Carn Voel & the house is very quaint the Floors are Painted and Polished Orange and green just a few mats of all colours to match the Various Rooms.

Evidently Susan shared Dora's 'modern' taste for bright colours: Carn Voel also had lots of orange paint in the old days. The house she lived in, where we stayed, was at Truro; her other house, in Provincetown, was let to Edmund Wilson that summer. Susan had a cook called Isabel, a dog called Tucker, and a new car which she could not drive. As Griffin also could not drive (despite those lessons in the old Ford back in 1928), a local lad was employed to take us in Susan's car to the beach a mile away. With loaned toys and neighbouring children to play with, everything was set up for a marvellous holiday.

Susan and Mary Vorse were year-round residents, key figures in the Provincetown artistic community that had begun to colonise the area early in the century, just as artists also settled in Newlyn and St Ives in Cornwall. Mary was on assignment in Europe at the time we were there, reporting the ominous developments in Nazi Germany. Her house was let to summer visitors, but

Griffin mentioned her daughter Ellen living in a cottage nearby, 'writing stories'. In 1949 I stayed with Mary in her Provincetown home, Kibbe Cook's House, which she loved and wrote about with a passion like Dora's for Carn Voel. During another summer of my college years in America, Kate and her husband Charlie and I spent a week's holiday in Mary's barn, equipped in a basic way for unfussy guests. My adult memories, too, rate Cape Cod alongside Cornwall as a special place.

Griffin's description of Susan (see ahead) shows her at a low ebb, deserted by her husband Norman a year previously. In years gone by she had been a very successful playwright, a liberal and feminist who had migrated with her first husband, George Cram Cook, from the backwoods of Iowa to the *avant garde* intellectual circle of Greenwich Village. There she first became friends with Mary, and probably with Griffin too. As described in Chapter 1, Mary and the Cooks later moved to Provincetown, where in 1915 George Cook and others founded the Provincetown Players. In 1916, Eugene O'Neill was launched into fame from there.

A portrait of Susan Glaspell, in the Truro Historical Museum

The play-reading scene in the film *Reds* could well have been trying out a play by Susan, whose work was then considered as good as O'Neill's. Later Susan dropped into obscurity while O'Neill became the golden boy of American theatre (feminists would explain that in their own way). But interest in Susan's work revived in England many years later: one of her plays, *Inheritors*, was staged in 1997 in Richmond, Surrey, just as a new filmed version of Arthur Miller's *The Crucible* was making the rounds. Susan's play, written during the Red Scare of 1920, made the same points about freedom of conscience and the tyranny of the mob as Arthur Miller's play, written during the Red Scare of the 1950s.

No photos of our holiday in summer 1933 exist. This is Susan's house and a local beach in the 1990s.

    During this holiday, brief as it was and young as I was, a strong impression of My Daddy must have formed in my childish mind. After this summer I saw him only rarely and briefly until I was 15, but he was always a powerful presence in my imagination. Across three thousand miles and years of separation, his occasional vivid letters and, I can only suppose, my memories of Summer 1933, fed my little girl's romantic fixation on faraway Daddy. Here in Cape Cod, in the fragments of Lily's and Griffin's letters, I see my childhood psyche developing. In New York I had told a friend of Griffin's I had two homes, one English and the other ''Merican'; but it must have been the Cape Cod scene that came to represent my imaginary American home. There I had familiar security with Lily, lavish attention from Griffin, and, as Lily reported, a new focus for my affection in Susan: 'H. says she likes America & has made Herself very Charming to Susan which is about the only one person in our adventure she has taken to.'
    Not surprisingly, Griffin gave more attention to his walking, talking daughter than to toddler Roddy. He was less shy than me, and always a wow with strangers. When not at the beach with Lily, I spent my time sitting or

walking with Daddy:

> Harry is playing about my typewriter, asking me a million questions and when I tell her I am working asking the same ones over in a whispering voice... Everyone adores the great lusty Rod, who flashes smiles everywhere. I give H. one big hug every day, a ceremonial one, and it is then she tries to remember when I was in England. It is all tucked away in her subconscious I think – little thoughts she has thunk come out as we walk alone in the woods.

Yet it seems I had a clear idea of my double paternity, having told Griffin's friends my name was 'Harriet Ruth Russell Barry' (not quite accurate: Russell came last), and assigning different roles to Bertie and Griffin that perhaps parroted Dora's wishes – 'On a long walk yesterday through the pine woods she told me she would like "Mr" (stressing the mister) Russell for a daddy and me to play with.'

As the weeks passed, though always including happy news of the children, Griffin's letters to Dora became sharper, in response to hostile missives – or silence – from her. This extract, from a letter of 1 August, includes a sad view of Susan, who had earlier told him 'the children are bringing her back to life'.

> I think you owe Susan something more than the dry remark that it is good of her to have us followed by the instant suspicion that she'll steal your children. Most of her money has gone, though this place remains to her, yet she seems determined that we shall be her guests and daily, in her forlorn and old maidish way, she thinks up a new thing to do for your children. Next week it will be a children's party, ice cream freezer and all; she has given up her bedroom to them and her whole house is of course changed by them, including her dog Tucker who after days of jealous snarling has only lately made friends with Harry... Susan is over the worst of her rigors, I think, but is a shattered woman. She is twenty years older than you exactly [I think he meant ten]; and has nothing left save her writing ability... She has done no writing since Norman left but this week, to everyone's relief, has begun a one-act play. That will be her way out, if at all.[3]

Susan's plight echoed his own... 'Please my dear inform me as to the situation as it now stands. Surely you owe me that.' A few days later, bitterly complaining of Dora's 'stone-age treatment' of him, he is further down the road to despair:

---

[3] *Despite her reputation as a playwright, Susan thought of herself as primarily a novelist. Her novel* Fidelity, *first published in 1915 (in Britain in 1924), was re-published by Persephone Books in London in 1999. A new preface saw it as a landmark of early feminism, likening its heroine to Madame Bovary, or Nora in Ibsen's* The Doll's House, *and pointed out its influence on authors like Sinclair Lewis. Susan's depressed middle age seems especially poignant when we consider this lasting appreciation of her work.*

I must get rid as quickly as I can of the emotional drain to you. Until I do I am bled white. The children's being here and all the emotions that go to them, thence to you, continue the drain... The kids are unutterably dear to me, but their coming was another mistake among all those we have made – a mistake because of the expense and the delay in my money-making. A conference with you, even in a London park or at a restaurant table, might have been better. I fear words between us would avail nothing, though. They have all been used.

Missing letters leave me with few details of the last part of our stay. Earlier Griffin had asked, with Lily's endorsement, if we could all stay until 15 September, but Dora must have vetoed that idea. In early August, Jed Taggard had written to Griffin that as Marcia would not be returning to Beacon Hill for the coming year, would he like to use her return steamer ticket to England? This prompted another agonising letter of indecision to Dora. It was not good timing; he would have little time to seek work commissions before coming – but on the other hand, 'Seeing and talking with you...*might* make a change in our morale...it's up to you to say whether it's worth risking.' He asked her to cable 'something ambiguous' to indicate Yes or No, 'since the message will come over the phone of an old friend with whom I don't want to discuss the innards of our affairs'.

The answer must have been 'No'. In Dora's collection this is Griffin's last letter of the holiday before a tattered, browned-off, one-page bulletin dated 28 August, giving details of our sailing on 1 September and arrival on the 10th. It is a sad and bitter letter. He could find no words to reply to 'another statement of your attitude to me', but he could at least 'withdraw from the rat-pit where you return barbarity from B. with barbarity to me'. This he now proposed to do. The letter concludes:

> Nothing has shown your want of taste and insight more clearly than letters repeating that surely the children's visit will make me happy. Being with them has been the most painful experience of my life.
> G.B.

Blithely ignoring his other letters of the summer, and even other parts of this one, in *The Tamarisk Tree* Dora shamelessly used that last sentence to denigrate Griffin and make it seem that *she* was the injured party:

> I was distressed...by a furious letter from Griffin, angry at me for having sent the children to him, but still more for writing to say that I thought it must have given him great pleasure to see them. On the contrary, being with them had been for him, he said, a 'painful experience'. It seemed that I could do nothing right.[4]

[4] *Dora Russell, op. cit., p.271.*

As they always say, history is written by the survivors. At this stage in Dora's autobiography Griffin is already fading into an 'episode' that is now over. The passage above follows the account of her own activities in the summer of 1933 as she was whirled into a new romance – a love affair on an altogether higher plane than her relationship with Griffin, if we are to believe her own account of it.

PART II

TRANSATLANTIC VOYAGES

CHAPTER 10

DORA'S DESPAIR

After the memorable summer of 1933, for six years Griffin's only contact with Dora and his children would be a series of brief, often stormy meetings and sad partings, followed by the longer separation of the Second World War. Their love affair was over – though not on Griffin's side. For a while, in her distress, Dora selfishly exploited his undying love for her own purposes, and in so doing, kept his foolish hopes alive. When she no longer needed it, his fidelity became a tiresome burden.

✱ ✱ ✱

Griffin's summer ended miserably. I can only guess at the contents of a missing letter from Dora which seems to have included her long-term view of how to manage their joint parenthood, while living separately. Griffin's tight-lipped reply was carefully matter of fact, outwardly accepting her message, 'it's all over', but unable to resist the usual point-by-point rebuttal of her 'reasons' for rejecting him. Forlornly he continued to hope Dora could be *argued* into loving him again.

His earlier remark about the 'painful experience' of seeing us was explained in follow-up letters. How could it not be bitter-sweet, he laments, to have his children in his care just when her letters were expelling him from their lives? All this inclines me to forgive his parting view of three-year-old me as a belligerent little feminist:

> Harry, looking so much a Barry, seems very like you. She asked me categorically as she left if I was going back to "promisetown" to sleep with Susan and when I said "no" invited me courteously to come to Telegraph to visit "us". That "us" smote me; it had your very tone. I saw the women behind her [in your line]...who've suffered from male

tyranny and how this last mite, all unconsciously, revenges them on me with that cool invitation to call on her in a place apart...

Oh come now, Dad, I was only trying to be polite!

...Harry is wilful, intelligent and warm and I like her companionship better than anybody's. But it was Rod who touched me direly. Such a shouting, free, dancing, careless boy. Susan called him "a golden boy". He's beautiful and he looks more like you than like me. He'll overestimate his strength and rush into follies later as I think Harry may not. You must steer him away from those that will cripple him...

These last sentences were uncannily perceptive of Roddy's adult character, and the more cautious element in mine. How could Griffin have sized us up so accurately on the acquaintance of a few weeks?

By now he was back in New York, looking for work. Both he and Bunny Wilson were so broke they couldn't afford coal for heating and nearly got evicted for overdue rent. They quarrelled, and Griffin felt he should leave... But where could he go? His mood was black and his fingers stiff with cold as he answered a letter from Dora: 'You intimate you are looking for another man. If he lives with you, this means another father for my children. It is all a queer, queer history. I don't understand you.'

Before long he did understand, all too clearly, for Dora's next letter was a bombshell – One, *Paul Gillard is dead!* Two, *I loved him more than anyone else in the world!*

I have never been able to believe in Dora's fantasy figure, Paul Gillard, the man she always claimed was the true love of her life. The man himself existed, of course – here's a copy of his photograph from *The Tamarisk Tree*; but the young demi-god of supreme beauty and rare artistic sensitivity she describes there is simply too good to be true. Only Dora's romantic nature and her habit of self-delusion can explain her girlish notion that this unlikely suitor, had he lived, could have brought her lifelong happiness. How could she have held to that belief for the rest of her life?

That she could see him in that light *at the time*, I can understand; and having read through

Paul Gillard

her letters to Griffin, and his to her, I understand it even better. Her unhappiness over Bertie, and then Griffin's 'desertion', the strain of running the almost-bankrupt school, the tortuous and humiliating legal tangle and her anxiety about John and Kate, all combined to unbalance her emotionally to the point of breakdown. This personable young man, who suddenly revealed his admiration for her, could easily seem like a white knight to a very distressed damsel. When her plan 'to escape from reality' (Griffin's words) by running away with Paul was blocked by his tragic death, it's not surprising she fell over the brink into utter despair. Her half-crazed behaviour in the following months – briefly described in her own book and graphically shown in her letters to Griffin – depicts a state of complete mental collapse.

It was during the Easter holiday in Cornwall that Dora first came to see Paul as a soulmate, although by her own account she only discovered his love for her when he was acting as school secretary during the summer term. In August, with all four children visiting their fathers, she went to see him in Plymouth. In *The Tamarisk Tree* this is when she gets lyrical, recounting the discovery of their love as they explored the Devon lanes in her Austin 7. Apparently they had both been smitten at their first meeting in 1930, when Dora was heavily pregnant with me, and had hidden their love – in Dora's case even from herself – until now.

What was this paragon like, to deserve such adulation? Handsome, everyone seems to agree; and ambitious. Striving to escape from his nondescript life in Devon, he had reached the shallow end of Bloomsbury society in London, where in 1930 he met Griffin, then Dora – and shortly afterwards, inadvertently came to Carn Voel (as recounted in Chapter 5). Having previously worked for a bank in Paris, he had given up regular work to write a novel. He was active in the Communist Party in Plymouth, and with the 'rough trade' of the gay scene there. All in all there seems little to explain Dora's admiration beyond his personal charm – and Griffin also attested to that.

Dora doesn't make clear either in her book or letters to Griffin, whether she and Paul ever actually made love. Since he was homosexual and had never had relations with a woman (at first he told her he had, but later admitted he'd lied), this would have been a matter of some importance in the future relationship she was anticipating. It is also unclear how far Paul reciprocated her feelings, or believed they could 'make a go of it' together.[1] What *she* was planning, she later told Griffin, was to go with him to Paris at Christmas, taking me and Roddy along, 'and the divorce would then have to take its chance'.

---

[1] *Ray Monk, in his trawl through* all *the documentation relevant to these events and relationships, found 'no indication whatever that [Paul] was interested in Dora romantically'. Unlike Dora's, his account of the Gillard affair is full and impartial, and quite intriguing – see* Bertrand Russell: The Ghost of Madness, *op.cit, p.150 et seq. From my reading of Dora's letters to Griffin, I'm inclined to agree that the infatuation was on her side only – but my concern is with her feelings for him, and thereby the effect of the affair on her relationship with Griffin.*

Apart from a few days in October, when she went to Plymouth to try to persuade him to come back to Telegraph House, the summer holiday was the only period Dora spent alone with Paul. On the night of 31 October 1933 he died by falling down a railway embankment – whether by accident, suicide, or even murder, has never been fully established. (Further speculation on this point will be found in the next chapter.) At the time, Dora convinced herself he had a 'death wish', and that if she had insisted he return to the school she could have saved his life. Later she came to think he had been killed by Fascists, perhaps while spying on their activities. Thus she added to her own grief in the months after Paul's death, and in later years dramatised it as the Great Tragedy of her life. Paul had offered her hope of 'an un-dreamed-of personal and mutual fulfilment', she tells us in *The Tamarisk Tree*, and when he died this hope was lost forever.

Friends and admirers of Dora are bound to wonder why she accorded Paul Gillard such mythic status. At first the romantic legend may have been a useful fender against Griffin; but later, I believe, she needed to perpetuate it for another reason – as a lifelong excuse for her failure to find a worthy replacement for Bertie. Dora had to triumph over adversity – it was not in her nature to admit defeat; yet having been ousted so cruelly from the marriage she felt she was 'made for', she never formed another relationship she could be proud of. Paul Gillard was held aloft ever afterwards as The Reason Why.

Griffin knew nothing of Dora's new passion until her letter of 5 November, ten close-written pages relating the whole saga of her relationship with Paul. The key phrases must have run through his heart like icicles:

> ...after a time I found how much he loved me, had loved since the first moment he set eyes on me and had never felt such a feeling for a woman... I found I loved him too, discovered that in a way I always had done...

The shock sent Griffin reeling. His letters of the next few weeks are almost as distraught as Dora's, many scrawled in pencil, words almost falling off the page or fiercely crossed out as he veered between tender love and venom.

> I had thought you had a lover, but put the thought out of my mind. Couldn't face any more agony. Now suddenly I have only pity and love for you, my own dearest, and a desire to protect you from further sorrow, if I could...[Sympathy and affection for Paul follow, but he couldn't keep it up]. Now jealousy has me by the throat, as it inevitably would. And hatred, and contempt. I see that your hungry ego is getting some satisfaction out of these details so carefully stated to me. I cannot undo the day when I placed myself in your power... There's only Paul's way out...

And of course he saw a plot in the way she 'flung the children to him last summer' so that she could spend the time with another man. 'Well, he's dead now, and has missed the torture that he would have met' if he had lived, and, like Griffin before him, 'had failed to serve your diverse needs'.

Griffin was apparently surprised to learn who 'the other man' was, although Dora claimed Paul had told him he loved her. This Griffin–Dora–Paul triangle was indeed complicated. Griffin, as we know, was bisexual, and it seems that he too had at one time been attracted to Paul. Yes, he was a fine person, he agrees with Dora, 'though I didn't love him'.

> But I did make gay homosexual proposals (which didn't mean much in themselves to me) because his quality was irresistible as a person. When he conveyed them underhandedly to you I ceased to like him; I'm always bewildered and put off by intrigue – not that this one mattered as between you and me. Now I see he did that because he was deeply drawn to you –

Really? Was Paul deeply drawn to Dora? Ray Monk suspected, after reading Paul's unpublished novel, that he was more deeply drawn to Griffin! Be that as it may, Paul's role in my story derives only from the fact that Dora loved him, and then he died.

Dora's first letter, telling Griffin 'the whole story', was written in one swoop, without hesitation or correction, and no recognition that its contents might upset the recipient. Griffin can be excused for thinking her deliberately cruel, but I see this and other letters from her half-demented state after Paul's death as a kind of stream of consciousness, in which she was hardly aware of the reader at the other end.[2] The letters are full of inconsistency and wild exaggeration. Most pitiable is her difficulty in coping with the school while she feels so alone and bereft. The children swarm around her 'like cannibals'; even Harry and Rod demand more than she can give. Griffin had better take them when he's sorted himself out; he'll manage them better than 'a mother who is no more than a ghost'.

Such 'normal' manifestations of grief Griffin could respond to with sympathy; it was the endless eulogising of Paul that got him down. More than once he begged her to spare him – 'This murdering by letter must stop.' He wasn't immune to wild excesses himself, though. In response to Dora's musing that she might seek solace with other lovers, he worked himself into a froth of jealousy, warning her with Victorian thunder to turn away from 'the promiscuous path'.

---

[2] *Further evidence of her distracted state of mind is the letter she wrote to Bertie on the day before the one 'confessing all' to Griffin. This too was a cry of distress, recklessly throwing herself on his mercy at a time when he had none for her. Without replying, he sent it to his lawyer in case it might be useful in the forthcoming divorce proceedings.*

In calmer mood, however, he recognised the irrationality in her letters and tried a little tentative psychotherapy:

> It is against reason that a relation with a divided and inverted boy should have given you permanent happiness, but to think so, in loneliness and sex starvation, at nearly forty and in the middle of a costly break in your whole life through the desertion of a husband and a lover both – all that makes me think it must be complex determined almost wholly. I do not think you would have lived with Paul for long...

'Cannibals' at play. School life went on as usual, but Dora was too distraught to care.

Despite Dora's hysterical letters, such are the wily ways of the enslaved heart that within a few weeks Griffin was saying to himself, 'OK, so there was another man, but now he's out of the way, maybe there's still hope for me...'. And there was sense in this view: how *could* this brief affair have blotted out his own five years and two children with Dora? Once over the shock of her betrayal, he came to see her obsession with Paul as a 'neurosis' that would pass, and cautiously resumed his own wooing. He urgently needed to regain some emotional stability himself. Just as the news about Paul reached him he'd landed a job, and was having to learn difficult new work while every letter from England further undermined his morale.

During the New Deal, and then the Second World War, government jobs were relatively easy to find. Washington now became Griffin's base, starting with a job in a key New Deal agency, the National Recovery Administration (NRA). Its role in restoring some kind of economic balance to America was to regulate industrial production through agreed 'codes' for each trade which would stabilise prices for the products and also guarantee fair wages and working conditions. Griffin was employed by the NRA's Labor Advisory Board to promote and safeguard workers' interests at the hearings where these codes were being formulated. Like so much of the New Deal, this was experimental work, begun at a time when there was a widespread feeling that the god of Capitalism had failed. As 'Labor's attorney' versus the wicked capitalists, Griffin felt he was in the front line just as much as his radical friends organising farmers' strikes out west.

He'd been recruited by a friend hastily gathering a team for this new venture, but felt ill qualified for the work: most of his colleagues were 'economists and lawyers from the universities'. Even so, he thought he could 'fake it' for the few months the job was expected to last (if only Dora's letters would let him sleep at night!). Meanwhile his higher hopes were fixed on the American embassy in Moscow, soon to be re-opened as Washington finally accorded diplomatic recognition to the Soviet government. Failing that, he hoped to get abroad as a foreign correspondent, the work he felt best suited his talents. His new flat-sharer (at 1620 P street N W), Henry Collins, an old friend with whom he'd been to Russia in 1927, had told him there was an appointment coming up soon at the *Washington Post*.

Unfortunately none of these lines landed a fish, despite two friendly interviews with the new ambassador to Moscow, William Bullitt, another old friend from Griffin's past. But he was determined to get to England next summer, come what may, and began saving every penny for a steamer ticket.

As Christmas approached, he received some gifts from his mother to be sent on to the children. He was touched that she'd sat up all night sewing doll's clothes for me ('Think of the far-off day when Harry at 75 will be doing that for her grandchildren...'). On impulse he included in the parcel a dress for Dora (it was too small, as the clothes he sent her always were, but she responded gratefully anyway).

Evidently he'd now made peace with his mother after a ticking-off from her some weeks earlier (he sent that letter on to Dora for its appreciation of *In Defence of Children*, which Mrs Barry had had to queue for at the public library in Portland, Oregon).

> I say 'finished, reading it but that is far from true. I want it permanently on my table where I can take it up every day for a browse here and there. I shall when I can afford to buy it. I think it a great book, radical and all as it is. probably the radicalism in it is what holds me. But is its so intensely from a woman's standpoint and is so discerning, free and honest as well as replete with wide experience and knowledge, that it goes into my inner consciousness in a great way. Knowing through you when and how she wrote it and under what circumstances I marvel at her strength and versatility.

The two women in Griffin's life were on the same wavelength

Knowing she couldn't afford to cross the continent to see us, Griffin hadn't told her about our visit to America, only giving Susan Glaspell's address for himself 'for a month'. Six weeks later his mother was waiting impatiently for further news:

> What *is* the matter? You know there is really a substantial reason for me to be anxious during any lapse in hearing from you because of your experimental manner of living, and of life in most ways. I watch it all with heart and brain keenly tuned to all you are developing through these processes and, mostly, it all inspires me with new and bigger vision. But the experimental nature of these things with you is always present and I can never figure out on usual lines what you may be doing or just how life as a whole is going with you...
> Now, Griffin, I am going to submit this to the wide wide world and send it to the place in Mass – not knowing when or where it will reach you...
> I SHALL LOOK FOR IMMEDIATE REPLY NO MATTER WHAT ABIDES.

Poor Harriet Barry. All mothers know how she was feeling. No doubt Griffin would have written to her more often if he'd had happier news to impart.

At this stage he didn't know whether he was coming or going. After 'another recital of the divinity of Paul', three lonely Christmas days were spent writing vitriol back. By mid-January he was optimistic again: 'What steals over me like a sweet drug in your last 2 letters is the assumption of some community between us still.' A week later he was flattened by 'the most disastrous letter of all'. Pleading for his own peace of mind, and worried by Dora's morbid moods, he begged her to make no plans or decisions until he could get to England. He had long since conceded her argument that he should never have left her alone in 1932: how 'abundantly right' was she, and how 'tragically wrong' was he – or some such words – creep into every letter.

It's true that Dora had never forgiven that 'desertion', but Griffin was foolish to hope he could make up for it now. She still needed him as confidant and scapegoat, and would continue to use him for both purposes for some time to come, but by this time she had firmly decided against him as a future partner. That decision had little to do with Paul Gillard, but it suited Griffin to think it had; for if Dora's 'irrational' fixation on Paul had caused her to reject him, it followed that when she came to her senses, he'd have a chance to win her back.

By mid-March Dora seemed to be over the worst of her grief. After months of prevarication, she had at last filed a petition for divorce, and at first was confident that, as the 'innocent party', she'd be granted full custody of John and Kate. When she heard that Bertie, anticipating that claim, had had them made

Wards of the chancery court, she was thrown off-balance again.[3]

Some letters to Griffin in April and May were almost hysterical, lapsing into wild reveries about Paul and portraying herself as a tragic heroine broken on the wheel of Love. Children have always bored her, she doesn't want the bloody school, only to be a loving wife to 'a real husband' who will bring her 'answering love that is divine and unafraid...'. This soppy Dora cannot be taken seriously. It is contradicted by everything we know of her life and character before and after this sad period of emotional disorientation.

Some changes in her thinking at this time did have a lasting effect. Her association with Paul pushed her closer to the Communist Party, and to take up a deliberately 'proletarian' outlook in politics. She never joined the Party, but became and remained a fellow-traveller, always ready to trumpet the good and overlook the bad in Communism. She explained to Griffin her new feeling for working people:

> I have been thinking lately of how people used to come to our house in Chelsea for help when we stood for Parliament, poor people of all kinds in difficulties, and how they were never human beings to us or we to them because of our class and position. And how really I belonged with them, like the lady who wanted to run away with the gipsies. When I went lately to the Hunger Marchers congress in London I felt I was really seeing my own people for the first time – no longer helping them as oppressed inferior people – though of course lots of them are, as lots of the bourgeoisie are – but as my own people, and friends. Their faces were lovely, Devonshire men, Welshmen, Cornishmen, pale mothers from Scotland. I feel like them and I am like them, and like all the people one meets in pubs, or like the real artists and writers, not the fake snobs in Bloomsbury. And so was Paul.

Just as Bertie the aristocrat had to be written out of this new philosophy, so Paul had to be written in. He was not working class – his parents had both been schoolteachers – but Dora could see him as a man of the people 'corrupted by middle class values', just as she had been corrupted intellectually by her association with Bertie. How different her life might have been if Bertie had not 'caught and jailed me when I was young', if she had not been 'messed about by the intellectuals who as Lawrence says have "sex in the head" and do not live below the waistline'. As for Paul –

---

[3] *Chapter 5 of Ray Monk's book on Bertrand Russell, op.cit., gives a full account of the divorce proceedings. The issue of custody was crucial. By making John and Kate Wards in Chancery, Bertie aimed to achieve a tricky double purpose. The divorce court must be convinced that Dora was a blameless wife deserving the divorce he wanted; but if the chancery court were given jurisdiction over the children, different judges could be persuaded that she was morally unfit to have sole custody. My next chapter includes another instalment of this sub-plot.*

He was all that is lovely & fluid & creative in England twisted by the Puritanism of middle class culture, & by the cheap cynicism of the boulevards. Corrupted by his ambition to be smart like the rest, as I was corrupted by Bertie's intellectual nonsense.

Note the tie-up with D H Lawrence, more explicitly stated in another of Dora's letters to Griffin. *Lady Chatterley's Lover* was first published in 1928[4] and Lawrence's earthy philosophy had been a hot topic of drawing-room discussion ever since. Dora, who felt she'd been deprived of sex in her youth, could easily see herself as the sex-starved Lady C married to her impotent Lord, though I'm not sure the poetical, homosexual Paul was fittingly cast as the lusty gamekeeper (Griffin might have played the role better, but of course he was out of the running now).

Dora's allegiance to 'proletarian values' was heartfelt, but a bit phoney. She was not a snob of any kind, and over the years many 'ordinary people' became her close friends; but all were either political connections, or, like Lily, tied to the family by a personal connection. Dora was no better able than other middle class people to empathise with the 'broad masses', and would have recoiled from the philistinism and reactionary views of lumpen *Sun*-readers, if she'd ever known any. Like other socialists, she deplored the lack of 'revolutionary consciousness' among the British working class, and at the end of her life was dismayed to see them seduced by Thatcherism (weren't we all).

Thus the departure of Bertie from her life marked a change in Dora's personality to the mother who brought up Roddy and me, slightly different from the one John and Kate had known when they were small. In rejecting the 'aristocratic airs' she attributed to Bertie, she also denounced the 'bourgeois values' of Dartington Hall School, where John and Kate were sent in 1934.[5] If Beacon Hill had to close, she told Griffin, she wanted Roddy and me to go to a 'proletarian school'. Yet another facet of her new consciousness was a dyed-in-the-wool Englishness: when visiting Paul and his family in Plymouth she had discovered the 'ancestral magic' which bound them together and, by the same token, ruled out a future with Griffin.[6]

This slightly-different Dora emerging from an emotional whirlpool in the spring of 1934 was the person with whom Griffin would have to negotiate in future years: embittered towards men (except dead, saintly Paul, and yes-men who wouldn't cross her); near-communist in politics; and with a romantic

---

[4] *The full, unexpurgated version could not be published in England until after the memorable 'obscenity trial' of 1960 – a landmark step towards the permissive society of today.*

[5] *Her personal antipathy was exacerbated by professional jealousy and envy of Dartington's wealth, more fully explained later.*

[6] *As I have remarked before, there was a fundamental incompatibility between Griffin's archetypal Americanness and Dora's romantic Englishness. Curiously, although he often railed against English conventions and behaviour, this gulf between them never deterred Griffin in his pursuit of her.*

attachment to 'the working class' which made little sense to an American, even an old-time radical like Griffin. I remember as an adult being conscious of this political difference between them, but I doubt if it affected their relations in 1934. More personal matters were on the agenda when they met that summer for the first time since their tearful farewell at Southampton in October 1932.

Awaiting Giffin at Telegraph House, June 1934:
Joy Corbett and me with the Russells' dog Sherry.

CHAPTER 11

THE DIVORCE AND AFTER

By 1934 Dora knew her affair with Griffin was over, albeit leaving consequences still to be coped with. In kindness to him she should have tried harder to convince him of that, instead of keeping him in perpetual uncertainty with letters blowing hot and cold by turns. But in the aftermath of the Paul affair, and with the anguish of divorce proceedings ahead, she still needed him for moral support and as an outlet for her turbulent feelings. After bearing her troubles alone for so many months, she looked forward as eagerly as he did to their reunion that summer.

There are few surviving letters from which to reconstruct this visit. Griffin seems to have left America early in June, and was back in New York by 5 August. His job at the National Recovery Administration having ended, one purpose of going to Europe was to look for work (he found none, but luckily was able to return to the NRA when he got back). Meeting Dora in England may have been a furtive secret, mindful of the separation deed designed to show her as a chaste deserted wife. Unusually, several letters are addressed care of Dora's mother in Edgware, from where she wrote to him, back in New York, in mid-August. This was probably their illicit trysting-place out of sight of 'spies'. Bertie and his lawyers were now sniffing around for evidence to blacken Dora's name in preparation for a showdown over custody of John and Kate. Affidavits about her immoral character had been obtained from staff at Telegraph House, and Griffin's arrival in England had been noted.[1]

While still regretting having agreed to the divorce, in more rational moments Dora now accepted the inevitable. The custody of John and Kate was her main concern as she waited apprehensively for the case to come to court. She was painfully aware of the muck-raking going on behind the scenes, but

---

[1] Dora's relationship with Paul, as well as Griffin, was of interest in this enquiry: if necessary, Bertie was ready to use her demented letter written just after Paul's death to prevent her getting sole custody.

she couldn't afford the legal costs of a counter-campaign. In May, she tried to enlist the support of Ottoline Morell, but found her unsympathetic ('you see what these aristocrats are', she commented bitterly to Griffin).[2] During the summer they both talked to Francis Meynell, a friend of all the parties concerned, who had been appointed as one of John and Kate's Trustees; and later, with some trepidation, Griffin wrote to him supporting Dora's case for full custody. His intervention had no effect.

Also at issue was the question of John and Kate's schooling. Dora could not prevent Bertie from sending them to Dartington in September 1934, but she still hoped to get them back when – if – she was granted custody by the divorce court.[3]

One of her tasks that Griffin shared that summer was house-hunting for the school, as Bertie now wanted Telegraph House for his family home. He had expected Dora to close the school, but she was determined to keep it going and show the world it could thrive without him. Rightly so, for she was a born educator, and loved the work. Luckily Beacon Hill still had some good times ahead. In September 1934 the staff and children moved into Boyles Court, a beautiful Georgian house with magnificent grounds, near Brentwood in Essex. I still remember the look and feel of that lovely place, which like all the premises of the school was also our family home except for holidays in Cornwall. In spite of the looming cloud of the divorce court ahead, Dora wrote to Griffin in peaceful contentment from there in the first weeks of the new term, while he equally delightedly could picture her 'in that lovely yellow room with many cupboards'.

It seems all the wrath and insults hurled across the Atlantic in the past two years were set aside for a rare period of harmony that summer. They even shared a bed again, although Dora 'spitting venom' after an affectionate night made their last day miserable, Griffin complained in a rambling letter written on the voyage home. Nevertheless in her first letter after his visit Dora wistfully toyed with the idea of 'dropping everything' to bring the children and Lily over to America: 'I'd almost come if you cabled me now.' *Almost* – that's the key word, for in the next sentence she was fretting about John and Kate's clothing list for Dartington, and the still-incomplete negotiations for Boyles Court. Yet Griffin *almost* took that letter seriously, wondering in his reply if he should cable, even now...? But no, it's better as things are, as she has work in England she does so well, and he can live more cheaply on his own in America, sending

---

[2] Lady Ottoline Morell had been one of Bertie's grand passions in the pre-Dora era, and remained a close friend of his. Dora hoped she would take 'a mother's view' about custody, but Ottoline, after consulting Bertie's lawyers, said she thought Bertie should have custody and Dora only rights of access.

[3] Later in 1934 John and Kate would become 13 and 11 respectively, a good argument for sending them to Dartington, although Dora presumably thought she had the resources to continue teaching them. There were a few older pupils at Beacon Hill in the early days, but it was essentially a primary school.

A MAN OF SMALL IMPORTANCE

To advertise the new home of Beacon Hill Hill School, Dora had some publicity photos taken: a biology lesson; gardening with a group of younger pupils; fire drill from a bedroom (opposite).

her money when he can. All this was play-acting: he knew there were insuperable barriers to her leaving England at that time. But the confident tone of these letters suggests renewed hope (unstated, for fear it might vanish again) that he and Dora would eventually end up together.

As so often in this turbulent correspondence, these few kindly letters in September–October were the calm before the storm which convulsed Dora when the divorce came to court in November 1934. In the run-up to that event, writing two or three times a week, Griffin played his usual role of support and reassurance: of course B is a fool, so dominated by that girl; don't worry, John and Kate will still love you...; and oh yes, you're right about Dartington – he had met a teacher who worked under Curry (Dartington's Head) at his former school in America and wouldn't want *her* children educated by him: 'she thinks him a nice little man but a snob'. At the same time, with an eye to the future, he begged her to 'keep the door open', and could not deny an occasional impulse of fellow-feeling for Bertie... (careful, Griffin, that's dangerous ground!).

The fateful days of the court hearing sent Dora over the edge again. The pressure she was under shows clearly through an 18-page missive written over two days while the lawyers wrangled in court. Starting calmly with news of the school and the children, then the arguments being deployed by her counsel, how she's resting up carefully so as not to appear 'bedraggled' in court – then off we go into six pages of eulogising Paul, the unique love they had found and lost – on to her financial worries about the school (and if it fails through the divorce scandal, what other work will she find?) – then back again to 'this legal chess game' and the humiliation she's suffering, not only from the questioning in court but newspaper reports in which she sees herself 'made a scapegoat on account of Harry & Rod & you and B. don't get blamed...'. Predictably, Griffin found himself demonised along with Bertie and all other Men:

> You speak of grieving for me before Harry was born. Well you can grieve now and with cause – for Bertie & you finally led me up the garden & cheated me & then turned me over to the mercy of your patriarchal instincts & the patriarchal law... While the press twist it as if I were being protected because I'm a woman... Always men do women down while pretending to protect them. When did you protect me ever? By going away, I know you think – but look for what? to have the gentlemanly Bertie, protected by his title & money & the law & separation deed, nobly let his erring wife divorce him – she declaring her babes & he suppressing all his behaviour. And you write of "forgiving" me Paul – But you left me, Griffin. You showed yourself as worldly & cynical as B. himself...
>
> ...I'm sorry, I mustn't keep raging and hurting but there's a sort of corruption about this whole $2\frac{1}{2}$ years that stinks in my nostrils.

Poor Dora. The well-intentioned scheming of lawyers to avoid displaying dirty linen in open court all came to nothing when the judge ruled to let it all hang out.[4] For the press it was one of those juicy sex scandals the tabloids love. A further blow for Dora was the decision that John and Kate would continue as wards of the chancery court, in the custody of Trustees (a fate they did not enjoy), and as pupils at Dartington (which they did). For Dora this was not only a personal but an ideological battle lost, as she explained with heavy sarcasm to Griffin:

> Francis and Lloyd [the two Trustees] won't take J & K from Dartington. Why should they? They are bourgeois & they like to see riches spread in buildings & equipment to prepare a lot of ineffectual people for a world which won't exist when they grow up.[5]

---

[4] *At the time of the separation deed, a 'discretion statement' had been drawn up allowing both parties to overlook past infidelities, so that they need not be raised in court. But the judge now decided this should be disregarded, and custody decided in the light of 'all the facts'. Dora had amended her claim for full custody, so Bertie did not need to use the 'dirt' he had gathered for a chancery court action – but the divorce hearing was hurtful enough. Ray Monk's full account of the proceedings explains all the details in the light of English law at that time. Dora's retrospective view of it is gets a spirited airing in Vol. 1 of* The Tamarisk Tree.

[5] *Dora never hid her jealousy of the generous funding bestowed on 'bourgeois' Dartington by the Elmhirst family, while her 'revolutionary' school had to struggle to survive. Over the years she sank all her inheritance from her father into Beacon Hill School. Later she complained to Griffin that other (unnamed) schools were 'poaching her teachers' and 'giving scholarships to her ex-pupils'. A S Neill, founder of Summerhill, a progressive school similar to Beacon Hill in style, shared Dora's envy of well-endowed Dartington but was not so vituperative on the subject. Both Neill and Dora would be gratified to know, had they lived to see it, that while Dartington closed its doors for ever in 1987, Summerhill has survived, and flourishes to this day (see Chapter 14, and Note on page 187).*

In Dora's mind ideology was always intermixed with personal relations, and at that time the shadow of Paul intruded into everything. If only she'd never embarked on that divorce 'you all drove me into'! –

> I should have seen more clearly, earlier, that the legal & economic fight for J & K was hopeless – & I could have fought the spiritual battle for them more gallantly with Paul to help. I know so much now of his life & death that he has grown to tremendous proportions. He was a great man & might have lived to prove it had I known more fully what he was facing & dared to try & save him.

Poor Griffin too. What could he make of all this, except to protest at its effect upon him. 'Please do not write me any more bad letters for the evil they do lives long after them.' Through the winter and spring Dora's letters gave him no more comfort than her grudging 'I'm sorry' in November. In replying, he did not rise to the Paul bait regularly offered, and failed to notice significant references to 'new information' about his death that Dora had learned from a friend of Paul's. Wishfully thinking that event was past and gone, Griffin had pigeon-holed Dora's unreasonable passion for Paul as a 'neurosis' which would fade as she recovered from the distress of the divorce.

His letters of these months are tediously repetitious as he wearily defended himself against her accusations, and gnawed away at old bones of contention. In vain he tried to interest Dora in his work – 'this job I got on my wits and have held, precariously, during the storm of my private emotions when, often and often, my wits have gone completely'. Nothing could penetrate the wall of Dora's own preoccupations. Her letters showed him she had 'lost all sense of the history of these years and of me as a person'; they made him realise 'I have cast my manhood away for a woman who will never know what I gave.' Thank goodness for Lily, who continued to write and send him letters and pictures from me, through all these bleak months. 'Her letter <u>warmed</u> me so.'

In the spring Griffin's letters became calmer in tone. Perhaps he was benefiting from conversations with old friends. At that time Mary Vorse was living in Washington with her younger son Joel and had recently started a job at the Indian Bureau. Griffin's visits to the Vorse household, and other refreshing social discourse unrelated to Russell affairs, must have done him a power of good. His cringing subservience towards Dora was surely in part the result of so many long periods of solitude: his self-esteem was always a weak plant, needing friends around him to nurture it.

He had been sending Dora money intermittently, and presents for the children, but had saved his fare for a visit to England when his temporary job ended. This happened earlier than expected when he heard in mid-May 1935 that the NRA was being dismantled. Letters from Dora still banished him from her life – 'I decline to live with any man who shows the whining bourgeois attitude of Bertie and you' – but repeated wild references to Paul kept him secretly hoping it was just her 'neurosis' talking. Outwardly, he accepted her dismissal. A cool letter about his forthcoming visit announced that his long 'immolation' to her was over; now it was just a matter of managing their joint parenthood in a civilised manner. Surely 'even our strange circumstances can be arranged somehow if we have goodwill and kindness to one another'. And don't worry, he'd have money in his pocket, so he wouldn't be sponging off her. 'I'll take care of myself emotionally and in other ways.' Brave words, which as usual Griffin would find it hard to live up to.

Griffin's folder of Dora's hand-written letters, the first dated July 1932, ends with two fierce diatribes of February and March 1935. Presumably he didn't bother to keep any later ones. From about the same date, Dora no longer kept his letters in their envelopes (maybe in a box tied with ribbon, as lovers do?) but flattened out, in a folder, ready for the filing-cabinet. Her letters to him after that date, surely an incomplete collection, are only recorded by the carbon copies she kept. She still typed them herself, but her correspondence with Griffin had become an item of business for the working day rather than the outpourings of her heart in privacy.

The divorce had left her emotionally drained, and it is perhaps not surprising that she wanted to bury Griffin along with Bertie. She had only ever wanted him as a side-show to supplement an imperfect marriage; any later thoughts that he might become 'something more' were born of her distress and loneliness when first Bertie and then Griffin left her. In *The Tamarisk Tree* he is written out of her life story at this point in summary fashion:

> Griffin Barry, who awoke to a belated realization of his need of his children and me, came over from time to time and saw the children as they grew, but did not receive a permanent welcome from me.[6]

Alas for poor Griffin, her 'side-show' had become the all-consuming drama of his life, with many scenes yet to run. Despite so many rejections, he arrived in 1935 with hope in his heart to play out the next one, all unaware of a new rival blocking his path to Dora.

*** * * ***

The new man on the scene was Pat Grace. He was not yet Dora's lover, but something she needed even more at that moment: a companion who shared her obsession with the ghost of Paul Gillard. Pat's arrival in her life in November 1934 is dramatically described in *The Tamarisk Tree*: how he approached her,

---

[6] *Dora Russell, op.cit., p.289*

pale and dishevelled, at a meeting in London where she was speaking; how she took him back to Boyles Court to feed him up and listen with rapt attention to the murky tales he brought from his home town of Plymouth. This was a time of political tension in many British cities, echoing the trouble brewing in Germany as the new Nazi government flexed its muscles. Pat had been a disciple/comrade/boyfriend(?) of Paul, active with him in the street politics of the city. He was convinced that Paul had been murdered by Fascists; and worse, that he, Pat, who worshipped this fine man, could perhaps have saved his life if only he'd been with him on the fateful night, or had known of the plot to kill him. All this Dora drank in eagerly, for she too felt guilty about Paul's 'suspicious' death, and felt she could have saved him – if only, if only... Now here was this brave young man who had been at the barricades of the revolution with her beloved Paul, to prove she was right after all! Of course the fall down the embankment was no accident, she always knew it!

Whether there was any truth in Pat's version of events hardly matters now.[7] In 1934, at any rate, he convinced Dora that Paul's death was a dastardly deed by political enemies – perhaps because this chimed in so well with her own taste for melodrama, and seemed to vindicate the ineradicable grief she could not shake off. Now Paul's death was not just a drunken mishap to befall a charming nobody, but the political murder of a Great Man! – as she continued to believe for the rest of her life.

Whether Pat ever believed it we also cannot know; but the story of his and Paul's comradeship, and its unhappy end, provided a useful entrée into Dora's life, where he lived out the rest of his days in modest comfort. To justify his presence at Boyles Court, Dora made him school secretary – a job briefly held by Paul before his death, and which she had once urged upon Griffin. Some time later Pat became her lover, and eventually her second husband. He was surely a poor substitute for Paul, and in no way a replacement for Bertie, but at least a more biddable helpmeet for Dora than Griffin would have been.

Pat's arrival in 1934, and the news he brought, gave Dora new confidence in facing the outside world. She was no longer alone; she had someone at her side who not only believed in *her* uncritically but fully endorsed her moral stance in defence of her dead hero Paul Gillard (not a *cause* exactly, but it served that function in her psyche). How dare anyone trivialise such noble feelings as 'neurosis'? This is the gist of a brief correspondence with Vera Meynell (wife of Francis) in August 1935, which also provides the only evidence I have of

---

[7] *In* The Tamarisk Tree, *written in the 1970s, Dora's account of visits to Plymouth with Pat, searching for evidence, and the interest taken by the local police in Pat's arrival at Boyles Court, deliberately leaves the reader guessing about these 'mysterious' events. In the 1990s Ray Monk also visited Plymouth, but unsurprisingly could find no conclusive evidence about Paul's death. A drunken fall, possibly after an encounter with political (or homosexual) opponents, seemed to him the most likely explanation. Monk also casts doubt on Dora's view of Paul as a doughty fighter for the Left; in fact, there is some evidence that he may have been a 'mole' for MI5 in the National Unemployed Workers' Movement (NUWM) and other left-wing organisations.*

what passed between Griffin and Dora that summer. Dora's two letters, so typical of her intemperate character, also show the communistic slant of her thinking at that time.

On 1 August Griffin was staying at Boyles Court when Dora overheard him speaking to Vera on the phone and at once rushed to her typewriter, impelled to add her comments on what he'd been saying, 'the more so as he had been down to stay with you recently and had discussed our affairs with you' (an indiscretion she deplored). Evidently Griffin had appealed to Vera as a mutual friend to mediate their quarrel, seemingly still hoping for an outcome long ago ruled out by Dora: 'I cannot go to the States with Griffin, nor marry him, I do not love him.' She is quite willing for him to see his children, and later may consent to their going to the USA. If she avoids going out with them and him now, 'it is because he quarrels with me in front of them, as he also quarrels with me in front of strangers...'.

Next! Apparently Griffin has been telling her friends she is 'neurotic' or 'hysterical' in her behaviour; and 'when I have my living to get' she cannot allow 'suggestions that I am unbalanced and wicked and so forth, to pass without comment'. This is her launch-pad for a self-righteous personal credo, leading inevitably to Paul:

> I have always held that there was more to life than just getting on in the world, and sleeping around with people, the ideas I had, and thought others shared, I put into practice. For me a human being belongs to himself or herself and cannot be the property of another human being, except in so far as he or she owes work or help to the whole of the rest of human beings... The fact that I did not meet until late, the man who embodied for me all that I believed about life, and that he was murdered by the rotten society in which we all live, is my deepest misfortune. There is however, nothing neurotic about honouring and cherishing the memory of one who might have been a great leader, and wishing to see things changed so that his tragedy might not be repeated for other people when they grow up...

Vera should not think her differences with Griffin were merely personal: there were larger issues at stake:

> Griffin is, and always has been, an individualist, and a spectator of political events. He does not think in general terms, or seem able to bother about people in general. This more than anything else has always been the division between us, ironically too, for I was first drawn to him by the fact that I thought he admired and understood the Russian revolution. I did not realise that his interest was purely that of a journalist. And journalist [sic] appear increasingly to have a kind of cynicism for which at present there seems to me to be no place.[8]

THE DIVORCE AND AFTER

Vera must have replied to this long declaration with a placatory telegram, answered a week later by Dora. Griffin has not sailed yet, she tells Vera, but she holds out no hope for him except 'a possibly amicable settlement of our differences'. Then follows a dose of bitterness towards Bertie, and a plea that if he is now 'held by you all to be free to readjust his own life... then why do you not permit the same liberty to me?' As for Griffin,

> Short of giving [him] my whole self to bolster up his life and work, I did all I could to preserve him to build up life and work himself, and this I feel is all one can do for another, for we cannot live on one another's blood, only children should be allowed to do that.

There may be some justice in that summary of their relationship, but of course no recognition of the 'bolstering up' Griffin had been doing throughout the sorry mess of the Russell divorce. There is also no mention in either letter of Pat, perhaps not yet allotted a permanent place in Dora's life. But other evidence shows she was already using him as a guard-dog against Griffin.

Evidently Griffin's calm resolution of a few weeks earlier had melted away at the sight of Dora and the children – the family he so yearned to be part of. Vera's reply to Dora, excusing her intervention in their affairs, could have been his own words.

> It sounded to me as if your difficulties with Griffin this summer might be more accidental – due to misunderstanding & impatience, rather than profound incompatibility... That one of your families has been broken up seems to me no reason for breaking up the other; on the contrary, more reason than there would otherwise have been for seeking to preserve it...

Vera was not the only mutual friend who would venture to plead Griffin's case with Dora. But her heart was now closed against him for ever. With the divorce over, her need for a punch-bag diminished, and increasing intimacy with Pat provided moral support for her stressful life. From this point on, she did everything she could to discourage Griffin's interest in her, while still expecting he would keep in touch with his children and contribute to their upbringing when he could. This was simply *not enough* for Griffin. Some of his later letters seem 'realistic', seeking only to 'find harmony enough between us to do the best we can...instead of the worst'. Yet he could never entirely give up hope of winning Dora back, a persistent fantasy that continued to blight their relations in years to come.

---

[8] *As I indicated earlier, Dora's association with Paul, and now with Pat, pushed her closer to (though never into) the Communist Party. Seeing them and their comrades in the Party as frontline fighters for the betterment of all mankind, the implied comparison with Griffin the 'onlooker' is unmistakable.*

Easter or summer 1935 – we went to Cornwall as usual,
taking a group from the school.

The year 1935, marking the funeral of their love affair, is a suitable place to consider whether it could have ended differently. Without the emotional storms that threw Dora off balance, could she and Griffin ever have settled down to a happy life together? Objectively, a case can be made. Perhaps the dissonance of their different origins could have been overcome, as other couples have demonstrated. Griffin would surely have been more successful in his work, and happier, with the security and affection we all derive from a partner and family. Dora would have found him more stimulating than Pat as a companion; and Griffin's earnings, even if sporadic, would have been more useful than the few shillings Pat ever brought into the family.

But the two people I came to know as I grew up, no longer impelled by the physical passion of youth, could never have lived contentedly in the same ménage. They were just too bellicose – each of them separately, never mind together – and their differing needs did not match up. Dora may have looked up to Bertie as a father-figure, but Griffin was not in that league; and in all her other relations with men she had to be dominant. Griffin was not a macho man, but neither was he a door-mat. His ingrained masculine ego, so trodden upon by Dora, had to be given room to breathe.

In 1935 he was still only 50, young enough to have followed Fred Astaire's advice in a popular song of the time and 'pick himself up, dust himself off and start all over again'. But he couldn't do it. A rolling stone since his youth, he had no home base to return to, no relatives or group of supportive friends to help him make a new start. Dora – and, increasingly, his children – were the only fixed point in his vagabond life. He would spend the rest of his days trying to attach himself to them.

CHAPTER 12

WASHINGTON DC, 1934–36

Lacking any sign of interest from Dora, Griffins letters of 1934–36 say little about his own activities. What a pity. While the Russells were getting divorced in England, he was making history in America as a tiny cog in the path-breaking New Deal. Since his landslide election victory in 1932, President Roosevelt had been trying to get the nation on the road to recovery, facing down one crisis after another. In 1934 a period of bitter labour unrest began, when 'the thunder of mass revolt shook the nation', writes Mary Vorse's biographer, with four major strikes and many hundreds of smaller ones across the country. One aim of the National Recovery Administration was to avert this 'mass revolt', by giving American workers a voice in their conditions of work and pay rates – something trade unions had been trying to win for them, and mostly failing, for the previous 50 years. The NRA would soon be dissolved, when the Supreme Court ruled that federal 'interference' of this kind was unconstitutional; but its work led on to the historic Wagner Act of 1936, the 'workers' bill of rights' taking its place alongside other pioneering reforms of the period.

At the NRA's Labor Advisory Board, Griffin felt unqualified for 'civil servants' work that in Russia would be given only to heads of state – half judges, half advocates on wage boards', he told Dora. 'I may be sent to Tennessee in ten days to negotiate wages and hours for cotton workers and am eye-deep in documents.' Yet he seems to have satisfied his superiors, doing that work for most of the NRA's short life. He did go to Tennessee – an envelope from a Memphis hotel confirms this – and I'd be very interested to know what he did there. Overproduction of cotton in the depressed agricultural South was a major problem another New Deal agency was trying to solve.[1] But the envelope from Memphis

....

[1] In an effort to raise prices to give farmers a living wage, the New Deal invented the policy of 'artificial scarcity' now widely practised in Europe and North America – essentially, paying farmers to grow less. In 1933 the Agricultural Adjustment Administration ordered 40 million acres of cotton to be ploughed under, which had the desired effect, but also displaced thousands of tenant farmers and black sharecroppers. The 'cotton workers' Griffin was sent to deal with were probably processors of the crop, who must also have suffered mass redundancies and falling wages, which the NRA was pledged to stabilise.

contains only a familiar plea for mercy from Dora. Her latest 'barrage' had given him a sleepless night, followed by a day in bed to recover. 'Since then I have walked through my work like a husk.'

In another letter Griffin praised his current boss, 'unspoiled by his upper-class education', who had spent a weekend helping him 'to clothe feed and instruct a Communist from the Florida fruitpickers who's been living underground in small towns armed against the owners and preparing (I think) an explosion'. This must have been a clandestine operation, not part of the NRA's brief, but upper-class sympathy for that Communist agitator was not so surprising in 1934. The struggle for workers' rights was not yet won, and it was most vicious among downtrodden groups like migrant farm-workers, often led by the Communists and other militants Mary Vorse had been tracking through bitter, unsuccessful strikes in earlier years. In the early 1930s, the mood of public sympathy for the long-ignored victims of unregulated capitalism gave the tiny American Communist Party some influence beyond its own ranks for the only time in its history (though far less than was later claimed).

Another Washington agency striking out in new directions was the Indian Bureau, and Mary Vorse became editor of its journal, *Indians at Work*, early in 1935. Its director John Collier, in charge of Indian affairs from 1933 to 1945, opposed the then popular assimilationist or 'melting pot' idea that all ethnic groups should eventually merge into one homogenised American society, rather than retaining their distinct cultural identities. His controversial policies, encouraging respect for native Indian culture and giving them rights to self-government in their own reservations, started an argument which still rages today: are Americans just Americans, or Native Americans, Irish-Americans, Italian-Americans, African-Americans and so forth? To Griffin in 1934, American Indians were just Indians, or 'redskins'. He wrote appreciatively to Dora about an exhibition of their textiles, beadwork and jewellery, where he bought Christmas presents for all of us in England. I remember a leather belt adorned with silver medallions, and one or two wall hangings still among our household possessions in the 1960s. (I wonder what happened to them after that?)

When Griffin returned to Washington in August 1935 the NRA was no more, a victim of the Supreme Court's view that Washington was trespassing beyond its constitutional sphere. The NRA, and the equally important Agricultural Adjustment Administration, were disbanded. Under pressure from Congress and public opinion, however, the judges soon yielded to the argument that new circumstances of the mid-twentieth century justified an extension of federal power. Other agencies took up the work already begun, as the New Deal steamroller pushed ahead.

Conservation was an important concern of the New Deal. (The wildlife in the poster – actual size 55cm x 80cm – are all carefully identified at the bottom.)

Griffin got by on short-term jobs until March 1936, when he started work for the Department of Agriculture, publicising wildlife and conservation projects scattered across the nation. This job took him all over the country. One letter, from a Migratory Waterfowl Refuge in North Carolina, enclosed a colourful poster for the children (opposite). Another came from Kansas, en route to the Pacific coast.

At this time or earlier, Griffin forged a connection with a New York-based magazine called *Travel*, edited by his friend Coburn (Coby) Gilman, long-term extra-marital partner of Dawn Powell. An article by Griffin for this journal, 'America Protects her Migratory Birds', published in April 1937, may have been written as part of his job, or for himself, as a useful spin-off. It was the first of several articles he wrote for *Travel* in the coming years, helping to pay his rent between jobs.

Soon after starting work with the Department of Agriculture he was offered a better-paid job at the Social Security Board, just setting up to administer another key New Deal law, to begin on 15 June. Again his task would be to publicise the agency's work – a sort of press officer, I suppose. 'It's a grander job than this, with better educated young men to work with, socially educated I mean, many of whom in their thinking have gone over to Moscow.' The appointment was initially for three months, with the prospect of continuing indefinitely 'unless I fail completely to make good' – and above all, it would be in Washington, *the* place to be at that moment in history. The atmosphere of excitement in those early days of the New Deal seeps through even the scant information in Griffin's letters. 'Beneath the banal bourgeois politics Washington is in a ferment.'

Better than any factual account of the New Deal, a retrospective personal impression by Isaiah Berlin admirably fills out the fragmentary picture in Griffin's letters. 'Social discontent was high', wrote Berlin, and Roosevelt was 'providing a vast safety-valve for pent-up bitterness and indignation'. He was trying to prevent a revolution by providing greater economic equality and social justice –

> – without altering the basis of freedom and democracy in his country. This was being done by what to unsympathetic critics seemed a haphazard collection of amateurs, college professors, journalists, personal friends, freelances of one kind or another, intellectuals, ideologists, what are nowadays called eggheads, whose very appearance and methods of conducting business or constructing policies irritated the servants of old-established government institutions in Washington and tidy-minded conservatives of every type. Yet it was clear that the very amateurishness of these men, the fact that they were allowed to talk to their hearts' content, to experiment, to indulge in a vast amount of trial and error, that relations were personal and not institutional, bred its

own vitality and enthusiasm. Washington was doubtless full of quarrels, resignations, palace intrigues, perpetual warfare between individuals and groups of individuals, parties, cliques, personal supporters of this or that great captain, which must have maddened sober and responsible officials used to the slower tempo and more normal patterns of administration; as for bankers and businessmen, their feelings were past describing, but at this period they were little regarded, since they were considered to have discredited themselves too deeply, and indeed for ever.[2]

Just odd sentences here and there from Griffin – especially during his time at the NRA, where an office 'earthquake' every week was almost routine – show an insider's view of all this. The New Deal was unprecedented, experimental, unique in the history of government. I wish he'd told us more.

Griffin did take up the job at the Social Security Board, but to his disappointment, it lasted only until December 1936. After further adventures in Europe (recounted in my next chapter), in 1939 he was again taken on by the Department of Agriculture – yet after six months this job too came to an abrupt end. Why? Griffin's explosive temper must have made him a quarrelsome colleague, and an insubordinate subordinate; this may well be why he was eased out of *Newsweek* magazine, and perhaps explains other lost jobs over the years. But I suspect his failure to hold down government jobs was due to his left-wing political past. Before his appointment at Social Security he had written confidently to Dora: 'my record was combed and its left-wing chapters seemed not unwelcome' – but like many too-trusting liberals in those days, he was over-optimistic. The new dawn of liberalism they were basking in turned out to be all too short.

Already in 1936 Mary's boss John Collier and his colleagues were being smeared before a government committee on Indian affairs as 'Christ-mocking, Communist-aiding subversives bent upon finding a back door entrance for the establishment of Communism in the United States...'. Such absurd charges could surely be disregarded, just as in 1934 a howl of derision had greeted a rabid anti-New Deal tract called *The Red Network*, branding 460 organisations and 1,300 individuals (including the President's wife, Eleanor Roosevelt) as 'members of the international Communist conspiracy'. Yet in 1938, only four years later, its 'evidence' was being presented to the newly-formed House Un-American Activities Committee (HUAC), and thence was copied into FBI files on activists like Mary Vorse.[3]

[2] *Isaiah Berlin,* Personal Impressions *(London: Hogarth Press, 1980), p.26*

[3] *This information, and quotations from her sources, together with her phrase previously quoted, come from Dee Garrison, op. cit., pp.267–9. Mary's brief spell at the Indian Bureau was fateful in providing the 'evidence' for the FBI to start a file on her. Griffin was probably not prominent enough to have attracted the FBI's attention, but there is very likely still a US Government file somewhere, detailing the suspect associations of its one-time intermittent employee.*

Loyalty checks on 'reds' in government service began during the Second World War (despite the United States' wartime alliance with the Soviet Union). In 1942 Mary's close friend Josephine Herbst, whom Griffin also knew, was summarily fired from her government job for the activities of her Party-member husband at a time (1934) when 'not only was the Communist Party legal, [but] Communism was fashionable'.[4] Fashionable for a few, maybe, but never for most Americans. The reactionary backlash against the New Deal which began in the 1930s led straight to the Cold War hysteria of McCarthyism in the 1950s, when HUAC came fully into its own.

Following Griffin's personal story through his correspondence with Dora has become a dispiriting task. His movements are hard to track after 1935, when letters from both became less frequent. In Dora's case this was due to extreme busyness – and perhaps a deliberate desire to keep Griffin at arm's length; while on his side there would be long months of silent brooding until, by some mental gymnastics, he could kid himself that another approach might find the cold Dora of recent letters or meetings miraculously replaced by the old Dora, ready to welcome him. Time and again he would return, by letter or in person, to knock loudly, entreatingly, on her door, with increasing despair at every rude rebuff. This pathetic self-delusion had painful effects on us as children, and is still painful to read now in these letters. But they are still my main source for this sketchy biography until I reach a time when my own memory can help out.

In the winter of 1935–36 the letters were spiky with irritation about money, an overwhelming preoccupation for both of them in different ways. A terse note from Griffin enclosing a cheque informs Dora: 'This job ends December 1 and as yet I am not certain of another. When I am, I'll send you a share of the income... [signed] GB.' Later he demanded that she acknowledge the $650 he had sent her over the past two years. Dora replied that she *had*. In fact she had much bigger money worries than he did: the school was failing for lack of pupils, she was running out of personal money to put into it, and with negotiations about alimony from Bertie still dragging on, 'I do not quite see where bread and butter will come from...'. After months of anxiety, in August 1936 she wrote that the school might be saved by amalgamating with another one in their premises near Rye, in Sussex. There she would be employed as a salaried teacher, but would have to pay fees for Harry and Rod, about £120 each per year. Would Griffin be able to help?

Dora's financial and other problems were beyond Griffin's comprehension. (Neither he nor Dora had a realistic picture of the other's world.) In March he

---

[4] *Elinor Langer,* Josephine Herbst *(Little, Brown and Company, Boston/Toronto, 1984), p.155. Herbst's husband John Herrmann, who left her in 1935, was later implicated in the Hiss case of 1948 (see Chapter 19). Herbst always denied complicity in his activities, and eventually cleared her name.*

had suggested Dora should come over to start a school in New Mexico; an absurd idea, but he did not see its absurdity, and worked up a froth of resentment when she declined. His next ploy, on the strength of his forthcoming job in Washington, was to beg her to come over for the summer, bringing Harriet but not Roddy (could Lily look after him at home?). Dora protested at this favouritism (Griffin's idolisation of me, and 'neglect' of Roddy, was always a sore point between them) – but in any case she couldn't come: the school was playing host to an educational conference, she had another one to go to after that, and John and Kate would be home for the holidays. Instead, why didn't Griffin come over to stay with Harry and Rod (Lily would help), so that she could give John and Kate the mothering they needed? Griffin replied through clenched teeth: had she not noticed that he was starting a new job in June? 'Therefore your proposal that I come over to stay with the children while you absent yourself is out. I will reply to the remainder of your letter shortly. GB.'

The only kindly words exchanged in these months concerned Griffin's mother. After suffering two hip fractures in the space of a year, she died in September 1936. Griffin had hoped, after the first break, that she would recover sufficiently to visit England, to live near her grandchildren for a while, on her income of £8 a week (another crazy notion). Dora's file includes a touching letter from her last convalescence, dated 16 June, sending gifts for Roddy's fourth birthday in March and my sixth in July. 'If they make them know their Granny in America has not forgotten them I shall be most happy.'

The merger of Beacon Hill with Brickwall School took place in the autumn term of 1936 – a short-lived disaster for the school, as it turned out, but with the happy side-effect of nearby Walnut Tree Cottage as a rented family home. Relating these developments to Griffin in her letters about the children, Lily also tactfully conveyed that the core of this 'family' was now the shared bedroom of Dora and Pat. Griffin's heart went cold. In October he wrote a long, systematic indictment of Dora's 'theft of the

Walnut Tree Cottage, 1936

children I love and the theft of a father from them' – a letter he did not send.[5] With his Social Security job in Washington expected to continue, what could he do about this latest turn of events in England? Then in December the job suddenly ended. Griffin wrote at once that he was heading for London:

> I would dearly love to spend Christmas with you and the children. Only one thing stands in the way – the household which Lily writes you have established at the gates of the school with the young man with whom you were living when I last saw you. I can't see you nor the children with the obtrusive young man about. Perhaps I shall have to wait in whatever lodgings I find in London for you to send – or bring – the children there... I will let you know where I am in London, unless I hear from you when the boat lands...
>
> [A scrawled postscript adds] I expect to stay abroad.

This letter introduces a new phase in Griffin's relations with Dora, even more desolate for him than the preceding years. Its tone of seething impotence, amplified in later letters, vividly recalls the father of my childhood nightmares: the spitting, raging ogre shouting insults at Dora, and she raging back at him – I knew not why!

But now I do. For Griffin the worst had happened – not only a rival in Dora's bed, that repulsive creature he'd met at Boyles Court, but a usurper-stepfather of *his children*. The un-sent letter is explicit: 'Harry and Rod go to the first home they have ever known outside a school. Their feelings are being moulded for all their lives.' Alongside his concern for the children are the glints of raw, macho jealousy of the two *homosexuals* (he uses the word as a term of abuse) who have supplanted him in Dora's affections – first the unconsummated affair with Paul, now this 'new homosexual' even *in her bed*.[6] It was intolerable to think of this 'parasite' playing Daddy to his own children. But he wouldn't give them up without a fight! These were the jungle feelings that brought him hammering on the door of the next home of the school and the family, a time I've come to think of as The Siege of Kingwell Hall.

But that was a few months ahead. First he went off to another hot spot of twentieth century history, the Spanish Civil War.

---

[5] *It only came into Dora's hands two years later, when at another moment of extreme bitterness he 'found it in his trunk' and sent it to her. The letter runs through the course of their relationship since he left for America in 1932: a relatively calm statement of his point of view on these events until he reaches the latest 'outrage', when his language becomes poisonous.*

[6] *This demonisation of 'gays' is odd for a man of liberal views, especially one with Griffin's sexual history, but I can find no other meaning in certain passages of this letter than the conventional hetero's contempt for 'poofters'. Did he feel his long association with Dora had qualified him as a fully-fledged heterosexual, entitled to share their disdain for 'the other sort'? Did he feel that to be replaced in Dora's bed by a homosexual was a special humiliation for a 'real man' like himself? Or beneath* her *dignity? I cannot fathom these subtleties of male psychology...*

A MAN OF SMALL IMPORTANCE

POSTSCRIPT TO CHAPTER 12
Our caravan holiday in 1936

At Easter 1936 Dora hired a caravan for a holiday touring Sussex, which remained a happy memory for years (see Chapter 18). We stopped at The Royal Oak, near Telegraph House, to see Alf and Carrie Ainger, who had been loyal friends to Dora during the divorce.

From left: Pat, Kate, Alf, Lily, Roddy, Carrie, John, me (kneeling at front).

172

CHAPTER 13

GRIFFIN IN SPAIN

I don't know whether Griffin succeeded in seeing us in the few weeks he spent in England before leaving for Spain in January 1937, on a new and unexpected mission. My recollections of Walnut Tree Cottage are few – we lived there less than a year – but the one event I do clearly remember must have overshadowed our Christmas. While out with Lily and other children, Roddy, aged 4, walked into the still-hot embers of a Guy Fawkes bonfire. Hot ash spilled over the top of his wellington boots and before Lily could pull them off, his left ankle was badly burned. I remember the fear and drama of that moment, and the lifelong scar Roddy bore, but little else of the brief 'Brickwall period' of the school's history. By the summer term of 1937 we were ensconced at Kingwell Hall, near Bath in Somerset, where the best years of Beacon Hill School were played out, and my own clear memories begin.

I have even less direct evidence with which to reconstruct Griffin's activities during these months: just one photograph, cracked and worn from being folded into an envelope, with an inscription on the back in his handwriting: 'Daddy interviewing Italian prisoners in Valencia with Lady Hastings March 28 1937'.[1] It shows a group of men in conversation with two women (whom I guess to be Lady Hastings and her interpreter); and in the background sits Griffin with a pad on his knee, taking notes. The only sight I have of my father at work! Of course there would have been a letter with the photo, and others: I vaguely

---

[1] *Lady Cristina Hastings (later Countess Huntingdon, when her husband inherited his father's earldom) was the daughter of an Italian aristocrat, the Marchese Casati of Rome, and wife of Viscount 'Jack' Hastings, an artist who worked as a muralist with the Mexican master Diego Rivera. Hastings was also a musician and writer. At this time they were both active supporters of the Republican cause – she as a member of the Spanish Exhibition Committee, along with the MP Ellen Wilkinson, Fenner Brockway, Emma Goldman and others; and Jack as an artist. A mural by him can be seen today at the Marx Memorial Library in London. (Later, with a second wife, Lord Huntingdon moved rightwards into orthodox Labour politics.) In a letter to me in 1939, Griffin said 'Cristina' would come and visit us, but if she did, I don't remember the occasion.*

remember receiving them, and the 78 rpm record he gave us of the songs of the International Brigade (maybe brought back when he returned?) – but alas, none of these souvenirs have survived.

Having no full account of his time in Spain, I must rely on glimpses of Griffin from strangers – two women, unconnected with each other, who both knew and worked with him in Valencia. These sources are wonderfully evocative, not only of a very characteristic Griffin Barry, but of the confused and tragic historical drama which they all witnessed.

The Spanish Civil War began in July 1936 with a revolt of army officers, led by General Franco, against the elected Republican government. It arose from turbulent Spanish history, and Franco had purely national aims – to restore and maintain the 'old order' dominated by the Catholic Church, the Army and other conservative elites, by defeating the diverse and competing ambitions of democrats, socialists, communists, anarchists, and local nationalists in Catalonia and the Basque region. But Franco's fascistic tendencies, and the help he received from Italy and Germany, countered by arms to the Republican side from Stalin's Russia, turned a bitter civil war into an international contest between Left and Right.

Left-wingers in Europe and America, already alarmed by the rise of Nazism, saw the 'non-intervention' policies of their own governments as tantamount to aiding Franco, and thereby assisting the onward march of Fascism.

International Brigades of volunteers went to Spain to help the Republican forces: about 50,000 men and a few women, from 50 countries. Many were killed. As the war intensified, every self-respecting lefty unable to fight did their bit for The Cause in other ways: protesting, publicising, raising money. Concerned Americans, disgusted by their own countrymen's lack of interest in world affairs, rushed to Spain in 1937 as they had rushed to the Western Front in France in 1915 (and a few, like John Reed, from there to Russia) – just as a later generation would rush to help the Sandinistas in Nicaragua in the 1980s.

The sense of excitement and urgency in this great crusade can be felt across the years in a letter to Dora from 'Helen' in Paris.

> Then came a cable from America asking George and me to go to Spain and make an objective report on what we found there. That being the entire purpose of my trip to Europe this winter (going to Spain), I was able to convince George that we must rush off at once without delays. In the meantime Griffin turned up at the Liberia Hotel where we were staying and announced that he had gotten the proper credentials in London and was off for Spain the next day accompanied by Muriel Draper. (As to Muriel, this all having taken place at least six weeks ago, she dashed to Madrid for a day and dashed back to Paris to get a boat for America loaded with propaganda posters and enthusiasm but leaving behind in Valencia her silver fox scarf which I foolishly offered to evacuate and which is now hanging limp and useless on a hanger in our room at the Liberia.) Three days later George and I received an enthusiastic letter from Griffin from Barcelona urging us to get down there as soon as possible. The next night, Feb. 26th we left [Paris]... We arrived back from Spain two days ago and having [sic] been mailing out articles ever since. All this long explanation, Dora dear, to explain why you haven't heard from me before this...
>
> [She and George will shortly be returning to Spain "as correspondents for a bourgeois New York paper"]... We have already sent out eight articles to New York which will be published in the New York Post. Later we do some articles for Harper's Magazine but now it is advisable to hit the daily papers. We were in the Madrid trenches for a solid week and that is where I want to go back. First Bilbao probably to settle the Catholic Church which is acting as chief reactionary censor at present to American newspapers. Spain needs arms, petrol and transportation, not food or money...[2]

So it looks as though Griffin had met up with friends in London already on their way to Spain, and got himself hired as a reporter to join them. Off he went to Barcelona.

---

[2] *Helen and George were a pair of American journalists, Gilbert (also known as George) Seldes and his wife. They were old friends of Griffin's whom Dora had met in Majorca just before Roddy was born. Muriel Draper lived next door to Griffin and Edmund Wilson in 1933–4 (see Chapter 8).*

Franco's rebellion had started in Spanish Morocco, from where his forces were airlifted to the mainland by the obliging German Luftwaffe. In the early months of the war the Nationalists cut a swathe from south to north alongside Portugal, controlling about half the territory of Spain by the end of 1936. The ensuing fighting was not a clean sweep in any one direction but a series of battles for strategic cities and areas. About one-third of Spain in the centre and south-east, including Madrid, was still in Republican hands when they eventually surrendered in March 1939.

Helen's letter is undated, but it must have been written in mid-April 1937. By that time Franco had already launched a major onslaught on the Basque Country and its industrial heart, the northern port of Bilbao. On 26 April the German air force pulverised the town of Guernica, the Basque spiritual capital, with the loss of over 1,500 civilian lives (an act of savagery commemorated by Picasso's painting of the carnage, which became a symbol and reminder of the Spanish war ever afterwards). Soon Bilbao, an important supply route for the Republican forces and escape route for refugees, had fallen to Franco's army.[3]

In the spring of 1937, however, the outlook was still hopeful for the Republic. The government still controlled more economic resources, and more people, than the enemy. Against all expectations Madrid had withstood the Nationalist siege, in large part thanks to International Brigaders, including the British. Their heroism also contributed to two famous victories in the early spring: the Battle of Jarama in February and the Battle of Guadalajara in March.[4] Many hundreds of prisoners were taken at Guadalajara (including those being interrogated in Griffin's photograph).

Fearing Madrid would fall, the government had fled to the east coast port of Valencia in November 1936. Apart from occasional bombing and shelling from the sea, life in Valencia was relatively normal compared to Barcelona or Madrid. Some of the sociable occasions described by my second source, Kate Mangan, sound like holiday activities. She was a Londoner who had gone to Spain to find and rescue her lover, Jan Kurzke, badly wounded in the early months of the war. To support herself she was working as a secretary/translator/interpreter at the Press and Censorship office in Valencia. Griffin was one of the many people she met, both famous and anonymous, who earned a mention

---

[3] *Just ahead of Franco's army thousands of refugees left by sea, including the 4,000 'Basque Children' reluctantly accepted by Britain 'temporarily', at the insistence of a Committee set up to arrange the evacuation. Among them were 'the Spannies', Carito and Marina Rodriguez, both on the staff at Dartington Hall School when I was there, along with two other teachers who were Republican refugees from Spain, and another from Nazi Germany (see Chapter 18).*

[4] *Of the 526 British Brigaders killed in Spain, 167 fell at Jarama. A volunteer from Glasgow, Alex McDade, himself killed in a later battle, wrote the song* There's a Valley in Spain Called Jarama *that became a kind of anthem of the Brigade: another evocative reminder of the war in later years. By one of those sad ironies of history, the defeated 'Nationalist' forces at Guadalahara were mainly Italian troops sent by Mussolini, pitched against the Garibaldi Brigade of* anti-Fascist Italians.

Kate Mangan

in the account she later wrote of her adventures.[5] His first appearance there dates from early February 1937, after the southern city of Málaga was overrun by Franco's troops on the 8th.

The day after the party Griffin Barry got back, looking very dusty and worn. He was another middle-aged, loose-end intellectual, Irish-American who worked for one of the news agencies. He and the Reuter man shared my services to go through the Febus [news agency] sheets and translate daily... Barry had started off to go to Málaga but had been too late to get there. He had been caught up in the retreat and delayed.

He brought back a hair-raising and picturesque story, he had more literary talent than most of them and far too much for a news agency. He told of pathetic families with their donkeys loaded with household goods fleeing from the fascists and it seemed it had been a major exodus and a shocking one.

This is the closest we'll ever get to a sample of Griffin's war-reporting. The words of a more eminent writer on Spain give some idea of what he witnessed. She was Katharine, Duchess of Atholl, whose book *Searchlight on Spain* was part of her vigorous campaign to make the world take notice of what was happening there. Perhaps what she wrote about Málaga drew on Griffin's report, who knows?

> What the world did hear with horror when Málaga was captured, was that thousands of non-combatant refugees who fled from thence along the coast to Almeria were bombarded from German and Italian warships and machine-gunned from low-flying German aeroplanes, during the four, five or six days of their flight. The rain of death was so incessant and deadly that there were women who preferred to plunge with their children into streams by the way and drown rather than continue to face the pitiless hail.[6]

---

[5] *Through one of those circuitous links that delight researchers, an American who knew Griffin in the 1940s put me in touch with Charlotte Kurzke, the daughter of Jan and Kate, who has an unpublished manuscript by her parents describing their experiences in Spain. Kate's part of the manuscript includes several vignettes of Griffin. All the extracts I quote come from there.*

[6] *Katharine Atholl (Duchess of Atholl),* Searchlight on Spain *(Penguin, 1938), pp.178–9. The author was the wife of a hereditary peer and herself a distinguished MP. One aim of this vivid contemporary account was to expose the extent of German and Italian aid to Franco, in violation of international agreements. She was also instrumental in persuading the British government to accept the Basque children.*

Having started off in Barcelona, north of Valencia, by early February Griffin was reporting from Málaga in the south. As a news agency reporter[7] he would have been based in Valencia, making expeditions to Madrid or other fronts as necessary. Behind the front lines of any war, of course, journalists spend a lot of time just hanging around waiting for something to happen. In Valencia the hanging-around place was the Victoria Hotel. Kate Mangan was rather put out when she had to give up her single room at the Inglés Hotel to the convalescent British Battalion commander, Tom Wintringham (who had been badly wounded at Jarama), and share a room with an American friend at the Victoria. But her friend Poppy was lively and gregarious:

> She got to know everyone who spoke English and at meals we were generally six or more, celebrities, nonentities, all sorts. The hotel was the rendez-vous of journalists, and the official place to lodge visitors invited by the Government. The waiters were superlatively rude and furious at the excessive number of chairs we gathered round one table. As we could not have it in our room, even breakfast was a social meal. We generally had it with Barry... I translated for him and went through the first set of Febus sheets before going to the office.

So that's how their working day began. Long evenings could be more depressing:

> Sometimes in the evening, at the Victoria, as we sat in the lounge, with its oil paintings of sunny Spain on the walls, Barry would say the place reminded him of an ocean liner on which we were all bound on some interminable voyage with no prospect of ever reaching port.
> "This place is hateful to me," he said, putting down his empty glass and vainly trying to attract the attention of a waiter to order another drink. The waiters were expert at avoiding one's eye and sometimes told the guests that they had had enough to drink already.
> "This is not Spain, nor America, nor England", he said, "it is just Limbo."
> "Yes", I said, "'embryoes [sic] and idiots, eremites and friars'."[8]
> Poppy went off into a peal of loud laughter, other people looked round and I was sorry I had spoken as I caught sight of the Canon of Córdoba sitting in a corner. He was in lay dress but I knew him.
> A waiter came up and said, "You should ring the bell if you want anything."
> "I did ring it," said Barry, "I want another whisky."

---

[7] *Helen says he worked for Reuters, as I always thought, but Kate seems to think it was another agency.*
[8] *This is a quote from Milton's* Paradise Lost, *Book III, line 474, listing the inhabitants of Limbo.*

The waiter looked at the clock. "It's too late," he said, "we've decided not to serve drinks after eight so that people will go into dinner on time."

Kate Mangan's laconic style makes for entertaining reading, especially in her hilarious account of another social occasion shared with Griffin. Someone called Geraldine had borrowed a summer villa outside the city and invited a group to dinner there, including the two of them and a 'very important' political commissar from the Brigade, an 'aggressively virile' Italian called Gino. Having missed the last train back to town they all had to stay the night, mostly in some discomfort, though Griffin, with his greater experience of such emergencies, had craftily secured one of the few beds. Next morning they all piled into Gino's small car for the return journey. Jolting over the cobblestones, they were treated to an outburst of Gino's offended machismo:

"It's an outrage", he said, "never have I been so treated."

"Yes," said Barry, "too bad not to tell us the time. Getting stuck like that. It would be just my luck to get scooped."

"That clown, Geraldine", said Poppy, wiping her glasses which had been misted by smoke.

"It's monstrous", went on Gino, beating his breast, "to sleep the night in a house, me, and not to sleep with a woman! Not only that but for all the women to sleep separate from all the men. I never heard of such a thing. Never before have I undergone such a humiliating experience, never. And before my driver too. You can see the boy is laughing at me; you can see it by the way he is driving."

"Yes," gasped Poppy, on whose knees I was perched and whose head struck me under the chin at a sudden bump.

"An English house-party, hein?" said Gino sarcastically, and relapsed into a moody silence, his phenomenal chest swelling still more with indignation and nearly precipitating Barry, who was but a morsel of a man, out of the window from which his head and arms were already hanging.

This jolly carousal, with food and drink a-plenty, sounds like just the sort of party Griffin used to enjoy in the 1920s, when he was the age of Kate and his other companions in Spain. Now he was middle-aged and melancholy – though still a night-owl, as Kate observed.

Some people were so accustomed to night life that they would never give it up. Barry was one of these. He would sit in the Wodka café until it closed at about half-past ten and had then discovered several other possibilities. In one sand-bagged building in the Plaza Castelar was the office of the Febus News Agency which was open all night, so he would look in there. Above it was an illegal café which I only ever visited at midnight and could never find again. Once we tried to get into a brothel by mistake as we saw lights under the door and heard sounds of merriment; we were on the wrong floor.

In fact Griffin probably enjoyed a few nights out in Valencia with old friends from the 1920s, for many of them passed through in the months he was there. Ernest Hemingway arrived with Martha Gellhorn, then an apprentice war-reporter (and later Hemingway's third wife), working with Joris Ivens on a documentary film, *Spanish Earth*, to publicise the Republican cause. Dos Passos came later, to work on the same project; and Josie Herbst, joining the leftist 'crusade'. The Republican side of the war was the setting of Hemingway's novel published later, *For Whom the Bell Tolls*.[9]

Kate Mangan met most of the visitors, sharply observant as usual: Hemingway 'always with an entourage', 'a huge, red man, in hairy speckled tweeds', while the Duchess of Atholl 'wore a coat and skirt of some rough durable material like the upholstery of a railway carriage'. She also remembered meeting Dos Passos with Griffin on a street corner, and the American Socialist leader, Norman Thomas. 'The summer of 1937 was the time when we were so inundated with visitors that Valencia might have been a tourist resort', she wrote. 'A lot of them were important people but some came for frivolous reasons because it was the fashion.' She was only roped in as interpreter when there was an excess of visitors, her Spanish being only so-so.

The tour usually included a trip to the front, either at Teruel or Madrid. One of her colleagues who regularly went to Madrid in the course of duty hoped the tourists brought their own food with them. 'Last time I was up there', he said, 'we had stewed cat one day and dog's head the next. It was a big dog and we pretended it was a calf's head.' The citizens themselves were stoical. 'Madrid was shelled every day but it was not dangerous to the residents as they knew the time of day to expect it and where the gun emplacements were, so they walked on the safer side of the street.'

Don't be deceived by the light-hearted tone here: this war was deadly serious. So was the in-fighting on the Republican side, as Dos Passos discovered in a tragic way. He had arrived expecting to meet his friend and translator José Robles, who had returned from the United States to support the Republic, only to find he had just been executed by the Communists on a trumped-up charge. This shocking event was a turning-point for Dos Passos. Thereafter he moved steadily from Left-sympathiser to extreme-Right, ending up a virulent Cold Warrior in post-war American politics. At the time, the

---

[9] *This novel of Hemingway's, later a film with Gary Cooper and Ingrid Bergman (somewhat mis-cast as a Spanish damsel), did much to publicise, and glamorise, the Spanish war, just as his earlier novel,* A Farewell to Arms, *had immortalised the First World War in literature – see Chapter 1.*

shrouded circumstances of Robles' murder caused consternation in Republican Spain and for the American Left, torn between die-hard Stalinists and others who had 'seen the light'.[10]

What did Griffin make of all this? I wish I knew. Kate Mangan's picture of him in Spain shows a man who could have been – *should* have been – back in the groove at last, helping to document the history of the twentieth century. He was good at the work, and used to enjoy it, even the longeurs of hanging-around that all foreign correspondents must endure. Yet in the confidences he bestowed on Kate on Sunday afternoon walks on the beach, we see not a man in his element, fired with excitement to be present at this crucial moment of world history, but a now familiar sad-sack Griffin, obsessed with his personal troubles.

> Barry, I gathered, had been unfortunate in his domestic affairs. In his wallet he carried a photo of his children which he showed to everyone. It was rather embarrassing to go out with him because he used to stop and talk to strange Spanish babies. He was particularly attached to a weazened [sic] little baby at the breast, which a gypsy woman used to carry round the cafés. He said it looked like Queen Victoria and always gave the mother something though begging was forbidden. He really should have been a mother not a father.

This pathetic picture was not just Kate's impression. It turns out that the real purpose of Helen's letter to Dora on her flying visit to Paris was not to plead the cause of Republican Spain but of heartsick Griffin Barry:

> Griffin was in Valencia when we left there and has taken on a job with Reuters Agency, cabling news every day... However, I happen to know that he is also in a state of almost complete melancholia about you and the children... My own instincts ... tell me that he is still very much in love with you, is simply mad about the children, and worried... There wasn't a time that we were together in Paris or Spain when he didn't talk about you and the children and ask my advice as to what he could do. I advised him to stay in Spain for the time being, make a good thing of his Reuter's job, which needs doing badly after all the phonies and spies they have employed there as journalists, learn Spanish, and stick it out. If Griffin doesn't stick it out it will be because of his doubts and worries as to you and the children. None of this is propaganda for Griffin, Dora, it is really what happened... Nor did he ask me to write this letter or say these things. I am only answering your own letter to me and telling you the truth about everything.

---

[10] *Stalin's henchmen were very active in Spain. George Orwell's* Homage to Catalonia *revealed how the Communist Party manipulated the Republican cause to suit Soviet foreign policy – see page 183. When it was first published in 1938, few copies were sold because it did not fit the Communist Party 'line' on the Spanish war, which dominated the left-wing press and the campaign to support the Republic. Later it became a classic.*

No reply to this letter exists, but I doubt if it had much effect. And of course Griffin didn't stick it out. Was he sacked by Reuters? I don't know. At the end of May he wrote to Dora, announcing his return to England:

> I am coming out of Spain late in June and shall want badly to see the children, in fact I am making the journey to do so, as I have made others across the ocean. I shall not seek them however in any house inhabited by you and your young man. Please let me know how this can be arranged.

Thus began another exchange of angry letters between this benighted pair ... and thus ended what proved to be Griffin's last chance to make a name for himself in work that was his true métier. The most crucial events of the Spanish war happened while he was there: the bombing of Guernica, the siege of Madrid, the infamous May Days in Barcelona. For six months he had witnessed history in the making, but no word he wrote about it has survived. At the time he knew Kate Mangan she was just as obsessed with her personal troubles as Griffin was with his; but she had the youthful stamina to enjoy her time in Spain, and in later years the tranquillity to write eloquently about it. Griffin never did. The sad truth is that by 1937 he was an empty shell, hollowed out by anguish, incapable of taking a serious interest in anything outside his personal life. We shall never know what he saw in Málaga, Madrid, Teruel, or what he may have known about the death of José Robles. What a shame.

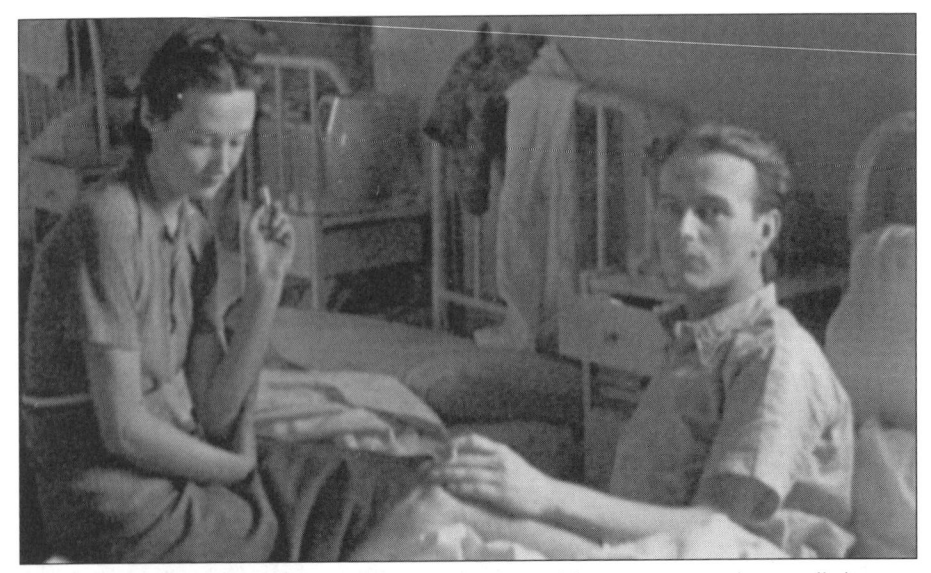

Kate's quest ended happily. She got Jan into hospital for treatment – and eventually home to England.

POSTSCRIPT TO CHAPTER 13

The Anarchist Revolution in Spain, 1936–37

While the politicians of the Popular Front government debated whether or not to oppose Franco's military insurrection, trade unionists from the socialist UGT and the anarcho-syndicalist CNT seized arsenals and fortresses for their own resistance to the generals and their foreign allies. Workers took over factories and peasants took over land in a genuine popular revolution – one which did not suit Soviet foreign policy. George Orwell's *Homage to Catalonia* describes how the revolution was betrayed, on Stalin's orders, by the Communists' suppression of the Trotskyists (POUM) and the anarchists (FAI-CNT) in the so-called May Days of 1937 in Barcelona. Ken Loach's 1995 film *Land and Freedom* tells the same story.

Peasants! Free yourselves through the collectivisation of the land, organised by your unions.
The Land is Yours!

Emma Goldman visiting peasants in the Valencia region, looking rather different from her last meeting with Griffin in 1920 (see page 25). I wonder if they met again in Spain?

CHAPTER 14

DORA'S SCHOOL

While Griffin was reporting world history in Spain, Dora was making her own contribution to history of another kind – the long struggle (still ongoing) to humanise the British education system. I hope Beacon Hill School will one day receive the serious study it deserves, to set alongside her own lively but uncritical account of it in *The Tamarisk Tree 2*. In the meantime I'm going to step aside briefly from Griffin's Story to pay my own tribute to Dora's achievement. Several former pupils, and a friend who was a teacher there – all, like me, looking back on the experience after a lifetime in other spheres – have contributed their recollections to this picture of the school as we remember it.

It is cruelly ironic that because of his fame, Beacon Hill was often referred to as 'the Bertrand Russell school', and widely believed to have closed when he left it. In fact he was only associated with the school for the first five of its 16-year life. By the time it was established at Boyles Court, having shaken off the Russell associations of Telegraph House, Beacon Hill was in every sense Dora's School.

Its prime of life was surely the period at Kingwell Hall, near Bath, from 1937 to 1940, years I remember well myself. But we can start a bit earlier than that. Suzanne Kalenberg (Sue Murray, when I met her in later years) was a pupil during the last year at Telegraph House and the first at Boyles Court. Barely able to read at the age of nine, after years of cruel child abuse (I don't know the details), she found her salvation at Beacon Hill. Later she gained a scholarship to Bedales, a more formal but still 'progressive' school.

> Day 1. When I arrived I saw a group of four boys playing 'tag' across the other side of the field. They called me over. "What's your name?" "Suzanne Kalenberg." "Saucepan? Come on, Saucepan, you're It then. Catch us!" We ran and ran all afternoon, and 'Saucepan' I remained for the rest of my two years at Beacon Hill School.

The boys (I had never met boys before) were freckled, tanned, shabby. They had not laughed at my red hair, my strange clothes, my foreign name. My sense of liberation at that moment remains a vivid memory...

Later, I knelt by my bed to say my prayers. "What are you doing?" My interrogator was a seven-year-old boy, jumping up and down on his bed. "Saucepan, what are you doing?" "Saying my prayers." "Don't you know there isn't a God?" I climbed into bed and again that sense of liberation overcame me. "Thank God for that", I thought. So ended the first day of my new life...

The next day classes began. The rule was that, if you didn't want to attend, you had to stay away for the whole day. Joyfully I went out to play on the huge swing under the great beech tree. It was a bit lonely. After a while, my class walked past me on their way to another classroom. They waved: "Hello Saucepan."

Of course I felt lonely and isolated, so the next day I joined my class. No remarks were made and I was helped to catch up on what I had missed... The teaching was arranged so that the information, stories and projects ran in sequence, so I never again missed a lesson, for fear of losing continuity...

One of the activities was writing the school play. Once a subject had been decided upon, characters were created to fit the available actors and each child was encouraged to invent their own lines. Betty, our teacher, would write it all down, giving only a minimum of guidance...

Although I was often cold and hungry, I do not remember ever being bored or lonely or unhappy; further, I never saw or experienced any bullying. Life at Beacon Hill was a constant exploration of the limits of my mental and physical capacities, of everything and everyone around me. It was an explosion of delight and discovery after my short lifetime of fear and bewilderment.

Every child's experience is different, of course – for example, Kate and other pupils from the Telegraph years remember serious bullying there. But Suzanne's memories neatly link up with the experience of another traumatised waif who came to Boyles Court in the spring of 1936, and left the school from Kingwell Hall in 1937. The intervening year rescued her from misery too. Coming from Nazi Germany to Beacon Hill was like 'coming out of a prison camp into a travelling circus', she wrote to me recently. Dora's school 'gave me a whiff of the excitement of life itself, the delight of being free, physically too, in a beautiful natural environment... and, most importantly of all: the idea that children's thinking mattered!'

Sixty years after she left Beacon Hill, now living in retirement in America, Ati Gropius Johansen wrote up her experiences there in an unpublished autobiography. In 1936 she was Beate Frank, nine years old, speaking very little

English, grieving for her mother who had just died, and not yet entirely secure as the adopted daughter of her aunt Isi and her uncle-by-marriage, Walter Gropius. He was the renowned modern architect and Director of the Bauhaus in pre-Nazi Germany, brought to England in 1934 and eased into a new life here by Jack Pritchard.[1] Jack and his wife Molly were staunch supporters of Beacon Hill, where their own children Jonathan and Jeremy were pupils from an early age. After Ati's first school-less months in London, Jack took her to Boyles Court to see if she'd like to join them there.

> Shrieking and giggling half-naked children raced randomly over the lawns, paying no attention to our presence, or that of any adults... There appeared to be no discernible discipline or order of any kind, and I knew instantly that I loved the place.
> Beacon Hill was a child's garden of earthly delights.

Timid little Ati was nervous at first. She was quite frightened of Dora, and even of Lily – 'Matron', charging around her domestic territory 'with the muted fury of a rhinocerous'. But she soon learned that Pat had no important role, and could safely be ignored:

> ...the young man with smooth black hair slicked back and wearing fire-red ties I had thought was a teacher, but... was, of course, Jeremy explained, Dora's communist friend. This last was his only distinction, at least in my eyes, who knew from my Nazi schooling that to be a communist was next to being Beelzebub. However the young man rarely spoke, at least to us children, and as a somber, mute shadow next to Dora [he] had no drama and even very little mystery to offer.

Classes were bewildering, until she entered into the spirit of the place. She found she could do well in mathematics; but in other subjects the required 'uninhibitedness' was elusive. 'It didn't seem to matter to anyone how conscientiously I worked. Only colorful, free bursts of expression seemed to make a dent on the community, and lifted one above one's peers.' Her previous training was no use at all in the artroom:

> With dripping brush I also learned to paint illustrations of Greek myths onto paper tacked onto the walls. The paint running down in rivulets and splattering all over the floor, the big pots of lurid primary colors were all heady stuff. I had never had anything but faint-colored pencils and little pads of thin, lined paper to work with. In art classes in

---

[1] *The Bauhaus was the revolutionary State School of Art and Design founded after the First World War in the Weimar Republic of Germany, which closed in 1932. It attracted* avant garde *artists in all fields and gave birth to the Modern Movement in architecture and design which gradually permeated the western world, despite the Nazis' attempts to kill it. Jack Pritchard, by rescuing Gropius, and his own work in architecture and design, might be called the midwife of the Modern Movement in England.*

The artroom at Kingwell Hall

German schools we carefully copied tiny reproductions of 19th century etchings with stubby pencils in total silence. Now I followed Jackie's undaunted lead as, with waving brush and hoots of enthusiasm, she attacked the wall and drew huge naked figures of the Gods upon it.

In her memoir Ati rightly fastens on the artroom as a centrepoint of the school. More attention was paid to all the Arts than was usual in other English schools at that time, which in this respect (and others) were not unlike her German schools. The educational establishment regarded places like Beacon Hill as a kind of lunatic fringe.

In her own book Dora explains the origins and ideas of the progressive school movement of the interwar years, from which the most radical school, A S Neill's Summerhill, still survives today.[2] Beacon Hill was closer to

---

[2] *The school is now run by Neill's daughter, Zoë Readhead. Needless to say it is still frowned upon by the educational establishment and in 1999 New Labour's OFSTED régime almost succeeded in closing it down. Their inspectors objected to the children's freedom not to attend lessons, a fundamental principle which the Head rightly refused to interfere with; but after a vigorous campaign (supported by the local Conservative MP), OFSTED backed down. This common feature of the more radical progressive schools has always alarmed outsiders – though unnecessarily, as Suzanne's experience shows.*

Summerhill, in theory and practice, than to any other progressive school, and Dora and Neill were personal friends; but both schools were also the product of their founders' own inclinations. From the start Bertie and Dora wanted the teaching at Beacon Hill to have a firm academic grounding, and Dora stuck to that practice. But there was a strong emphasis on natural history rather than kings and queens, and on learning from 'the world around us' as well as from books. Another of my contributors, David Correa-Hunt, who attended the school in its last phase, when Dora was almost the only teacher, vividly remembers this part of her curriculum:

> Nature-study involved exploring a nearby stream – collecting frog spawn. I recall discovering a colony of newts (I've never seen a newt since)...
>
> One of my fondest memories is of the Natural History lessons with Dora, based on study of that great tome "The Science of Life" (by H G Wells, Julian Huxley, & G P Wells). Dora encouraged us to question, to follow our curiosity... into all sorts of highways & byeways of phenomena of life; to speculate; to wonder... I remember sheer fascination and a sense of the infinity of the field of knowledge that was waiting to be explored.

The principle of 'learning by doing', also fundamental in progressive education, is neatly illustrated by the recollection of David's six-year-old sister Susan (now Downes), again from the last years of the school:

> I remember Dora letting us 'make' a ladder very seriously with all wood hammer & nails provided. It broke of course – six year olds not being technically very efficient, but I remember how excited and grown-up we felt being allowed to try!

Susan also remembered 'being taught French with words and pictures by Dora. She made it into an exciting game – very competitive! but fun.' I have the same memory from when I was six, at Boyles Court, though in my case Dora was teaching us German. She knew what is only now being recognised in Britain: that primary school is the place to start language teaching.

David was old enough to take part in the play-writing described by Suzanne, in his case our 1942 production, *Give The Devil His Due*. This was a feature of the school throughout its life, given prominence in Dora's account of it.[3] She mentions Suzanne and other children closely involved in the writing, performing, and then publication (by a small publisher, The Janus Press) of some of the early plays.

---

[3] *The Tamarisk Tree 2: My School and the Years of War (Virago, London, 1980), pp.114–15.* Chapter 10 of this book, *The Poems and the Plays*, reprints extracts of both, and gives a full account of how the plays were written and produced.

A meeting of the League of Notions, from a play performed in December 1937

This book appeared in 1934, entitled *Thinking in Front of Yourself* from one of the plays, and illustrated with lino-cuts by the children. How fortunate that Dora preserved a gem of a review of the book in the then *Manchester Guardian*. After a paragraph praising the worthy activity of school drama, and young dramatists who 'find their material...in the world in which they live', the anonymous reviewer warns us that 'these plays are strange and remarkable for their style and for their matter; they arrest the reader and make him think'. Just when Dora might have been expecting applause for their originality, came the sting in the tail:

> We believe that the average reader will be shocked that children whose ages range from five to twelve years should already be familiar with problems of breeding, of divorce, of social and economic distress and disorder, of the war supposed to be waged between 'science' and religion; we believe that he will think that other things should occupy children's minds and not these. And if he admires the wealth of vocabulary which these precocious children display he will simply be sorry that their language, if strong, is coarse; if fluent, nasty.

Reprinting this pompous comment in the 1970s, Dora was still indignant at the injustice of it. The word 'divorce' does not occur in the book, she protests, nor is breeding discussed, and the only swear word in the text is 'bloody'. How unfair! But the point she might have made, by that date, is that Beacon Hill was decades ahead of other primary schools in its curriculum and methods, and its concern for the needs of children. What primary teacher now, or in the 1970s, would be shocked by the subject matter of our plays? Helping children to cope, in the safe environment of the school, with problems of family break-up, of social and economic distress in the outside world, is just what caring teachers are supposed to do today.

In 1937 Kingwell Hall in its beautiful setting was a happy landing after the failed merger with Brickwall School. The spacious front lawn, facing south, and in my memory always sunny, ended with a 'ha ha', a short drop into the cow-field below. On the western side were greenhouses, gardens and woods beyond; and at the back, a swimming pool. With two new teachers, Geoff and Evelyn Brooks, Lily and Walter as matron and cook, and devoted Pat at her side, Dora must have thought her luck had turned at last. The extensive grounds and numerous sheds allowed her and Pat to indulge their own love of animals – cats, dogs, goats, rabbits and guinea pigs of course, plus Rasputin the Capuchin monkey (officially belonging to John), and even a tame jackdaw, Squawky, a fledgling swept out of the chimney by the sweep (and later blown away in a gale). For us kids the menagerie was a source of delight and of education, though somewhat out of control, as I recall. The cats had kittens indiscriminately and messed where they shouldn't; my rabbit ate her young because no one told me those little pink lumps shouldn't be handled. I suppose that was one way to learn rabbit-care, but I rather went off rabbits after that.

Although we had so little to rebel against, we had to test the limits of our freedom from time to time. Suzanne remembers abolishing all the school rules 'as an experiment', and how quickly 'anarchy' turned to boredom. In 1937 a similar episode at Kingwell Hall ended in the same way. I was intrigued to discover from Ati's memoir how the Bigs precipitated the 'Great Strike' I remember so well. For her group of rebels, 'it was the Children's Crusade of Beacon Hill, and its goal was food'. This is what happened (in my paraphrase, with Ati's words in italics):

> While indulging the Smalls[4], always her favourites, Lily had refused second helpings to the Bigs, *raising mutiny in our hearts*. What was to be done? *Clearly, as our education in communism had shown us, the thing to do was to go on strike*. So the Bigs, led by Jonathan and Jackie, set off to march to Bath (exact intentions unclear). They soon got hungry, and pooled their pennies for Jonathan to buy a loaf of bread. *It was still hot as we tore into it with our fingers, and its sweet smell and powdery crust remains unendingly in my mind.*
>
> Unsure of the route, the rebels began to flag. *To reach Bath by nightfall was clearly impossible. Our mission had failed.*
>
> "Come on," said Jackie, "we've got to get back. We'd better telephone Dora and tell her where we are."
>
> A lorry came by, and took the weary wanderers back to Kingwell

---

[4] Ati remembers them as 'Littles', but in fact the youngest class of children were called the Smalls.

Hall. There they found the kitchen closed and went to bed supperless, but still defiant, *with mute dignity*. Next day they realised the seriousness of the situation: all the teachers and the cook were on strike, *not counting terrible Matron and her flock of Littles. We went through the ghostly hours doing "as we pleased". There were no classes now, of course, to fill the time, and not fear but utter boredom slowly overpowered us. The day crawled by endlessly. When evening came and brought back the blithely cheerful adults, we were ready to negotiate.*

Ati may have forgotten one incident indelible in my memory from that endless, hungry day (or maybe she wasn't in on this piece of devilment). I was not a Small but a Middle, and must have had help to steal from the larder a huge tin of currants and a string of raw sausages to eat in the old railway carriage in the woods. I don't think we got far into the sausages. Like Ati, I was mightily relieved when Walter reappeared and cooked us all kippers for tea.

Readers who have been through teacher-training will recognise in this story Rousseau's 'discipline of natural consequences' – in essence, that kids who break windows must suffer the draught – as one underlying principle of Beacon Hill School. For Ati, it meant something more:

> Seated around a large table, the strikes were discussed, complaints heard, adult points of view aired and a sober reconciliation was reached. Though we knew we had ultimately been trumped by the adults, a brand-new feeling of strength and self-respect grew in us. We knew we had been taken seriously and treated like union strikers and not like little children. For me it was a turning point in my education. Never again would the nonentity of a child in a big institution be a role I could totally accept. Beacon Hill and Bertand Russell had had their effect. They had given me a sense of innate worth.

In retrospect, it must be admitted: food was a problem at Dora's School. Suzanne and Ati both remember being hungry, as I do; and the rock-hard baked bread at every meal – good for our teeth, I was always told, but probably a way to make it go further. Fresh loaves would have been wolfed down (as the Bigs wolfed theirs on the road to Bath). How we all fawned on Joy when she received a strange product called peanut butter in parcels from America! None of us hungry kids were aware of the school's financial knife-edge that gave us sparse rations at times.

Much of our learning happened outside the classroom, of course, as education authorities with their prescribed curriculum sometimes forget. Here's Ati again, recalling Beacon Hill's version of behind-the-bike-sheds sex education:

> The bathroom had several tubs in it, and two or three of us to a tub. Every evening, after the Littles had finished, we Bigs had a gleeful,

splashing half hour together with everybody hopping in and out of tubs, sudsy, slippery and screaming. It was here that I learned about the anatomy of boys and girls in great detail... Actually I had received at least a theoretical sex education in Berlin from my classmates, of which I hadn't believed a word – it seemed utterly preposterous [even when confirmed by her aunt]. Here at Beacon Hill, however, facts were facts in a very ordinary, unpreposterous sort of way. I came to accept the bathroom biology lessons in the same spirit as geography classes... all true enough, and quite acceptable, but of no lasting interest.

I too remember the matter-of-factness of our sex instruction – in particular, a Council meeting (of the whole school, pupils and staff) specially called to explain what a 'bugger' was, to counteract our casual misuse of the word. ('A man who loves another man instead of a woman', we were given to understand.)

When the Gropiuses emigrated to America in 1937, Ati was devastated to leave Beacon Hill. Once again she was imprisoned in a conventional school until she found liberation in 'a marvellous, mad extension of B H' – Black Mountain College in North Carolina. Readers who know about that experimental academy will recognise the echoes of Beacon Hill that delighted Ati as a student there.

In her book about her father, Kate has written an appreciation of 'her' Beacon Hill, the pioneering days at Telegraph House – which paradoxically broke up the childhood idyll she and John had shared with their parents before they opened the school. In my case – and probably Roddy's too, if he were alive to testify – the school *provided* the idyll which shielded us to a large extent from the parental quarrel raging over our heads. At Kingwell, where the quarrel reached a crescendo, distressing scenes which might have blown apart a nuclear family were quickly forgotten in the extended family of the school. These are the years when the figure of Lily is as important as Dora in my memory. As she bandaged our grazed knees with no fuss and bother, so she also provided a refuge from emotional storms – not with any comment on the dispute that caused them, just calm and orderliness to soak up the trauma.

It was only in later years, remembering the importance of Lily's Room in that vast barn of a house, that I recognised Lily in this role – played intuitively, unconsciously, as was her way. She was matron to the whole school of course, but Roddy and I knew we were 'special'. If she went to Bath on her half-day off, we could expect some little treat from the shops, and next day, before breakfast, would present ourselves at the door of her room. Perhaps the other children resented this favouritism, but Lily was always more than Matron to us.[5]

---

[5] *Having no home other than the school, Lily and Walter stayed on at Kingwell in the holidays, acting as caretakers when we went to Cornwall and often getting involved in family affairs.*

Barbara Wright – 'Baba' – recognised Lily's central place in the life of the school the moment she arrived. Barbara spent 1938 as class teacher of the Smalls. She came from a conventional background and has always insisted that for her, the enlightenment that took place at Beacon Hill was a two-way process: not only what she succeeded in teaching the Smalls (*if anything?* she agonised to the diary she kept), but her own introduction to the 'Real World', her 'Rite of Passage', the year that changed her life. Sixty years later her memories were 'still so remarkably vivid to me it's almost ridiculous'.

> I have heaps and heaps of sort of mental snapshots... From the poppies on the curtains in my nice little room... to Alison, being annoyed with me once (why?) coming down the stairs and me at the bottom being greeted with the filthiest insult she could possibly think up: "Barbara believes in God!"... And whenever Lily took a day or so off (which was practically never), everyone going down with coughs and colds and suchlike which, the moment she came back, disappeared like magic...

Lily's role, and the perpetual common cold, are recurrent topics of Barbara's diary:

> Lily: "If you children blew your noses you wouldn't get colds!"
> Roddy: "I blew mine this morning. I blow my nose <u>every</u> morning."

And her authority was not confined to the sickroom:

> My whole class of Smalls decides it would be fun to rush out into the garden. NOT with malice aforethought, I seem to remember, just for fun. My only response is to sit down on the floor in the corner and cry.
> Enter Lily.
> Lily, at the french windows: "COME ON BACK IN, YOU LITTLE BUGGERS!"
> Re-enter my whole class.

Poor Barbara was plagued by self-doubt during her first days in the classroom:

> <u>January 11th</u> [my sixth day at Beacon Hill]
> By devious means I made Roddy draw a parrot today of which I am pretty proud. I got it to go in his exercise book and I added the date myself so's to show that he has done something with me. I feel as if it's the last thing he might ever do with me...
>
> ...Evelyn told me I was lucky that they liked me; my god if they do, thank god they don't *not*... I wish I could force reading and writing down them on the strength of it.
> ["force"! I hadn't been there long enough to get the message.]

Evelyn was right. We did like Baba, and during that year she proved herself an inspired teacher in true Beacon Hill style. For the Open Day in June 1938 her Smalls produced their own play, *Cats Have No Fun*, in which she played the Great Clumping Giant. She also played the piano for the main production, *The Feast of The Gods*. Baba is a key figure in 'my' Beacon Hill, and has remained a lifelong friend. Nothing is more evocative for me than her collection of tiny sepia prints, a record of her year at Kingwell, which I have used to illustrate this chapter.

Barbara also confided to her diary a few comments about the Dora–Griffin relationship. Griffin's siege of Kingwell Hall (described in the next chapter) began as soon as he returned from Spain in July 1937, and lasted until he sailed for the United States in February 1939. Consumed with jealousy of Pat, and a passionate longing to be with his children, he pestered Dora endlessly for his parental 'rights'. The staff could hardly avoid noticing the rows, and newcomers would soon learn enough of the background to have some idea of what was going on. They were all very sorry for Griffin, and puzzled by Dora's attachment to this nonentity, Pat, who seemed to have no important function in the school. In the staffroom the joke was that Pat drank all the money the school desperately needed.[6]

For Barbara, the dilemma was acute. During her year at the school she fell under Dora's spell and, not unnaturally, swallowed whole her version of the break-up with Bertie – that Great Tragedy of Dora's life, for which, in her mixed-up emotions at that time, she also held Griffin responsible. How else to explain Barbara's diary comment – the accolade of a true disciple: 'I admire Dora for having the courage of her convictions in being beastly to Griffin – all the more so because he really *does* seem such a nice person.'

Sixty years later, Barbara and I agreed, it was not so easy to apportion praise or blame between the parties. But 'Dora being beastly to Griffin' was one aspect of life at Kingwell Hall I never forgot.

---

[6] *In a recent letter to me Barbara wrote: 'The ghastly Pat – I (and I think we – the staff –) imagined that Dora was suffering from* la nostalgie de la boue *– and that the mud most calculated to hurt and distress and damage Bertie was precisely the ghastly Pat.' This is a perceptive observation. It fits in with Dora's character, and her efforts to become 'proletarian' after the split with Bertie. I don't know whether he was offended by the mud on Pat's boots (figuratively speaking), but Griffin certainly was. He was always disgusted that Dora had 'stooped so low' in her choice of his successor.*

DORA'S SCHOOL

With the exception of the photo top left on the next page, donated by Jennifer Heseltine, all the photos here are from Barbara Wright's collection of 1938. As much of school life as possible took place outdoors – with an emphasis on 'keeping fit' and caring for animals. In fine summer weather we were allowed to sleep in tents on the lawn.

Rehearsing *The Feast of the Gods*

195

4 June 1937: Jenny and her sister Bronwen celebrate their shared birthday

A briefing by the teacher on a visit to Bristol Zoo

Dora with Raspy the monkey on her sholder

DORA'S SCHOOL

The 'Stop Me and Buy One' man biked up the drive regularly.

CHAPTER 15

THE SIEGE OF KINGWELL HALL

Griffin arrived in England in July 1937 in belligerent mood. His first salvo lobbed at Kingwell Hall is a reply to Dora's letter received in Spain.[1] Anxious to avoid embarrassing scenes like those at Boyles Court in 1935, and again last Christmas, she must have suggested a meeting with her solicitor to arrange a *modus vivendi* between them. Perhaps she had also intimated that, as Pat was still on the scene, Griffin had better learn to tolerate him. He replied through a red mist:

> If I want enlightenment on legal points I will get a solicitor of my own... I hardly need a solicitor to remind me what I have lost by having children with you outside the law and again by having sacrificed years of life with them in order that you should lose the least possible in your entanglement with Bertie. You are now enjoying the fruits of what I earned – the utmost control obtainable over John and Kate and the utmost lien on your husband's money – and are using the spirit of the laws whose protection I surrendered for myself and against which, when you were on the wrong side of them, I went into exile on your behalf, to deprive me of even a minimum of family life and to deprive the children of it too.

By now his endless reworking of old grievances had led him to believe – or so he pretended – that Dora had planned *from the beginning* to banish him from the scene so that she could live in luxury on Bertie's alimony (the absurdity of this idea needs no emphasis). As for Pat – ! Every unavoidable mention of this 'half-sinister, half-ridiculous young man' is suffused with loathing and contempt. Pat is an intruder, to be firmly ignored when arranging to see *his* children – preferably with Dora too.

---

[1] *Dora's letter is not here, so I can only guess at its contents. As Griffin no longer kept her letters, I now have only Dora's carbons of typed ones, usually brief and businesslike. Gaps in Griffin's sequence of letters also call for supposition to make a coherent story.*

THE SIEGE OF KINGWELL HALL

From then on his persistent aim was to engineer these cosy little foursomes of 'family life'. He first proposed a summer holiday, 'for whatever peaceful time you can manage and wherever; I can supply money if you want to go away.' Surprisingly, and no doubt with some apprehension, Dora agreed to a week in Devon with him and the two of us – duly recorded with her Kodak Brownie (see photos). This was the only holiday we ever spent together as 'a family', and I'm sorry to say I remember nothing about it except that smelly seaweed round my neck. Perhaps this indicates harmonious relations during the week (unlike other occasions I remember). It seems another plan also went well – until Griffin got the bill for it.

While she went away with John and Kate for a few days, Dora allowed him to use the services of a local chauffeur to run us about in her car. When Griffin queried the driver's bill Dora replied that it had at first been higher, but was reduced 'when Pat took up the matter vigorously with him' (ouch!). Now she detailed every penny for petrol, oil, and the driver's time. Never mind, she'll settle this bill, 'and I would prefer to have no further financial dealings with you at all'.

Poor Griffin. His few weeks of playing Daddy had cleaned him out. In October, while we settled in for our first winter at Kingwell, he hitched a ride with friends to the south of France and decided to stay there, as the cheapest place to live, until he had written something saleable. And he did produce at least one published piece that winter: a very competent article, *Changing Patterns in French Life*, which appeared the following summer in Coby Gilman's *Travel* magazine. It is a skilful mix of travelogue and social analysis, tailored for his readership by a practised journalist. Even at a low ebb Griffin was capable of good work – if only he could keep his mind on it.

Away from Dora, and the irritation of Pat, he was calmer – but alone; intermittently ill; and often very sad. Dora wrote to him a few times; so did I. In one letter to me I see him struggling to remember I'm only seven years old:

> ...I tell you all this not because it's very interesting but because it's about all there is to tell – except, of course, what's in my mind and some of that you wouldn't understand though I think you would understand nearly everything if I could see a lot of you and talk to you a lot.

Having no other grown-up to confide in, his letters to Dora, his once-beloved, were still his only outlet for heartsearching. Can she have been unmoved by these rueful reflections?

> I found I was doing journalism like a dead man, with a spirit gone deaf and dumb. When my heart or my imagination was moved by a woman or a job very soon Harry's image came between me and the quicksilver I should have seized – Harry's or yours or a fragment of the deep biological life I began to live with you. This was not only during the years I kept afloat in Washington but alarmingly in Spain – a job cut out for what was once my temperament...
>
> ...And I know that unless I strike pay dirt in my writing soon I shall come to the end of life with nothing of my own, not the companionship of my children and their mother... probably not even a job.

Touched she may have been – but Dora had her own concerns. The finances of the school were perilous, as usual, and despite the devoted work of her staff, she carried the burden of worry alone. She also cared deeply about national and world affairs, as anyone who knew her will recall. Dora took politics *personally*: to her dying day she seemed to feel that all the tragedies she'd witnessed in her lifetime might have been prevented if she had tried hard enough. And there was plenty to worry about. Among my clear memories of these years are her pacing up and down the lawn at Kingwell in grave discussion with Important Visitors;[2] and her stricken face, newspaper in hand,

---

[2] *The only one of these I can positively identify is Wal Hannington, leader of the National Unemployed Workers' Movement. The NUWM organised the dramatic Hunger Marches of the 1930s, the most famous being the Jarrow Crusade of 1936.*

when the Spanish Republicans surrendered in March 1939.

At a domestic level there was continuous tension with the Russell household as John and Kate were shuttled to and fro. And now here was Griffin again, with his imperious demands and accusations...

While still in France he again accused her of denying her younger children 'parental care' – by which he meant not the *separate* attention bestowed on them by two loving parents, but this mystical 'family life' they should be jointly providing for us. But the wretched Pat is in the way! Since he is young and has no children by you, he wrote to Dora, he should just clear off and allow the two of us 'to mark out our destinies...'. Griffin seems to have thought that merely spending time together would re-ignite Dora's love for him – that despite all her rebuffs, and discounting his two successors, by some ruse, or twist of fate, or sheer will-power, *he could win her back.* In the spring of 1938 he returned to England to resume the siege.

He now had a room in some (unspecified) friendly household in London, as well as a useful base in Bristol, 12 miles from Kingwell, with his old friends Roy and Eugenia Baker. Roy was the US Consul, a man of progressive views, as befitted a New Deal appointee. Their two sons were at Dartington. I remember visits to their house and visits by them to us (usually Eugenia and Griffin, to take us out in her car). The weeks of April to June 1938 are punctuated by letters to and fro, arranging or rearranging such visits and excursions – businesslike on Dora's side, sometimes tetchy on Griffin's when his precise requests could not be met.

This photo was probably taken on a visit to the Bakers' in Bristol

As his funds trickled away, he became dependent on obliging friends with access to a car to get down to Somerset at all. In May he asked to come with Tom and Kitty Wintringham, friends from the Spanish war; and could they stay the night? Dora replied that in term-time every room was occupied, but she would book them in at a local B&B at 4/6d a night; will he let her know? Griffin exploded with rage: he could not afford 4/6d, and would have to stay with the Bakers. Then he fell ill, and didn't come at all.

In June – oh joy! – he saw a chance for another 'family life' interlude when a mutual friend, Portia Holman, invited us all to her cottage in Sussex for a week. Dora's letters wriggled and squirmed with objections, reservations, alternative suggestions... In the end we did all go, for a few days at least, but the visit must have ended with a flaming row. This phase of the siege was brought to a close with a sharp exchange as Dora prepared to take us to Cornwall for the summer holiday:

> *From Dora, 28 July* – As I told you at Portia's, I do not think our meeting is of any use; and it is better for you to arrange to see the children elsewhere in September or the autumn, and not come here at all.
>
> *From Griffin, 29 July* – I agree it is better for us not to meet – unless you and your young man can cease to frustrate a civilised relation between us...

It's difficult to assess at this distance how far Pat was 'frustrating civilised relations' between them. Dora certainly used him as a shield when meeting Griffin; several letters show Griffin's resentment at his presence. But Pat was not very assertive – by no means a macho defender of womenfolk – and would only have done what she asked. Griffin's jealousy of him as a pseudo-stepfather to us was certainly misplaced. Pat was a cardboard figure in my orbit at that time. Other adults – our teachers, Lily, and Dora most of all – were the people who counted.

Another question about Pat at Kingwell Hall concerns his effect on the fortunes of the school. Griffin's letters often claimed that Pat's presence was blighting the school in some way; that 'influential parents' were so put off by Dora's relations with him that the school's reputation was suffering. Even allowing for sour grapes, he was probably half-right there. Barbara Wright agrees that 'everyone' at the school despised Pat, as we have seen. Dora's admirers outside the school, and she had many, must have wondered at her association with someone so far below her own level.[3] But the difficulties of the school had other causes too.

Pat– 'a cardboard figure in my orbit'

---

[3] *I have pondered the same question all my life, especially as I grew up and came to dislike Pat intensely – as Kate did too. Kate offers the most charitable view of him, as Dora's 'faithful hound', obedient, loyal, reliable. He never questioned Dora's decisions, and over many difficult and lonely years he was* always there, *with moral and practical support. It was during this time at Kingwell Hall, as her problems worsened, that he established his indispensability.*

In September 1938 came the Munich Crisis, when for a week or two we all thought war would break out at any minute (until the British Prime Minister Neville Chamberlain flew off to meet Hitler at Munich, and allowed him to gobble up Czechoslovakia). Suddenly Griffin saw a way out of the fix he was in (not revealed to Dora at first) by offering his services at Kingwell Hall, which he assumed would be flooded with city children at the outbreak of war. On 24 September he wired Dora: EXPECT REFUSE PRESS OFFERS AND PROCEED KINGWELL HALL TO ASSIST YOU IF WAR COMES, followed at once by a note elaborating his offer and expecting to arrive the day after tomorrow. 'Reserve me some real work to do, please, and find me a place to sleep where you can.'[4] Dora replied immediately:

> I was very much surprised to receive your telegram... I cannot see in what way you could help us here... I do not expect that we run any serious danger down here... I'm afraid that just now I do not feel inclined to accede to your request.

Back came three close-typed pages from Griffin explaining in tedious detail why she *must* accept his generous offer. First, he owes money for bed and board and must leave his lodging within days: 'further credit is exhausted'. Secondly, an American journalist friend assures him he can earn a freelance living from anywhere in England... Thirdly – oh, here we go again: another recital of events since 1932, his longing to be with the children, his resentment against Pat (but he promises not to quarrel with him!), and how useful he will be when the 'influx of children fleeing from bombs' arrives. 'I hope to hear from you on Saturday and leave for Kingwell then.' Dora again replied by return of post:

> ...notwithstanding everything, I simply cannot have you here... when you come there are always disturbances... To do anything that would upset my own nerves or disturb the staff when they are faced with heavy work and problems is definitely bad for the school... We have tried the situation before and always with disastrous results...

Dora's picture of Griffin as a walking time-bomb was apt. But he was crushed by her refusal to accept his self-sacrifice. Picking up the bludgeon again, he fired off two letters announcing his intention to come and live in the nearby village *anyway*, so that he could have his fair share of association with his children. For Dora as Head of the school he was demanding the impossible: to

---

[4] *Griffin relished the atmosphere of urgency and danger in London at that moment – parts of this letter read like the report he must have wished he was writing for some American newspaper. 'It looks like war this morning... People here are being fitted with gas masks, young men mobilized, and girls. The town is waiting. But meantime all the children who can be got out of town easily are being got out – which means of course the well-to-do first. I am going up to help Tom and Kitty Wintringham dig holes in their North London park.'*

be free to pluck us out of the classroom at any moment that suited him. Luckily, at that moment came an offer of work which kept Griffin in London for a few weeks to pay off his rent arrears, and put him in a better mood.

This spat occasioned a long letter from Dora, dated 5 October 1938, which is a useful document of this stormy relationship. Its immediate purpose was to set out the conditions for seeing us in term-time. Holidays were different, of course: 'I have stated over and over again that you can have the children to stay in holidays, if you will make the necessary arrangements. My having John and Kate...rests on exactly the same conditions...' Then she patiently repeated what she had said to him in London:

> I explained to you that what you were asking...was something that I could not permit to any parent of children in the school, since if they all lived near and had the children out at odd times during the week, the school could not be properly run. Most of them...only see them about twice a term and then for part of Sunday...
>
> ...if any parent came here and expected [free access at any time] I should at once ask them to... send them as day children, or take them away altogether.

Fair enough. The letter then reminded Griffin of other uncomfortable facts about his situation as a parent. 'Had the arrangement on which these children were born continued, [they would have] lived in a home that was not yours, and you would have had to...see them...in a home provided by you.' But in the eight years since Harriet's birth, he had 'not built up anything for the children'. She appreciated it was difficult to make a living in England, but 'a steady job in the States' would have enabled him to come over every year to see them. If the school failed (as Griffin well knew it might), *she* would have to get a job and 'stick to it with all its limitations' to provide for the children. 'You cannot claim rights without accepting some responsibilities.'

Having fulfilled her obligations towards him, she now begged him to back off:

> You seem to me not to have the ordinary decent feelings even of those people who believe in free relationships, of which the essence is that one does not intrude on another person when that person has made it quite clear that things are ended. For married people there is provision in law for such circumstances; I do not see why those who profess to have a better morality than the law should prefer to persecute rather than behave like decent human beings.
>
> I do not and will not intrude on you, and I have the right to ask that you give me the same courtesy.

Griffin's failings as a 'provider' are stated quite tactfully here; and it is a clear and reasonable statement of the terms for his present and future access to his children – as much as any separated parent could expect. This is the view Dora held for the rest of our childhood, and transmitted to me as I grew up.

Did Griffin fully and finally accept those crucial words *'things are ended'*? A few weeks later, making plans to move to Somerset, he was at least conciliatory: 'I should expect to see the children only by arrangement with you; once or twice a week would not disturb their routine, I'd think.' And how he was yearning for those visits!

> ...I long for the sight, sound and smell of my children, unforced, casual and in my own place or under my own wing; I've never had it since Harriet was 2 or 3, nor she of me, and Roddy has never had it at all in an atmosphere unpoisoned by the long and dreary row between his parents. If I had a well-funded existence of my own, I know you say we could have that away from you from time to time, but I have not got that existence – not yet...; meantime I feel I cannot go on without more of the children than I have had...

Of course the friendly mood did not last. For a while polite letters tripped back and forth, arranging this or that outing... But the strain of regular contact, exchanging us at the front door, was telling on them both. On 18 December some kind of explosion occurred. Four days later Dora wrote to say, 'We have decided after all to go away for a few days over Christmas... There will be an opportunity for you to see the children when they get back....'

Catastrophe! Griffin was devastated to be shut out of our Christmas *again*. (How typical that Lily, who recognised his needs as she recognised everyone's, went to visit him in his lonely bed-sit on Christmas Day with a present of cigarettes.) He poured out his grief in a letter to me at Carn Voel:

> ...It's not a very grand present but next year I will try to make the handkerchiefs all diamonds and pearls, somehow, and maybe I can unless I commit suicide before next Christmas – which would only slow up matters, really, for I'd manage to get in touch with you from Heaven or Hell or maybe it would be Limbo I would find myself in...
>
> I was terribly sorry to have you whisked away for Christmas because I came to Europe specially to be near you and Roddy at such times... It sort of left me on my bottom but I picked my bottom up on Christmas Day and put it on a chair and worked. (There! I laughed for the first time since I knew you were gone)...

... and more of the same. Despite his attempts at childish badinage, adult misery keeps bubbling up – 'I mourn your going like a beast', 'my old heart is full of grief'. Letters like this help to explain the sick dread I still feel when I try to recapture my eight year-old self. Such depth of feeling after so long hardly seems justified by the few quarrels I actually remember.[5] Somehow I felt his terrible sadness was *my fault*.

Of course I was absorbing the constant tension, as children do (Roddy less so, being younger, and because Griffin's attention was always focused on me). Looking back now, I see him lying in wait for me like the Ancient Mariner – waiting until I was old enough to hear out his endless tale of woe. And waiting so impatiently!

A few months later Dora wrote to reprove him for a letter to me written in terms 'likely to cause the gravest upset to such a young child, who ought not to be troubled by her parents' disputes'. I had brought her this letter saying I did not understand it, Dora wrote, but after reading it herself she had decided to confiscate it.

Feeling the effects of the siege?

> I must ask you not to write to her like that; it is really not fair to her or to you or to me. She is interested in childish things, and she rather expects us to take an interest in her doings and the things that she likes. I do not think children ought to be asked for the kind of sympathy that one tries to get from a grown-up.

Well said, Mum. And throughout our childhood she never did burden us with 'her side' of the dispute – but of course as the victor, in possession of the prize, she did not need to.[6] Moreover her rebuke to Griffin is a little disingenuous: the offending letter, carefully worded for eight-year-old eyes, naturally shows *her* in an unfavourable light. She must have been glad of an excuse to hide it from me.

By the time I received that letter the besieger of Kingwell Hall had retreated, defeated. An angry exchange in January 1939 conveys the mood of his departure:

---

[5] *A spitting row at the front door, me clinging to Dora's legs, "Stop! Stop!" (Daddy had arrived unexpectedly with a car, wanting to take me out for a ride, and was refused because Roddy was out and 'it wouldn't be fair to take me and not him')... A dreadful scene in a Bristol theatre where we'd all gone to see* Peter Pan, *the two of them shrieking at each other, everyone staring, me trying to hide myself and my shame. Years later when I saw* Peter Pan *in a West End theatre, it all came flooding back...*

[6] *Dora was not so restrained in her dispute with Bertie, where she was the one who had lost out. In her book about her father, written after his death in 1970, Kate has recounted the emotional blackmail to which she and John were subjected by both their parents.*

> *From Griffin, 8 January* – Since you made your scene and departed with the children, I have seen a solicitor...
>
> *From Dora, 12 January* – I cannot discuss arrangements in reply to a letter of abuse, and in future if I receive such letters I shall not reply to them.
>
> *From Griffin, 24 January* – I have decided against the legal steps which I have been advised are possible. They would certainly destroy the school, which is a protection to the children if it can survive.

This was an absurd pretence. Griffin could not afford lawyers' fees, or anything else. He was in debt, and by now had realised he must return to the United States 'to restore the prosperity I now lack and to share it with [the children] from far off'. The tone of this bitter letter is almost suicidal, even to the last request of the condemned man: could the children come next Saturday to the Bakers' in Bristol, as 'I should like very much to spend my last night with Harry and Rod under a friendly roof'? The histrionics are almost comical until you reflect that, just as he feared, this would be Griffin's last experience of 'the sight, sound and smell' of his children *as children*. Every parent will know how desolate he was feeling.

Griffin wrote me a long letter on his voyage home, mainly about the 50 Mexicans on board, returning from service with the Republican forces in Spain. Their commander (I later discovered) was David Alfaro Siqueiros, a famous mural-painter, one of the 'Big Three' Mexican muralists, with Orozco and Diego Rivera. He gave Griffin a copy of his book *Art and Revolution* to read, in French. 'It would sound very dry to you now', wrote Griffin to me, 'but later on it wouldn't and perhaps you and Roddy will live to see what he means, all worked out for everybody to see.' Alas, by the time that book was translated into English, in 1975 (when I might have read it, but didn't), the spirit of socialist idealism that united Griffin and those Mexicans had long since faded.

The cheerful tone of this letter must derive from the whiff of his homeland across the last stretch of water. Griffin was always glad to get home. But the next day he was a sorry sight to old friends in New York, as we learn from Dawn Powell's diary:

> *16 February* [1939] – Griffin Barry, sad, dried up, desperately miserable at 54, once a pretty boy, once the lover of all the famous women and even of their lovers... – he appeared at 10 o'clock, forlorn, somewhat drunk on Pernods. He had been weeping over them at the Lafayette.

Not until I'd worked through all these sheaves of letters did I realise why Griffin was so forlorn in February 1939. It would be seven years before he saw us again.

Dora, by contrast, must have been immensely relieved to see him go. For her the coming year of 1939 was a succession of crises, the school sliding towards bankruptcy as American pupils headed home, anticipating the war in Europe which broke out in September. A month earlier, John and Kate had left for America to join Bertie and his wife, a departure bringing great joy to Kate, but great sorrow to Dora.[7] That summer she had a spell in hospital with severe eczema, surely made worse by her many anxieties. And there were more to come. A brief, failed attempt to amalgamate with a school evacuated from London brought outbreaks of diptheria and scarlet fever to Kingwell. The winter of 1939–40 was bitterly cold, the frosty lawn crunching under our feet, trees crashing in the woods under the weight of ice (I remember it vividly). Yet the lessons were taught, the pictures painted and hung on the walls, the plays and dancing rehearsed, the vegetable garden planted and the animals tended.

Until it all came to an end in the summer of 1940. Two mainstay teachers of

August 1939. The send-off party for John and Kate as they embarked for America: Pat with Raspy the monkey, Dora, Dora's sister Mary Unwin, Mary's twin sons Fisher and Harold (see Chapter 17). Myself and Roddy in front.

---

[7] *At this time Kate's loyalty lay firmly with Bertie and elegant, womanly Peter. At 15 she was glad to get away from the scruffy, impoverished and often embarrassing home-life provided by Dora to set sail for glamorous America – just as I was, when Kate assisted my escape eight years later. Dora was naturally grieved in 1939 – and deeply hurt to read Kate's frank account of how she had felt to 'escape' in her book published after her father's death (but before Dora's). Years after that, Kate felt ashamed of her teenage lack of compassion at a time of such stress for Dora – see Ray Monk, op.cit., p.227. I too have regretted my unfeeling treatment of her – continued into adult life, when I should have known better. For all her faults, Dora was a better parent than many.*

the school, Paul and Grete, Austrian refugees from Nazi persecution, were whisked away into internment – one of those daft 'mistakes' of the government's preparations for a feared enemy invasion.[8] Then, just after the Army requisitioned Kingwell Hall, empty Carn Voel was saved from the same fate by Dora's heroic dash with children and animals in her old Armstong Siddeley – 'Dora's Ark' in its last weeks of active service (its final journey was a return trip to collect the goats). Frantic letters exploring the possibility of evacuating us to America all came to nothing. Having few other options, Dora decided to carry on with the school in the relative safety of Cornwall. With a handful of children – seven boarders and a few day pupils picked up later – Beacon Hill School reopened at Carn Voel in September 1940.

Lily and Walter went 'home' to Southport, in Lancashire, where Lily's brother Len lived with his family. For a few years they lived and worked up there, until in 1943 they once again came south to help us out.

The tail-end of the school, and our seven-year separation from Griffin, belong to the next chapter. The part of my childhood it describes is no longer centred on the school, which had been my whole world up to then. Those years at Kingwell Hall were the happy prime of life of Beacon Hill School, as Dora has recorded, and the archives show. Whatever hidden damage Griffin's siege may have done to my psyche, it did not spoil my enjoyment of the experience.

Paul Gelb with a group on the 'ha ha' overlooking the cowfield. Me in striped skirt, Roddy on my left.

[8] *Under Regulation 18B, as it was called, nationals of enemy countries (and some British fascists or sympathisers, notably their leader Oswald Mosley) were imprisoned to prevent them assisting the expected German invasion. The hasty rounding-up was so badly managed that many of the internees were* anti-fascist refugees from Nazi or Italian Fascist tyranny, *later released after indignant protest against this clumsy measure. Paul and Grete were interned separately, but later reunited in London, where they married and were allowed to do 'war work' for the duration of the war.*

CHAPTER 16

THE YEARS IN BETWEEN

In my memory there's no continuity between the Daddy I knew and wrote to as a child, and the Dad I came to know when I was 16. They are two separate people. During the seven years of Griffin's absence from my life I hardly thought about him at all – out of sight out of mind, it seems. At least that's what I recall *now*; but letters from him to Dora, and from him to me, show that we did correspond fairly regularly at least up to 1943, the year I became 13.

As I grew older and more aware of The Quarrel, I tried to set it aside from my relationship with Griffin. It's easy to see why. That upsetting letter Dora had confiscated (see page 206) was apparently provoked by me, writing that I hoped 'he wouldn't lose the next grand job he got'. He saw this as Dora's propaganda which had to be rebutted with a long tale of self-justification and absurd charges against her. At that age I was not yet aware of his acute sensitivity at suggestions of 'failure', and as Dora was the parent caring for me day by day, naturally I resented his attacks on her. Later I drew up a Non-Aggression Pact for them both to sign. Dora sent him two copies, already signed, for him to counter-sign and return one. Evidently he didn't, writing to me that he 'didn't want to sign too quickly', and adding enigmatically that Dora 'might have weighed her signature a little more carefully before she put it on'.[1]

My letters to Griffin are lost, but from his to me I can see I sometimes wrote hurtful things that make me wince today, implying that he was 'useless' as a Daddy for not being around to provide me with baubles and sweeties. Of course he should have been big enough to overlook such childishness and to understand why I hated being dragged into the never-ending row with Dora. But at every opportunity he felt compelled to 'put me right', to make sure I grew up thinking well of him and convinced, as he was, that the failure of their

---

[1] *Unfortunately this historic document has been lost. It was clearly inspired by the Non-Aggression Pact signed by Hitler and Stalin in August 1939, which Hitler tore up two years later. Mine was also ignored.*

relationship was *her fault*. In a strange way the quarrel with Dora, and his need to explain himself to me, had become his *raison d'être*. Being forbidden to mention it gave him nightmares!

> One of your letters was about not criticising your mummy and saying you would not write to me any more if I did. Very early the next morning I had a dream and your face...was saying you were not going to write me any more letters, and you cried, and then I cried, and then I woke up and got a-hold of the cold water pitcher to wash off the tears, which I found were real ones.

Among the painful letters of these years is the diatribe against Dora which delayed for so long my exploration of this archive. That too was provoked by a sentence from me in typed capitals: HOW STUPID ARE FAMILY QUARRELS. Reading it again now, with others of this time, having worked through Griffin's sad life up to this saddest period of all, I am touched rather than repelled. His letters are so full of yearning for the physical reality of his children, growing up out of his sight, so far away. He begged for measurements, and photos, and was distraught when some snaps Roddy said he was enclosing *were not in the envelope*!

> So I was very sad, because I wanted so much to see what you look like in that suit, remembering that it went from my hand to your body and that it fits you, unlike Harry's poor too-small red velvet dress.

I don't remember that suit, or the red velvet dress, and photographs were few in wartime, when films were almost unobtainable. He must have had some from Kingwell days, but the ones he cherished most were those from the time when Dora still loved him –

> I carry your baby pictures about and put them up on the wall in whatever dreary lodgings I am in. Three are before me as I write; two of you on the lawn at Telegraph, a chubby baby looking like all my people as you so remarkably did ... one with a huge black cat in your arms [yes, I know the one]... and another impish one of Roddy entirely without clothes standing on the seat of a bike and making a little imp's face into the void... Your mother becomes the woman I remember then, too; not wearing the agonized and cruel face that has come between our children and their father.

Another recurrent theme of these letters is work – the next job he's hoping to get (and usually doesn't); or apologies for long silences when he was jobless and penniless. The worst disappointment was a chance to go to England that fell through.

I had been inching toward it ['a grand job that would bring in money'] for a long time. When your letter came I expected to write you within a week when I would set out; or perhaps to go suddenly and surprise you... Then, tragedy. A slow tragedy it was, going on for weeks, because no answer came and I couldn't find out why and I borrowed money (I was very poor) to go to New York to find out why the appointment wasn't made, and couldn't – and, well, that's all, to this day. I never found out why.

To take him overseas in wartime, this must have been a government job. The long wait to be appointed, and then never knowing why he wasn't, tells its own story. Like his friend Josephine Herbst, whose fate I described in Chapter 12, Griffin could not survive the security vetting for 'important' government work, or for permanence in a lesser position. There were civil service jobs to be had – but he couldn't hold them.

Each time he landed a job, he would pay off his debts and hasten to send us goodies from the shops. (Like many Americans he thought we were suffering more hardship in wartime than we were; but these occasional gifts were very welcome in our spartan life at Carn Voel, and later in London.)

Griffin's memory was stuck in 1932 (see page 112) but by 1941 we looked like this. Roddy has borrowed the Highland dress of a Scottish pupil.

With long gaps between letters (some perhaps sunk by U-boats), it's hard to follow Griffin's career through the war years. During 1939 he seems to have had no work except freelance writing. I have seen three *Travel* articles which appeared that year, all thoroughly researched and illustrated, and in good company in that magazine, to judge by the Contents page. In June there was *Swiss Democracy Goes Into Action*, examining the Swiss tradition of neutrality, and the people's militia which may be called upon to defend it in the coming war. In August, *The Problem of a Wandering Race*, a discussion of gypsy culture, also with a topical slant: they are migrating north-westwards out of Germany, fearing what's coming there – some even arriving in the United States. Then in November, *America's Busses are Going Places*, a fascinating history of American motor buses from their beginning in Minnesota in 1913 to the long-distance Greyhound bus (which became 'respectable' in 1934 when

Clark Gable and Claudette Colbert had a love affair on a bus journey in *It Happened One Night*). This piece includes a prescient passage towards the end:

> Bus travel is precisely the creature of our time. Air travel is still only for the rich; it will take the speeding up of invention inherent in another world war and an increase of wealth in the hands of the masses so great that a changed social order is implied, before the four million can fly. The private automobile? The individual car has penetrated as far into universal use, roughly, as it can unless there is a decided rise in the purchasing power of the multitude. And unless provisions are made for traffic in urban centers that would change the face of urban life at what looks today like a prohibitive cost.

In the post-war boom of the 1950s, based on Cold War arms production, all those things happened in America – transcontinental flights for all; cars, cars and cars; and freeways taking them into every city centre. Despite the spread of car ownership, the Greyhound Bus Company lives on today.

By December 1939, Griffin was again working for the Department of Agriculture, doing publicity work as in 1936, attested by the poster he sent me for our wall a newspaper, *The Beacon Hill Pioneer*. Once again, the job lasted

Griffin's contribution to *The Beacon Hill Pioneer* (a publicity leaflet dating from the New Deal period)

only a few months; no doubt because he failed to get security clearance.

The summer of 1940 was spent recuperating from a bout of ulcer trouble on Bear Island, off the coast of Maine, owned by a friend of his.[2] Most of 1941 must have been another round of job-hunting – sustaining himself with more articles for *Travel*, and perhaps others – until in November he found himself back with another former employer, the American Red Cross. (Did his service in 1918 help him into that job, I wonder?) The job he hoped would take him to England, but didn't get, seems to have been at the US Embassy in London. One he did get, in January 1943, was mediating industrial disputes – another echo of his New Deal work; but again it lasted only six months. He soon had another one, however, for an international news agency, by the sound of it: 'I shall work all night by the big tickers that bring in broadcasts from the warring world and which it's my job to edit.' This job too might take him to England, he thought... But it didn't. How long did it last – and what happened next?

The rest of Griffin's war work will remain unknown. His letters to Dora had ceased in 1941, and this one, of July 1943, is the last from him to me that has survived. All I know is that he later worked for the Office of War Information in Washington and New York – presumably the 'series of special war jobs since 1943' mentioned in a letter to Dora in 1945, which he was glad to leave behind when he finally set sail for England the following year. These jobs were either temporary ones never confirmed, in the familiar pattern, or so menial as not to require security vetting.

* * *

So much for Griffin's wartime years. Now what about mine? (Notice that I'm moving over from Dora to me as the other half of this transatlantic relationship.) At this distance it's impossible to reconstruct my side of our correspondence, but I'm afraid all Griffin's appeals for sympathy and understanding would have rolled off my 12-year-old shoulders like water off a duck's. 'Dad is a fool', I wrote in the margin of one anguished screed. I just didn't want to know about all that! His only place in my consciousness was as a fantasy figure – a big, strong Daddy who might one day re-enter my life with hugs and gifts like the daddies in the Stories for Girls and suchlike romantic tales I was reading.

Other aspects of my Lolita years can be conjured up from the contents of Pandora's Box. A small postcard collection, mainly from Kate in California, whose big sister letters were full of good advice ('Give up the idea of being

---

[2] *Griffin spent about two months on Bear Island and wrote several times from there. Two letters include a reference to a cache of Barry family papers which I have copied into a Bibliographical Note, to keep it on the surface of history, so to speak, before these letters are re-buried in Dora's archive.*

My birthday tribute to Pat, 1942

another Shirley Temple – you wouldn't enjoy living here')... Poems and letters to and from me, correspondents whose names mean nothing now (writing letters was 'my thing', and anyone whose address I could discover might get one)... A most touching letter from Paul Gelb, while we were still at Kingwell, who had been sent into internment in Australia (while Grete, his betrothed, went to the Isle of Man) – 'I hope you will write once a letter to me, what happened with all the plants in the greenhouse and garden, the cucumbers, tomatoes...' A handful of wonderful Lily Letters that bring tears to my eyes, remembering her... Two to me and Roddy from Pat when he was away in the Army – affectionate and amusing letters, with jokes worked in, proving Kate's recollection of him as a funny man, which I had entirely forgotten... Even more surprisingly, pictures and poems to Pat *from* me, showing that for a year or two at least, I felt something akin to filial affection for him. If Griffin ever had cause to feel jealous of his relationship with Roddy and me, this was the time.

But not for long! One incident of these years is burned into my memory – the accidental discovery, when I was about 12, of Dora and Pat's marriage certificate. I believe my loathing of Pat began with the realisation that he was officially my stepfather, actually married to Dora, when up to that time he'd been just a man about the house. Of course I knew they shared a bed, and by then I certainly knew what a shared bed signified; so I find it hard to explain the cold disgust that overcame me when I came across that document on Dora's desk. To make *that man* her husband! – a favour never granted to my father – and not even to tell us about it! I confided the secret to Roddy, but to no one else, and ever afterwards tried never to acknowledge Pat's official status in the family.[3] This act of betrayal by Dora led me to question her judgement for the first time – my first step towards independent thinking, I believe.

Years later I learned that they had married for practical reasons, to claim the marriage allowance when Pat was called into the Army in 1940. But he was soon invalided out; and with little paperwork to occupy him at the shrunken school, and no physical skills to offer, he readily lapsed into his true nature, a boozy Irishman most at home in the pub. Our move to London in 1943 gave him full scope for this role. He was a born spiv, a useful breed in wartime, and could be counted on to find some black market cigarettes or a turkey for Christmas – but that's about all he was good for. Thus he became as I remember him (though Dora would disagree) – nothing more than a millstone round her neck.

I can just about recall my Beacon Hill companions at Carn Voel: Jackie Gordon, who at 14-plus was no longer a pupil but came to help Dora for a while; two Scottish lads, John and Jimmy, sons of a Cable and Wireless engineer, who lived at neighbouring Land View; Sally and Gay Galsworthy, descendants of John Galsworthy,[4] whose father also worked for Cable and Wireless; Mark and Leo, two scruffy boys who came from I know not where; and one or two boarders like Susan Correa-Hunt and her brothers Tim and David (see Chapter 14 for their recollections of these years). Their mother Gwen was one of a succession of temporary helpers who partly relieved Dora's labours in these exhausting years. As the main teacher, cook and housekeeper most of the time, she carried the school almost alone.

Back row: Jimmy, John, Harriet; front: Mark, Leo, Roddy

---

[3] *Since parting from Bertie, Dora had continued to use the name Russell professionally, as she did for the rest of her life, so her marriage to Pat passed almost unnoticed by the outside world. After that event, however, which took place some time in 1940, she was legally Mrs Grace.*

[4] *In the 1970s we all got hooked on the BBC TV dramatisation of his most famous work,* The Forsyte Saga. *The Galsworthy children, and their friends the Correa-Hunts, were the only day pupils whose parents had any understanding of 'progressive education', and were pleased to enrol their kids at Beacon Hill. For the other few who came, it was just a convenient alternative to the local primary school at Bottoms in Crean.*

Yet all of these are reconstructed memories. What comes to my mind unbidden, when I think back to living at Carn Voel from the age of 10 to 13, is falling in love with Cornwall. Despite the wartime coastal defences (concrete look-outs on the cliffs, barbed wire on the beaches), and 300 soldiers guarding the vital Cable and Wireless installations in Porthcurno Valley, there were very few restrictions on local residents. Dora was too busy to keep tabs on Roddy and me, so we were free and unwatched to roam the Valley and the beaches by ourselves. We befriended the locals who went fishing, and learned to use their 'long rods'.[5] Joe Trelawney, the blacksmith, made us eel hooks to catch sand eels at low tide for bait (if we didn't catch any mackerel we could fry up the eels). In the spring we picked up new potatoes at Trewey Farm – more loot for the dinner table. We discovered from Mrs Bottrell, whose husband mended shoes at Polgigga, how to make Cornish cream in a wide enamel bowl, and tried it out at home – but a mouse fell in and drowned. In 'the classroom', hardly distinguishable from the rest of our lives, we made bar charts of the egg production of our hens, Carrots and Goldie, and wrote stories for *The Beacon Hill Pioneer*. When someone gave us two fertilised duck eggs we put them under a broody hen, but she abandoned them before they hatched, so Dora had to finish them off with a hot water bottle in her bed.

My pre-teen years, with every sense receptor wide open, were full of vivid images and feelings. Collecting the milk from Trewey Farm, warm from the cow, in the dark of a winter's morning. A group of long rods jogging up the hill from the fishing rocks, pencil marks against the pale evening sky. Baby rabbits scampering around in the field over the front wall – and their half-chewed corpses at the back door. Dazzling sun on the sea as I ran over the rocks to inspect the big rock pool at low tide (is that pool still there? – I haven't looked for years). The smell of wet earth and primroses in the woods at Tresidder, where we kept the goats and Stella, my horse (she looks stumpy and knock-kneed in the one dim photo I have – not at all the fine steed I remember). These were my girlish preoccupations as I approached the even more breathtaking teenage years ahead – just when Griffin was trying to enlist

---

[5] *These were flexible bamboo poles, 12–15 feet in length, without reels, which depended on their own length plus the fishing line to hold the float and hook out beyond the weed. I forget whether we acquired rods of our own, or 'borrowed' them from the rack which used to stand on the path to the fishing rocks, where fishermen who did not want to carry them home left their rods between sessions.*

The shortage of family photos in wartime was made up in the commercial studio. We are 12 and 10 here.

my sympathy for his lifelong personal tragedy. *Please, please, I don't want to know all that!*

By the age of 12 I had outgrown the primary curriculum of Beacon Hill, and became a day pupil at Penzance County School for Girls. Far from feeling ill at ease in a conventional state school, I revelled in it, and was very disappointed that due to wartime clothes rationing, school uniform rules were relaxed – no blazer or hat required, just the navy blue gym slip over any old blouse. How proudly I wore my House ribbon and cheered on our hockey team, how lustily I sang the hymns at morning assembly! – as though born and bred to these rituals of English schooling. I made friends among local children on the daily bus, and exchanged visits with a classmate who lived at Marazion. With these first steps out of the cocoon of school and family, I began to realise for the first time that we seemed 'odd' to outsiders (though not in Porthcurno, where the oddness of the Carn Voel household was long established and no longer remarked upon).

My attention was now turned to the outside world, my head full of boys, films, make-up and clothes – and ballroom dancing. The highlight of my week was the Saturday morning lesson in the one-time schoolroom, then the village hall, from a teacher who came on the bus from Penzance. There I learned to foxtrot, quickstep and waltz, not to mention the Palais Glide and various novelty numbers classed as 'old-time dancing'. Jitter-bugging (jiving) had not reached Porthcurno; and so far as I know, it never did. Dances at the Exiles Hall in the Valley were staid, all-age affairs, where my best hope was a soldier partner, despite their toe-crushing army boots.[6]

Self-absorbed, I was scarcely aware of Dora's financial problems as Beacon Hill dwindled away at Carn Voel. The last of her personal money, inherited from her father, had been swallowed up in the rent arrears on Kingwell Hall that had triggered her bankruptcy. Since then the school and household had limped along hand to mouth, but Dora realised she had to make a break. In 1942 John had returned from America, a Harvard degree in his pocket, to join the Navy. He was now on a course in London learning Japanese, in preparation for being sent out to the Far East. They calculated that if Dora could get a job there – not so difficult in wartime, for someone with her education and talents – they could maintain a joint household, where John could live for the duration of his course. So in 1943, leaving Stella and the goats in Cornwall, we packed up the dog and cats and chickens and ducks and moved to the north-west London suburb of Willesden Green. At the age of 13, after a blissful country childhood, I became, as I had been born, a Londoner.

In 1943 empty houses were easy to find in London because so many Londoners had fled the terrible Blitz of 1940–41. The one we rented, number 72 Dartmouth Road, was big enough for lodgers as well as the family, at that time consisting of Dora, Pat, Roddy and me, plus Rover the dog and several cats. I believe the chickens we brought from Cornwall lived out their days in the back garden, but I'm not sure

72 Dartmouth Road, Willesden Green

what became of the ducks, last seen lodging with Paul and Grete Gelb, now released from internment, happily married, and living near our new home. John, a subaltern in the Navy, lived with us while daily attending his course at

---

[6] *The pre-war 'quarters' of Cable and Wireless students was now an army barracks housing some 300 soldiers. Access to beaches was not much hindered by the rolls of barbed wire placed there to deter invaders; in fact, we locals enjoyed having them all to ourselves 'for the duration'. Porthcurno's vital wartime role as a channel of telecommunications is now commemorated by the Cable and Wireless museum there, and the ivy-covered pill-boxes still on the cliffs.*

the School of Oriental and African Studies. Kate too joined the household in 1944, when she graduated from Radcliffe and came home to a civil service job – just in time to experience a few months of that second Blitz which took everyone by surprise. We had all thought it was now safe to live in London, but we were wrong.

Dora had a full-time job in the Ministry of Information, and Roddy and I were sent to conventional day schools in London. This was easier for me after the little grammar school in Penzance, but the huge scale of that school at Kingsbury was a shock of a different kind (making me a lifelong advocate of small schools). Roddy was far from happy at his prestigious grammar school, especially when he started to get caned for falling asleep in class – hardly surprising when we had spent the night trying to sleep on the platform of St Johns Wood Underground station, a regular practice among Londoners at that time, to escape the bombs. By the summer of 1944 ordinary high explosive and incendiary bombs had given way to V-1 rockets, the pilotless planes we called 'doodlebugs'. They came doodling overhead like a distant motorbike until suddenly the engine stopped and you held your breath, waiting for the bang which meant it hadn't fallen on you.

I vividly remember the day they first appeared over London: at school we were made to sit in the cloakroom all day, perhaps because there were no big windows to shatter on us, while the staff waited to hear from the Authorities what to do about this new menace – was it safe to send the children home through the streets? Doodlebugs were later succeeded by V-2 rockets, the forerunners of space travel, which in fact were less unnerving because by the time you heard the bang you *knew* it hadn't hit you. But it was a much louder bang.

All this was too much for Dora. She took us out of school before the end of the summer term and sent us to stay with Lily while she negotiated a deal with W B Curry, the Headmaster of Dartington, to send us there in September. I say 'a deal' because we couldn't afford the full fees, and furthermore the school was full (I spent my first term in a tiny laundry room). For the sake of friendship, and Dora's past contribution to progressive education – and with the help of scholarship money at that well-funded school – Bill Curry took us in at a reduced rate. Dora was grateful, of course, despite her long antipathy to Dartington, but she always disliked its middle class ambience – which I, on the contrary, came to enjoy.

I was blissfully happy at Dartington. Both the living and learning conditions at the Senior School were luxurious compared to our family's home life and the last days of Beacon Hill. Beautiful countryside, humane and stimulating company, every educational facility you can imagine and rare cultural treats at the Hall just up the road – what a feast for body and soul! Having been born and bred in a progressive school, I had no psychological adjustment to make – no running wild until I found the boundaries of the new freedom, the typical pattern for kids coming from 'normal' schools midway through their schooling. I was quite capable of Behaving Badly at times, and would have been queueing up to do so for a TV camera crew making a film about *The School Where Kids Run Wild!*, if there had been any such in those days. But at heart I was a goody-goody, always anxious to please adults and therefore susceptible to the cajolery and veiled threats of 'grammar school discipline', which was the unwritten code at Dartington too ('It's entirely up to you of course, but if you want to get anywhere in life...'). In fact I was a conceited little prig, and when I didn't get the five passes required for School Certificate in the summer of 1945, while people I thought stupid did, I couldn't face myself in the mirror until I'd caught up in the December re-sits.

Foxhole: The Senior School courtyard

Dartington Hall and gardens in the 1940s.

In truth I *did* run a bit wild during my first year, with my rather raffish girlfriend June. We spent every spare afternoon biking to Totnes or taking the bus to Paignton to go to the cinema. We also used to climb out of our rooms after Bedtime and spend hours up at Dartington Hall, chatting up American soldiers who were stationed there. I was sexually precocious (though quite wised-up to the dangers), and had already discovered while still living in Cornwall that 18-year-old soldiers far from home will eagerly fraternise with schoolgirls if there aren't any older ones in sight. In Porthcurno it was dancing partners at the weekly 'socials' in the Valley that I was after, but for June and me at Dartington the main attraction was cigarettes, Hershey bars and other goodies from the American PX store. In fact, we were under closer surveillance than we knew: when our GI boyfriends told us they'd been warned not to talk to girls from the school, and we were summoned for a Serious Talk with Curry, we knew the game was up. But my attention remained firmly focused on clothes, make-up, boys, film stars, dancing, the Hit Parade, and what might be in the next parcel from home – or better still, from Dad in America.

> *Saturday 3 February 1945* Daddy's parcels arrived – pr. of blue corduroy longs and another shirt for Roddy, & a BEAUTIFUL black silk skirt and a sloppy jo pink sweater for me. Also a tin of condensed milk.

> *Wednesday 30 May 1945* Received unexpected parcel from Dad – a striped dress, sort of silky 'celanese' material. Very cool, quite pretty.

Like many teenage girls, I kept a diary. Except for a kitchen calendar in later years, at no other time in my life have I kept any personal record of my activities, but for three years of my adolescence – 1945, 1946, 1947 – I wrote up a detailed account at the end of each day. I still have this well-thumbed record. It's no treasury of perceptive insights, no vision of an awakening intelligence, little more than a catalogue of self-obsessed daily trivia. Dramatic moments such as the Labour election victory of July 1945, which I remember clearly, get no mention alongside every detail of my scholastic progress, of letters received and written, of every book read and film seen – and above all, endless analysis of every amorous encounter.

Squeezed between the lines, however (and I do mean *squeezed* – my handwriting was designed for a pin-head), I can see even at this distance a dialogue with myself taking place, a process of self-discovery as psychologically important as the intimate talks with whomever was my current best friend. That was the role of this little book, in fact, alone in my room in the small hours. *It is beautiful*, I wrote of the green Diary for 1947 Dora had just given me for Christmas, *but I shall never love it as I love you, my lovely Red Diary*. These italicised phrases in the next few chapters are the authentic voice of my teenage self.

In September 1945 I began to try harder at school, as I'd been told to do, and became much more respectable. After the Christmas exams, June left the school and the new best friends I acquired were the clever girls bound for Oxbridge. I became a regular at Sunday evening Philosophy classes held at High Cross, the Currys' home, grappling with the momentous Moral Issues we discussed there. I developed a small passion for opera when the new Polish music teacher taught me some arias from *The Magic Flute* (which my thin soprano voice was quite incapable of singing). When elected to the School Cabinet, I took my responsibilities very seriously. Passing School Certificate in December (except for Maths) put me in the X Group (6th Form), but I wasn't quite sure if I *really* wanted to study for two more years to go to a British university. In case I should want to, Curry – as we all called him – began the patient one-to-one coaching which eventually got me through essential Maths the following summer.

I was now in that select group of senior girls who were obviously – and rather shamefully, now I think of it – Curry's pets, counselled and encouraged in every aspect of our lives, given special treats as a reward for personal achievement such as getting into Oxbridge, or as consolation for some family trouble. In my case, having to have my appendix out at Ashburton Cottage Hospital earned me an exhilarating drive on Dartmoor in his open-top two-seater vintage Bentley, followed by a grand lunch at a wayside hotel. Informality between pupils and staff was normal at Dartington, of course, but it was still a bit special, I thought, to be invited *so often* to tea at High Cross (unaware that several others were equally favoured). I adored and worshipped Curry and his wife Marsie, and looked to Curry, above all, for advice about my future. He was the *parent of my mind*, I confided to my midnight friend.

* * *

But I've jumped ahead a bit in this story. My appendix operation happened six months after the events I'm about to relate, which ended the long stretch of time when my father had been only a distant figure across the Atlantic. In the spring of 1946 I had almost completed basic school studies, and now had to decide whether to buckle down to *serious* study for higher education, still reserved for an intellectual elite in England at that time – or leave school in the summer. But then what? Was I ready for the world of work? If not, what else? One idea was to go to college in America, where a broader band of intellect was considered fit for higher education – a suggestion that came from Kate, now back at Radcliffe herself.

These were the things on my mind when Griffin arrived in England to reclaim his long-lost daughter.

PART III

DAD AND ME

CHAPTER 17

FAMILY LIFE IN LONDON – AND DUBLIN

This chapter introduces the last phase of Griffin's life, years of exile from America. Whether he expected or intended ever to go back, I can't be sure. One early letter among the sparse surviving correspondence of these years suggests that he did; but in the event, poverty and infirmity forced him to end his days in London.

I also cannot be sure whether he arrived in England still nursing the hope of a reconciliation with Dora. I suspect the thought was always at the back of his mind. Pat's death in 1949 encouraged him to try, twice, to 'help her out' by becoming a lodger in her too-large flat (both attempts failed).

But making it up with Dora mattered less to Griffin in 1946 than making friends with his two half-grown children.

* * *

I can still remember my breathless excitement as we waited at Newton Abbot station. It was 23 March 1946, Roddy's 14th birthday, when we met Dad for the first time since 1939. I had been a child when he left, but now I was Grown Up, or felt myself to be. I would be 16 in July, and was bursting to tell him about my plans for leaving school, and to show off the glamorous Dad who had reappeared in my life at last. An American, no less! And bearing gifts from the Land of Plenty (so I secretly hoped, and I was not to be disappointed).

I don't know how Roddy was feeling on that occasion. He must have been excited too, and Griffin must have been overjoyed to see him, too, but everything I remember and recorded about that time is focused on the two of us – Dad and me, me and Dad. His favouritism towards me throughout our childhood was still evident, and I was smugly aware of it myself. Letters were written to me – 'Hug Rod for me' – and answered by me; parcels of gifts were always weighted in my favour, as was the case at that first post-war meeting:

endless clothes and toiletries for me, a jersey and a penknife for Rod. If Roddy resented it, I don't recall him ever saying so. The generous lad who used to give me his sweet ration became the mature adult son who could handle both his parents – even together! – like a diplomat. But in 1946 I was still centre-stage with Dad, and determined to make the most of it. I was getting ready to start My Future, after all, while my little brother spent all his time playing cricket.

On that first day I was more than pleased with this exotic stranger, who reminded me of General Eisenhower (a familiar face from cinema newsreels). He was a bit older than I had expected, and shorter than his 14-year-old son, but never mind, he was *marvellous, a lovely little man*. Yet in my comments of the next few days I already see faint disappointment creeping in.

His visit to Devon was probably an anti-climax for Griffin too. He enjoyed observing our school activities – my singing practice, Rod playing football – but he soon tired of traipsing off to see films that bored him (*Blondie Meets the Boss*), and buying us ice cream at the Milk Bar in Totnes. There were a few explosions of temper over missed buses and other inconsequential matters: Griffin's irascible temperament quickly showed itself. That was partly due to his painful innards. Over a cup of coffee one afternoon he had a sudden attack of nausea, retching into his handkerchief in an alarming way, a sign of his chronic duodenal ulcer. To my diary-self I affected filial concern – *his little fit gave me a fright for a moment* – but what I actually felt at the time, I distinctly recall, was not compassion but dismay. Disillusion with my new-found parent was setting in fast, and for the most ignoble of reasons, as the dream-figure of my imagination was replaced by a real person not only old, bad-tempered, and too short for my liking, but *ill*.

What had brought Griffin across the Atlantic was a commission to write a book about Ireland. With an advance of £500 (seemingly inexhaustible!), he would soon depart for Dublin to begin his researches.[1] But he was still in London when we went home for the Easter holidays, a week after his visit to Devon. Our family life in Willesden Green was the other half of my teenage world in which I now had to find a place for my Dad, emotionally if not physically.

On the first day everything went swimmingly well. We arrived on 3 April, Dora's birthday, to be met at Paddington *by Dad and Mum*, says my diary, amazed. We all went home for a birthday tea – a delayed celebration for Roddy too – and then spent the evening at the house of Charles and Alison Gray, old friends of Griffin's with whom he was staying. *It's been such a lovely day –*

---

[1] *I always assumed that an American publisher had commissioned this book, but references in letters suggest that Griffin's 'advance' was in fact a loan from a generous friend, Eric Estorick, a cosmopolitan American based in London. Perhaps Griffin had proposed the book, and if one had actually resulted, so much the better; no doubt Eric would have helped him to get it published. This casual arrangement made it easy for Griffin to renege on whatever he had promised. At a later date Eric began a joint book-project with Dora, but this too was never completed.*

seeing Mum & Dad together & being with them – & them not quarrelling! The next day was equally congenial, meeting Dad in central London for lunch in a pub with Joel O'Brien, Mary Vorse's son, who was working for the BBC at that time. (Mary herself was touring devastated Europe for the United Nations Relief and Rehabilitation Administration – UNRRA. I would meet her too a few months later.) Dad and I met Dora after work and went to the pictures, but the evening ended on a sour note when he discovered the Grays had been expecting him for dinner, and were somewhat put out. That was our last sight of Griffin before the summer: the rest of the Easter holiday Roddy and I spent sailing on the Norfolk Broads with our family friends, the Pritchards.

My diary does not tell me what Pat Grace was doing on those two days. My contempt for him was now well-established, and references to 'His Grace' were rare. He was then employed as an accounts clerk in the government department where Dora had a senior position (the Ministry of Information had now become the Central Office of Information – COI). Most of his wages must have gone on cigarettes and beer. In Cornwall or London, his life centred on the pub, from which he would return late at night in a befuddled state to the meal Dora had been keeping hot for hours. Loud quarrelling would often ensue, echoing up the stairs as I drifted off to sleep. Every morning came the sound of Pat coughing and spitting to clear the phlegm from his congested lungs. I should have pitied him for that cough, which led to his early death in 1949; but instead, I hated him as another burden on Dora.

In our London household Dora was the dominant figure, as she had been throughout my childhood. But there were other important influences on my teenage development. Kate was my guide to 'feminine things' as well as my confidante in family matters until, finding herself unable to live in the emotional whirlpool of either of her parents, in October 1945 she had fled back to the United States. *Oh hell, why do you have to go, Kate?* I had wailed to my diary the night before she left, knowing how sorely I would miss her. Earlier that year John had been posted to Washington DC, supposedly en route to the Far East, but the war ended before he got there. Quite by chance he met Griffin

1944: All together again – but not for long.

on the street, and had taken the flat just vacated by Mary Vorse in the house where Griffin lived. From this distant vantage point he launched a brave, but misguided – and ultimately fruitless – campaign to reconcile all the members of the Russell–Barry 'family' with each other. His long, tortuous letter to me on this subject was greeted with dismay (*...depressing and disturbing... a lot of complex things about life in general from John...*), but I was too preoccupied with my own immediate concerns to take much notice.[2] Soon after this, John met and quickly married Susan Lindsay, a fateful step in his life which had repercussions on the rest of the family too, in later years.

At about the time Kate went away, Lily had arrived with Walter to run our household of lodgers and family. Her coming imposed order and cleanliness on domestic chaos – at last. Dora was always busy and overburdened, and had every excuse for her slapdash housekeeping. But those forgiving sentiments were not what I felt at the time. Domesticity was never her strong suit, and having little else to criticise as yet, I secretly despised her for this failing. In Cornwall I'd been too young to care, but now I was self-consciously aware that our home was 'different' from other people's – not only dirtier, and oddly furnished with a strange collection of ill-matched items, but without a proper sitting room or any communal life beyond the crowded kitchen. After meals everyone retired to their own rooms, in my case a dark cubicle looking out on the blank wall of the house next door. So I spent my leisure time in other people's rooms, playing endless rounds of Mah Jong in John's, listening to radio concerts in Kate's, or at a later date being sketched by our lodger Harold, who was something of an artist.

Looking dolefully at the dried-up cat mess under the grand piano in the hall (stored for Granny, untuned and never played), it never occurred to me to get down on my knees and clean it up. Like many teenagers, I preferred to nurse my grudges, and smouldered inwardly for years about the 'squalor' I'd had to endure in my childhood homes. But at Dartmouth Road, everything changed when Lily came. At her elbow I became an apprentice housewife and, in the fullness of time, a mother who drove teenage sons crazy with her obsessive need for a clean and orderly home.

This was not the first time Lily had come to our rescue, as we have seen – nor would it be the last. In 1945 Dora did her a good turn too, by finding Walter a job as a messenger in the COI – work which exactly suited his erratic temperament, and kept him happily employed for the next 30 years.

Another central relationship of my life at this time, and at all other times,

---

[2] *In 1944 the Russells and their son Conrad had returned from the USA to live in England. After their traumatic childhood, John and Kate's adult relations with their father and stepmother were proving just as difficult. John's 'campaign' led to even worse relations with his father and allied him more closely to Dora. This episode in the Russell family is related in detail by Ray Monk,* Bertrand Russell: The Ghost of Madness, *op.cit., Chapter 9.*

was with Roddy. Dora's busyness while running Beacon Hill had thrown us together perhaps more than most siblings, especially in the holidays, when the boarding pupils were swept off home. We fought like cat and dog at times, but we also had a very close private understanding, a shared view of the adult world around us – Roddy's a more charitable view than mine – and, when necessary, an automatic united front against outsiders.

At Dartington we moved in different circles, but some of Roddy's friends were mine too. In London our main pastime was going to the pictures, sometimes twice in one day. At the three cinemas on Kilburn High Road, including the Gaumont State, boastfully 'the largest in Europe', we saw just about every film in circulation, from Hollywood epics to the French classic *Les Enfants du Paradis*, made in Paris under Nazi occupation (as I know now, but didn't then). At the Gaumont State we also saw, after the glittering Wurlitzer theatre-organ had sunk into its cavern with a final chord, the newsreels of Belsen victims being shovelled into mass graves. Unaccompanied by any adult, we had only each other to help us come to terms with all that on the walk home.

We were well aware of world events, of course, and the Dartington community included many refugees from European countries. Roddy's inseparable friend Lukas Heller, from a German refugee family, lived near to us in London and was a frequent visitor to Dartmouth Road. At school Luke was a notorious Bad Boy, but I liked him a lot. In 1946 Roddy started to be coached at a cricket school in Chiswick – to the brink of a cricketing career, in fact: captain of the Young Professionals at Lords in 1948 (but after that, he changed course). If Roddy was busy with cricket, Luke and I would sometimes go to the pictures together.

Some of our other visitors stayed overnight in the cold, sparsely furnished 'living room', otherwise rarely used except when Granny and Aunty Bindy came to tea. We were a B&B for non-Londoners, John's and Kate's friends as well as ours, and most frequently of all, my diary reminds me, our twin cousins Harold and Fisher Unwin (who both hated their given names and called themselves Chris and Ken). Their mother, Dora's older sister Mary, had died of tuberculosis in 1941, as had her eldest son Hilary. This double loss, and other problems of the Unwin family, gave Dora a feeling of special obligation to her two nephews, at that stage just being demobilised from the armed forces; but she strongly disapproved of, and tried to frustrate, the romantic interest that both of them intermittently took in me. I could have told her they were only forced to stoop to their 16-year-old cousin for lack of other girlfriends to fondle, but I didn't admit that belittling truth even to my diary.[3]

---

[3] *When Chris and I met again several years later, our greater maturity engendered a different kind of relationship, to which Dora happily raised no objection. We were married in 1960.*

A MAN OF SMALL IMPORTANCE

Roddy was rarely seen without a cricket bat or ball.

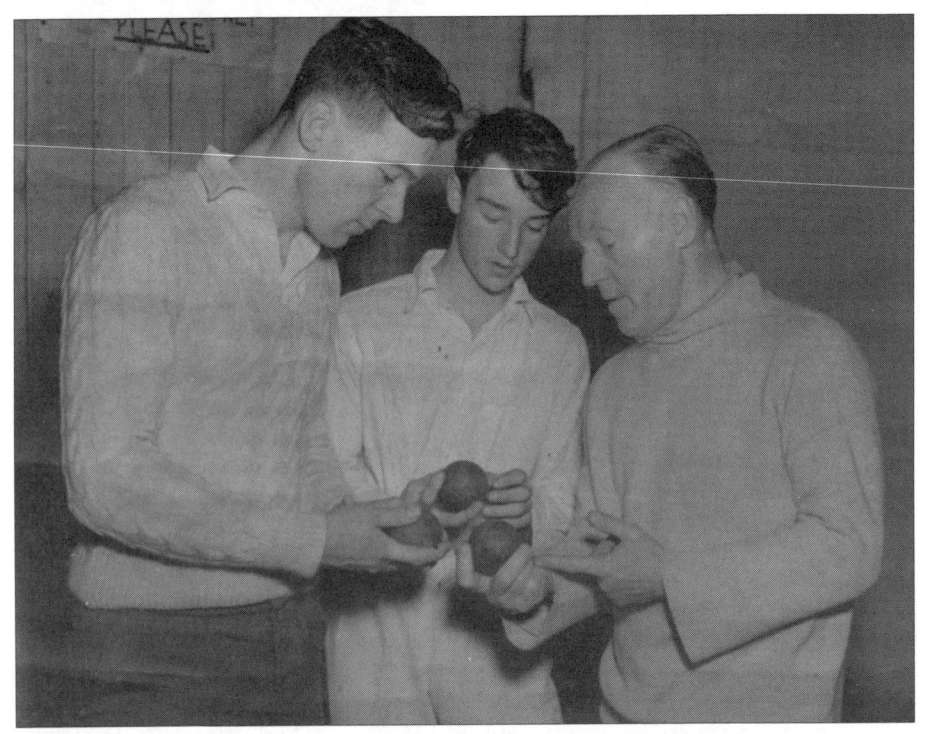

A publicity photo from the Cricket School where Roddy trained

What strikes me most forcefully, rediscovering the London of 1946 through the pages of my diary, is what a great place it was to be young in, even with little money. Queueing for almost everything was still normal, so 'Full' or 'Sold Out' sometimes meant disappointment, but that was the only brake on our activities. Not only Kilburn High Road but the West End was our oyster. Yes, you really could have a meal and take in a show for less than five bob! – well ten bob, anyway (that's 50 pence in today's money). Most of my trips to the West End were with girlfriends from school. We usually ate at the Salad Bowl in the Lyons Corner Houses strategically located in central London – all the salads you could eat for half-a-crown. One day Pamela and I treated ourselves to lunch there *and* a sherry at one shilling each. Finding we'd missed the start of our chosen film, we went round on the off chance to the Old Vic and got 4/6d tickets to the matinée: Ralph Richardson as Cyrano de Bergerac, a performance that stayed in my mind for years. I can't say the same for *Pick Up Girl* at the Prince of Wales, to which I took Mum, Lily and Roddy, with money I had earned for a book review Dora had put in my way.

I had a voracious appetite for entertainment, from high to the lowest-brow, depending on who rang me up to suggest what. One night *Don Pasquale* at the Cambridge Theatre; next day the Schoolboys' Exhibition at the Central Hall, Westminster. That expedition was business as well as pleasure, as it happens. Dora had asked me to write it up for the newspaper of which she was science editor, a journal launched by her Ministry during the war to encourage good relations with the Soviet Union, called, appropriately, *British Ally*. I had decided that Writing was to be my vocation, and was investigating becoming a journalist. Bold as brass, I wrote to Gerald Barry (no relation), editor of the liberal-left *News Chronicle*, to ask if he would see me to give me some advice. He did, the following week. It seems remarkable now that a chit of a girl could so easily get to see a Fleet Street editor 'for a chat'. Were human relations more open and civilised then, or is nostalgia clouding my memory?

I've departed from strict chronology to conjure up my 16-year-old world which now had to accommodate my Dad. On the day after his arrival in Devon, my diary tentatively recorded *He'll fill a big gap in my life, I think*. Was I play-acting to myself again? The very same entry includes my irritation at his presumptuous advice to 'stick to Maths' and re-take the coming exam – the same advice Curry had given me, and which I followed, but it was quite different coming from *him*.

Looking back, I see that any void I may have felt earlier in my childhood had by now been filled. Pat, unwelcome as he was, was in full possession of the place that in earlier days I had secretly hoped Dad would one day occupy (not knowing, then, how hard he'd been trying to do so). At Dartington I'd found a substitute father, now my careers adviser, who would have been stiff competition for any late-arriving Dad, let alone a grumpy, out-of-touch foreigner like Griffin. I had several other adult mentors, too, and was fiercely loyal to Dora as my chief protector, a role in which she never failed. In any case I was at the age when normal adolescents are growing away from their parents, and had bosom friends and siblings to confide in.

Griffin's entry into this picture would therefore be a matter of squeezing in rather than filling a gap. To work his way in would require tact and patience, qualities in short supply in his character. Nevertheless, I was still well-disposed towards him. He was what I thought I wanted to be – a journalist – and had many interesting and well-placed friends, I knew. He came from that land of milk and honey, America, where it seemed more than likely I would be going to college. Now was just the time to learn something about my American heritage. So when the summer holiday loomed, and Roddy and I had to choose between a school trip to Holland and a fortnight with Griffin in Ireland, we had no hesitation in opting for Dublin.

Dublin, 1946

Our trip to Ireland in August 1946 was Roddy's and my first venture out of England since our visit to America in 1933, which I scarcely remembered, and Roddy not at all. It was an arduous journey, still in the wartime pattern: a slow, overcrowded train with little comfort, and no refreshment en route. After a sleepless all-night ride from London, we boarded a ferry at Holyhead in the early hours and set sail at 6 a.m. In his typically muddled way, Griffin had mistaken the day we were coming and was not at the quay to meet us some three hours later. Nothing daunted, we took a *horse-drawn* taxi, relates my diary wonderingly, to await him at his flat.

That apartment in Dublin, two rooms and a kitchen on the attic floor of 26 Fitzwilliam Square, was the only home we ever shared with Griffin – for just two-and-a-half weeks. Domestically it was not a happy experience. But oh, life in Dublin was grand, just grand!

Griffin had assured Dora we would be comfortable there, 'up three very long flights of stairs through the house of Robert Collis, a famous Dublin surgeon who was lent to the Belsen refugee camp at the end of the war... and is kind enough to lend me books and ask me to dinner below.' It seems prominent Irish citizens were already being called on for sensitive international tasks, as they often are now. Southern Ireland, then known as Eire, had been neutral throughout the Second World War, although thousands of workless Irishmen had volunteered for the British armed forces, and no doubt all but the most fervent anti-British Republicans had privately supported the Allied cause. So closely tied economically and geographically to Britain as they were, the Irish had not escaped wartime privations similar to ours on the 'home front', and in 1946, as at home, there were still shortages and rationing.

But there were differences. I was delighted to see so many oranges in the shops, wonderful *tapioca!* on the menu for our first Dublin lunch, and greedily recorded all our meals of eggs (still scarce in London). As well as the food, another preoccupation of the visit for me were the tailor's fittings for a two-piece suit made up from a length of heavy tweed Griffin had found on a trip to the west coast. He had bought the cloth freely from a weaver's cottage in Mayo, but his women friends had to donate clothing coupons for the lining and other materials required by the tailor. How well I remember that suit, recorded photographically with my pre-war Kodak Brownie but hardly ever worn thereafter (the material was far too heavy, suitable only for an overcoat). In Dublin I was able to buy films, also hard to find at home, and a photography session on St Stephens Green provided the only photographs I have of Griffin in his later years – the Griffin I actually knew.

The pivot of Griffin's social life, and therefore of ours, was Harry Craig. He was tall, fair, pale-faced, with the profile of an eagle – no beauty! But Harry Craig was the most charming man I have ever met. From Griffin's correspondence I know more about him now than I did then. In a letter to Dora describing the social setting of our visit, Harry rated special mention as 'the real force behind *The Bell*, Ireland's best monthly', whose writings therein had lured Griffin to seek him out. By now they were firm friends, almost daily companions for the political and literary discussions that were bread and wine to Griffin (to Harry too, I would discover). 'He has his personal problems', Griffin had added, one of them 'an illegitimate child a month old unknown to the community, of whom he is very fond, as he still is of its mother...' Now that's something I didn't know in 1946, and might have been shocked if I had known, considering the lavish attention he paid to me – holding hands in the cinema, surreptitious cuddles walking home at night, bolder approaches when Griffin and Roddy were out of sight – all faithfully recorded in my diary.

Nor was Harry my only suitor. To my surprise and delight I found myself the centre of attraction in a social circle of young men and *older* women – no young ones. That was the key to my popularity, I realised later: not my irresistible charm but the rarity of a friendly young female, almost unchaperoned, in what was still a restricted and heavily Catholic society. Many of the young men hanging round the offices of *The Bell* and in the bars where we met Harry after work were themselves new arrivals in that free and easy, would-be bohemian Dublin circle. Like overgrown schoolboys, they drank too much and caterwauled in the quiet streets on the way home, enjoying the outrage of disturbed citizens. At a memorable party arranged to hear the reading of a visiting young poet, one Dylan Thomas, the company was so noisy and inattentive that the poet refused to waste his breath. Roddy got very sick, and some young man poured a glass of stout down the front of my dress. Only Griffin and Harry stayed sober to guide us all home.[4]

Of the physical Dublin I recall very little except a most congenial atmosphere. Harry took us round Trinity College, his alma mater, but did we inspect *The Book of Kells*? If so, I didn't consider it worth a diary entry. One afternoon he and I climbed the 167 steps up Nelson's Pillar, a kind of mini Nelson's Column commemorating the same historical event. It was in O'Connell Street, very close to the offices of *The Bell* as I recall, but Harry had never ascended it before, perhaps out of patriotic dislike of this symbol of British imperialism. We took photographs of the view, and of each other – but that film was defective, so nothing came out to remind me of what we saw. I do remember the elegant Georgian squares of the city, of course, and that everywhere we went was within walking distance except for a bus ride to visit Peggy, who had arranged the making of my suit. This was before the motor age – none of Griffin's friends had a car, and there were very few around, except on the main streets.[5]

Unusually for an Irishman, Harry was mad about cricket. Discovering Roddy's talent, he at once enrolled him as a temporary member of his own cricket club. With a set of borrowed whites, for the rest of our stay Roddy spent

---

[4] *When I saw the film* The Girl with Green Eyes *in the 1960s it seemed to me to depict the Dublin I had glimpsed in 1946. Based on a story by Edna O'Brien, it told the tale of two country girls arriving, all eager and innocent, in sophisticated Dublin, where one (Rita Tushingham) becomes the mistress of a middle-aged writer (Peter Finch) and eventually, finding herself pregnant, makes the inevitable journey across the water to England – a journey still made today by many Irish girls, for the same reason.*

[5] *In 1966 Nelson's Pillar was neatly blown up by Republicans, to mark the 50th anniversary of the Easter Rising in 1916. Since 1946, I gather, far worse desecration of 'old Dublin' has resulted from ruthless redevelopment and the proliferation of motor traffic.*

every available hour there – a great asset to the club, judging by the scores he recounted each evening.

Griffin dutifully struggled to understand the significance of '4 for 32' and '53 not out', but what he *really* wanted to understand was what made his daughter tick, something he'd been waiting years and years to find out.

A few days after we arrived he began the clumsy assault on my fragile adolescent psyche that ultimately killed any chance of friendship between us. Roddy was playing cricket as usual when –

> Dad and I 'had words' over the tea table – he did most of the talking. He's "very dissatisfied with our personal relationship". He thinks I only want his money and not him as a father. He wants "cooperation from me in revealing to him my personality". He was v. annoyed. I was keeping a barely restrained silence. I don't know quite what he wants me to do, & I'm not sure I can do it anyway. Damn him...

From that moment on, it was cat and mouse – me trying desperately not to be left alone with Griffin, he seeking every opportunity for a tête-à-tête. A few days later he caught me again, writing a long letter to Kate in America *all about school & Dad & everything*. Please could he read the letter? And couldn't he perhaps take a peek at that diary I was so devoted to? This affront led to more 'words' – then a sullen silence for the rest of the day. That was it! Finish! *After this I'll have to see as little as possible of my dear father, with whom "I have no personal relationship whatever". We are quite incompatible.*

It was not yet 'finished' of course; there would be other painful incidents later. But after those early spats I was always on my guard against Griffin's attempts to 'get to know me'. In Dublin, away from the protective adults who were helping me to negotiate the adult world, I felt trapped and vulnerable, 'found wanting' in some indefinable way by this gruff old man I was supposed to love as a father.

He was right that my interest in him was largely cupboard love, as I was guiltily aware even then. What basis did I have for any deeper feeling? He was patently not fulfilling the absurd childish fantasy of 'my Daddy', still in my mind when we had met him off the train in Devon. There were also real memories of his visits during my childhood; some happy, some traumatic, and those letters of moral blackmail that should never have been written. In 1946 – to judge by my diary – I did not hold these childhood traumas against him, or perhaps even remember them; yet combined with the sensitivity of adolescence, I believe this explains why I was so quick to slam the door in Griffin's face.

Of course those little talks in the bare-boarded attic at 26 Fitzwilliam Square (I still remember the dusty smell of that room) were not just about 'getting to know me'. The Ancient Mariner had finally caught me! Now he was going to explain *properly* – now that at last I was old enough to understand – the injustice done to him by Dora. Subconsciously I knew I was expected to make up for that injustice with an intimate father–daughter relationship that I felt incapable of sharing with him. Poor Griffin, how misguided he was. At 16 I was not really old enough to 'understand'; and in any case I was sick of that old family quarrel, wanting nothing more than to get away from it. A genuine love for him could not just be conjured up; it had to grow naturally from closer acquaintance.

The irony is that I *was* beginning to admire and respect him, when his attention was not focused on me. Through meeting his friends, and noting their regard for him, both in London and Dublin, I could see he was someone worth knowing. My faithful diary witnessed several animated late-night sessions in Dublin – Harry, Griffin and others arguing politics, or everyone listening entranced to Harry's declamations of Auden and Dylan Thomas. I was sometimes bored on these occasions, as any frivolous-minded teenager might be, but I was beginning to get a sense of 'the best of Griffin' – an intelligent, humorous, cultivated man, insatiably curious about human affairs and with a sage appreciation of intellectual quality in other people. What a pity that through his ineptitude, and my youthful inexperience, the goodwill I felt towards him in 1946 so quickly turned to resentment and dislike.

For the rest of our stay I avoided further confrontation, taking refuge in childish sulks and petty spitefulness, such as going out all day when I knew Griffin was ill at home and might be glad of my company (*running away from the unpleasant in my usual manner*, I was honest enough to admit to myself). His ulcer often troubled him; he was also worried about money, as usual; and I'm sure – although he never admitted this – also fretting about his work. To his credit he did not burden us with these worries and was determined to 'show us a good time'. Entertaining us was also, of course, an excuse to escape the lonely agony of writing and do what he enjoyed most of all – socialising with sharp-witted people.

It was characteristic of Griffin to have found his way to the heart of Dublin's intellectual life. Coming from Washington, and with such a wide experience of the world, perhaps he brought a certain glamour to what was still a provincial society, where at that time everyone with talent and ambition knew they would eventually have to 'cross the water'. Another friend who used to accompany us to parties and the 'fillums' was Vincent Crotty, quietly spoken, serious and rather shy. He was older than the rest, still blinking in the glare of normal society after spending his youth in a monastery. Now he was training as a psychiatrist, and soon to be married. Ten years later I knew him and his wife in the north of England, where he was a resident consultant at a large mental hospital and Mary a psychiatric social worker. Back in London a few years after that, I used to listen to The Critics on the radio and vaguely knew that the soft

Irish voice of H A L Craig must be the Harry we knew and loved in Dublin, but at that time I was too busy with motherhood, and then widowhood, to try to reconnect with him. Another acquaintance of 1946 who also moved to London and achieved fame of a different kind was a young radio commentator called Eamonn Andrews.

On 25 August we said our farewells, and the next day returned to London. I was glad to be relieved of the psychological pressure of Griffin's interrogations, and eagerly looking forward to the new term at Dartington.

Glad to be going home

Since 1946 I have visited Ireland only once, in the summer of 1963, when I took a week's tour by car with my two-year-old son Barney, and an Australian cousin as co-driver. We spent half a day in Dublin, where I looked up the Crottys, now back in their homeland. Mary took me to a special shop where I bought a length of beautiful Donegal tweed, and in London had it made up into a suit I wore for years. Vincent had just been diagnosed with inoperable cancer, and died soon after my visit. The news of his impending fate was a shock, but my own husband, Chris Unwin, had just died far too young, and I was having to get used to the meaningless cruelties of life. I hope Vincent didn't see his cancer as God's punishment for renouncing his vocation all those years earlier. He had loudly declared his atheism in 1946, but with cradle Catholics you can never be quite sure.

I often wondered what became of Harry Craig. Recently I asked a literary friend familiar with London cultural life of the 1950s and 1960s, had he ever known H A L Craig? Oh yes, he replied, a charming Irish poet and critic of plays and films, who was also a keen cricketer. Sadly he had died young, 'about 30 years ago'.

CHAPTER 18

ALMOST FULLY FLEDGED

Returning from Dublin, we still had three weeks before school started. At the end of August reports of John's marriage in Washington, and photographs of him and his bride, appeared in the London evening papers (there were three of them in those days, the '*Star-News-'n'-Standard*' shouted by vendors on every street corner). Eagerly we pored over the photographs. Only Griffin, before he left Washington, and Kate, now living in Cambridge, Massachusetts and working for her PhD at Radcliffe, had met our new sister-in-law. One report, connecting the event to the scandalous views of John's father, so amused me that I pasted it into my diary, making clear my own disdain for strait-laced *Evening News* reporters and their readers:

No "Trial Marriage"

VISCOUNT AMBERLEY, 24-year-old son of Earl Russell – Bertrand Russell – now honeymooning in America with his bride, poet's daughter Susan Doniphan Lindsay, is optimistic about the future of their marriage, in spite of his father's views on matrimony.

Thrice-married Earl Russell is an advocate of trial marriage.

Lord Amberley tells my New York colleague, Leonard Wibberly, that his father's ideas are irrelevant to his own case.

The Amberleys met last January; their marriage in Washington, where Lord Amberley is serving as a sub-lieutenant in the British Admiralty Delegation, was the culmination of a secret engagement.

I showed it to Mum & she roared with laughter. We all knew the couple had been 'living in sin' for months: Susan was already pregnant with Sarah, their first child, who was born the following January. Evidently the *Evening News* reporter did not, or he'd have had an even more interesting story.

That night *Roddy & I sat up late talking – about Pat, and Mummy & everything. Mostly about Pat and how much we hate him. Rod is wonderful – what would I do without him?* Solidarity with Roddy was crucial to me. I was much more concerned about family problems than he was, and more affected by quarrels and tension. Was this a gender difference, or just that his cricket took him out of the house more often? Roddy's special genius for human relations came in useful a few years later in managing both our difficult parents. At this earlier stage he was blessedly free of adolescent angst, but seemed to know I needed his help in coping with mine.

In mid-September Dora, Roddy and I took a nostalgic two-day trip to Sussex – fortunately without Pat (his presence spoiled any outing for me). We stayed the night at the Royal Oak pub at Hooksway, near Harting. Mum and I shared our double bed with *a huge black cat as big as a terrier!* The Royal Oak was near Telegraph House, the first home of the school, reached from there along a lane through the woods. The landlady had become a special friend of Dora's when she was there; throughout my childhood, Mrs Ainger had been an almost mythic figure in her reminiscences of the years at Telegraph, which had been at first the happiest, and then the unhappiest, of her life. Now here was the real Mrs Ainger, and her husband Alf, greeting us warmly. I was only four years old when the school had moved away in 1934, so the cry of joy in my diary – *I remember it all now!* – probably derived from our caravan holiday of 1936 (see page 172).

John and Susan

Bertie and his new wife were then living at Telegraph House, reclaimed as the Russell family home, and we had called there to collect John and Kate for 'Dora's half' of their school holidays, camping for the night at Hooksway. Shadowy pictures of other places we visited on that trip – Bodiam Castle, Battle Abbey, Pevensey – remain in my mind to this day, not to mention the excitement of fielding pots and pans flying out of cupboards as the caravan swayed round corners (we were unwisely riding in it, as there wasn't room for everyone in the car).

Later on that day in 1946 we went up the hill to look at the house, no longer owned by the Russells and at that time for sale (*only* £20,000! – an unimaginable sum to me). Next day we called on Mr Pullen at the Ship Inn, and Mrs Head at the Post Office. *They all remember Mum down here & all love her.* The locals of course knew about the scandalous divorce that had ended the idyllic Telegraph years for Dora – more than I knew about it in 1946. Later she recalled Mrs Ainger panting up the hill to warn her of 'snoopers' on Griffin's trail in 1934, loyalty which meant a lot to her at the time.[1]

I don't know if Dora ever re-visited Hooksway to see the Aingers and their big black cat. I hope so, because she loved the place, and for the rest of her life kept on her mantelpiece a cracked old photograph of the little inn, taken about 1910. When I paid a fleeting visit in 1961, with Chris Unwin, we had to search for the narrow road that led down to the Royal Oak, because the only route I could remember was the path through the woods, strewn with fallen beechnuts. The Aingers were still going strong, and the pub still had its *Cider With Rosie* character: a tiny bar-parlour with one wooden bench along the wall, another bench outside facing the duckpond, even the huge woodpile at the back where I remember hunting for little sugary Easter eggs on that holiday in 1936.

The rest of our holiday was spent in London, the usual round of visits to the cinema, and friends coming to call. Peter Swann, John's Navy friend just

The Royal Oak, Hooksway

---

[1] *Dora Russell*, The Tamarisk Tree, *op.cit., p.263. For this sordid aspect of the divorce see p.152.*

returned from Washington, passed through on his way to begin an academic career at Oxford. I was rather disappointed by his account of John's wedding, at which he was a witness and the only guest (at that time I was more interested in weddings than living in sin). Another event typical of the times – and our family – was the occasion when Rod went missing until after midnight. Mum and I sat up anxiously, waiting and talking... I thought he might have been stopped by the police, as had happened a few days earlier (*They must have thought he was a homo!!* said my diary gleefully).[2] Dora had similar fears for this pretty young boy, with his overlong hair in the age of short-back-and-sides. Had he been waylaid by a prowler in the West End? As it turned out, he'd gone to a dance hall with a friend, and had omitted to phone home his plans. Amazingly, as I look back on our free and easy teenage life in London, that's the only time I remember Dora thinking either of us might be in moral danger.

✳ ✳ ✳

I returned to Dartington for the autumn term of 1946 on slightly false pretences. It was now definite that I would be going to college in America. I had not embarked on Higher School Certificate with my age-mates, as an American university would require only School Certificate and satisfactory results in their College Board examinations. These exams, which I would take the following spring, had no set curriculum, so there was really no need for me to be at school. As I did not want to leave Dartington, Curry obligingly arranged a timetable of 'general education', while thinking up other ways to occupy me after Christmas. I'd have plenty of time for the Artroom, for singing and clarinet lessons, bookbinding, Philosophy classes once a week, and the new wall newspaper to write for...

In fact, I spent much of that term in the sickroom, nursing my grumbling appendix, and then convalescing from the operation to remove it. The sickroom was at Aller Park, then the Junior School, about a mile from Foxhole, the Senior School, where all my friends and activities were. For some weeks I was an ambulatory patient, using it just as a dormitory.

The startling news that rocked the school community that term was my best friend Jenny's betrothal – at age 17, and forsaking a scholarship to Oxford – to a former Dartington pupil who lived in South Africa. She was staying with her mother near Paignton (one of the family homes I used to idolise for its neatness and normality), awaiting a passage to South Africa.[3] Curry drove me over one day to see her. He was concerned that one of his 'pets' might be making a

---

[2] *At a time when homosexuality was illegal, and bored bobbies always looking for an 'easy cop', that was the most likely reason for young men to be stopped and questioned in the street.*

[3] *Jenny and her sister Bronwen had been at Beacon Hill briefly, and their mother Luned on the staff there. See photo on p.196.*

Jenny with her future husband Bryan Heseltine

youthful mistake – needless concern, for the marriage has lasted to this day – but my feelings were selfish. Oh, I wished them well of course, and envied Jenny the excitement of Getting Married – but how could she desert me like this? First Kate, now Jenny – it was all too much to bear!

Before long the hole in my heart had been partly filled. My weeks of semi-illness led to a matey relationhip with Dodie Kabraji, in charge of the sickroom, and a closer friendship with her daughter Etain, just then taking and passing the necessary exams for Cambridge. Etain was a year my senior, and I was somewhat in awe of her. She was much cleverer than me; her other friends were also Oxbridge-bound and they all had highbrow interests that I didn't completely share, but felt I Ought To. I was plagued by such doubts at that time. Both in my family and at school there were brainy women whom I knew I should emulate – and I was trying, I really was! – but secretly I was beginning to fear that my own intellect wasn't up to it. True, I hadn't yet been tested intellectually – perhaps I would surprise myself – but I did know how shallow-minded I was. *Is it very frivolous and useless to love dancing? I hope not, because I don't want to be a fritterer but I do love dancing...*

Family conflicts continued to simmer away in the background. Conrad Russell, Bertie's son by his new wife – and therefore a half-brother of John and Kate – had recently started at Dartington's Junior School, and I was understandably curious when he arrived as a fellow-patient in the sickroom. One afternoon Dodie asked me to divert him with a game of chinese checkers, and to make conversation I admired a paint-box by his bed. 'Yes, isn't it nice,' he said, 'my half-sister in America sent it to me.' I was bursting to tell him she was my half-sister too, but Curry had warned me he wasn't supposed to know about 'us'. To make sure he didn't, Bertie and Peter had insisted that Roddy and I should cease to use the name Russell. We had arrived at Dartington as Russells, but now we were Barrys.[4]

In later life, John and Kate were closer to Roddy and me than to Conrad. I met him again only once, in the 1970s – and by this time he knew who I was –

---

[4] *For many years Griffin had also wanted us to be Barrys, but was powerless to arrange it without Dora's agreement. The change was made informally at the start of our second year, in September 1945, but the Deed Poll by which I formally renounced the Russell part of my name was only effected in April 1947 – see p.250. (For Roddy, never registered as Russell, this was not necessary.) I must confess that at 16, just becoming aware that Bertie was really famous, I would have liked the whole world to know of my connection with him. In later years, I wanted only to disown the link. I remember in 1962 being hounded by the* Daily Express, *in pursuit of some current scandal, because at that time I was still listed as Bertie's daughter in Debrett, though he had managed to get me expunged from Burke's Peerage – see p.121 of Ray Monk, op.cit. (Monk's version of the paint-box story, op.cit., p.292, has become inaccurate in the re-telling.)*

when we had a family conference to discuss the problems of John's daughter Sarah Russell, a half-niece of both of us.

Over Christmas there was another crisis in my relations with Griffin, which took me rather by surprise. Now, reading my diary entries consecutively, I can see how it happened. The story begins while I was in hospital, recovering from my appendectomy.

> **Saturday, 30 November** ... *a nice postbag – a roll of magazines from Pat, a letter and a parcel from Lily and 2 letters from Pat. One of them was quite incredible – <u>he</u> suggested that Daddy should join us all for Christmas! Coming from Pat that's extraordinary to say the least! What's come over our family? They are all reforming! It would be lovely, but wouldn't they tear each other's eyes out?*

Roddy and I discussed the idea. We agreed that any 'trouble' would come from Griffin, not Pat, but we were expecting John and Susan to be home by Christmas and as they already knew and liked Griffin, they would be useful social balm in the motley gathering. But when we heard from Dora a week later that their return would be delayed – Susan had had a near-miscarriage and wasn't fit to travel – we decided not to ask Griffin after all. The risk of embarrassing rows was too great.

By mid-December we were back in London. The house was delightfully uncrowded with the student lodgers away, and we began to think again about the month's holiday ahead. After talking it over with Lily, and then with Dora and Pat – (*who were both very nice about it all – the whole atmosphere seems to have changed over-term!*) – Rod and I decided, with some trepidation, to ask Griffin for a fortnight after Christmas. *Oh God, I <u>do</u> hope it will be all right...*

> **Sunday, 15 December** *This morning I wrote to Daddy setting out the suggestion and warning him not to accept unless he was sure he could control that evil temper of his. If he comes, and doesn't, I'll break every bone in his body, old man or not!*

I dare say I added, for good measure, that the invitation had originated with Pat, just so he'd know how grateful he should feel. How I cringe, now, to think of that poor old man in his lonely Dublin attic, unfolding this tactless letter in his beloved daughter's hand...

> **Friday, 20 December** *A telegram from Daddy – he can't come, is writing. I rather expected that.*

I certainly should have expected it, and I hope I had a twinge of guilt for the tone of my invitation. But I was quite unprepared for the missile on its way.

Monday, 30 December This morning I had the most <u>disgusting</u> letter from Daddy. It was quite horrible & I was so impressed by the ghastliness & futility of this family mess that I sobbed my heart out into my pillow for about half an hour before getting up. It was an "explanation" of his refusing our invitation. Oh, it was awful. The things he said about Mummy. He is quite inhuman. I hate him. Oh God, I do try to be impartial & not take sides, but Daddy is making himself so unbearable that I am leaning further & further towards Mummy. I went down to breakfast but my tear-swollen face gave me away & I wept some more. Mummy must have a 6th sense or something [!] – at once she said, What's Daddy been saying now to upset you? She wanted to see the letter but how could I let her? I just cried & cried & cried. I showed it to Lily & Rod. Lily & Mummy both say take no notice of him, but how can I? I want to hurt him to the roots of his soul. I shall take the letter to Mary Vorse tomorrow, who is after all his oldest friend, & ask her to write to him. I shan't write until I get some sort of apology.

Such histrionics! I had not then seen the kind of letters Griffin wrote to Dora in the depths of their quarrel, and must have thought his invective had been specially worked up for me. Nor did I yet fully realise the explosive nature of his character, which his friends knew all too well. When I met Mary Vorse the following day (for the first time), she laughed off the letter as 'typical Griffin' and advised me either to ignore it, or ask him not to discuss Dora with me (*I think I'll do that*). This must have been the occasion when she told me the tale I've already quoted, about receiving a postcard from Griffin: 'After last night I never want to see you again. My next address is Oslo.' True or not, I always tell this story when people ask, What was your father really like?

I was also strangely naïve about the relationship between Dora and Pat as a couple, and Griffin the 'outsider'. On the day I received it, after recounting a shopping expedition, my diary returned to 'that revolting letter'. *Lily says he always wanted Mum to marry him, and has consequently always been terribly jealous of P.* Had I really never thought of that before? Even more puzzling is what I wrote next: *He has no other cause to hate Pat as he does. Pat has never harmed him except in diverting Mum's affections.* If Griffin needed a 'reason' to hate Pat (though I didn't need one myself), surely diverting Dora's affections was enough! However grown up I thought myself to be, my diary reflections on this incident show otherwise.

After Christmas I returned to school no longer just a pupil but a part-time member of staff – as assistant housemother in a residential House of the Junior School. This was a stop-gap arrangement until a job helping in the Nursery School became vacant after Easter. Thus Curry enabled me to mark time at

Dartington, where I was happy, instead of at home, where I was not. I was now working for my room and board – a routine I would become familiar with in the United States – while still having time during the day, and most evenings, to pursue my studies and cultural activities.

I was slightly ill at ease in this half-way role between the grown-ups of the staff and my schoolmates at the Senior School. That spring I developed a new friendship which helped me through this awkwardness. Carito and Marina Rodriguez, 'the Spannies', were sisters, pre-war Basque refugees (along with others on the staff at Foxhole), who had ended up as teacher-training students at Dartington and had then joined the staff.[5] Both of them lived and taught at Aller Park, and Carito, especially, became my new pal. The only problem was that I couldn't join the White Hart Club, the centre of Dartington young folks' night life, until my seventeenth birthday. On that happy day, 8 July 1947, I joined my friends at the White Hart for celebration drinks and a thrilling game of shove ha'penny.

Before that summer, we had all endured a very harsh winter, scored into the memory of everyone who lived through it. Exceptionally cold weather while Britain was still flattened by the war led to a national fuel crisis – electricity cuts during the day, I recall, and buildings barely heated, though there was snow on the ground. Oh, the torture of ice cold bed-sheets! I remember the night I struggled home from a Philosophy class at High Cross through deep snow, too deep for Curry's vintage Rolls Royce to venture out. Snow is a rarity in Devon, and it didn't last long. But I ended up in the sickroom with bronchitis, and in that weak state I was hit by another Dreadful Letter from Dublin.

Carito during the terrible winter of 1946–47. Aller Park in the background.

When I answered the Christmas bombshell along the lines Mary Vorse had suggested, I was still hopeful that if I asked Griffin not to burden me with his grievances, he would desist. It seems this letter did make some attempt to be reasonable – *he has obviously tried not to hurt my feelings, & I'm grateful to*

---

[5] *As explained in Chapter 13, their coming to England was a result of the Spanish civil war. They were among a few hundred of the 1937 child refugees who settled in England, although they moved freely back and forth to Spain once the Franco régime had ended. Adrian Bell tells the full story of these exiles in* Only for Three Months: The Basque Children in Exile *(Norwich: Mousehold Press, 1996).*

him for that. Nevertheless he had to go through, yet again, *a detailed recital of his persecutions and miseries since about 1930, with the accent on the brutal treatment he received at the hands of Mum & Pat.* With the wisdom of years, and when it no longer matters, I now recognise Griffin as a paid-up member of what cynical journalists call the Green Ink brigade – 'people who have devoted their whole being to some injustice they have suffered, real or imagined, and who write long letters in green ink explaining every last detail of their complaint'.[6] Oh yes, Griffin to a T. The injury to his feelings was obvious – *oh, I feel so sorry for him* – but although I was indirectly the cause of his misery, by having been born, that was hardly my fault. I could not feel responsible for his plight – yet somehow he made me feel I *was*.

'Green inkers are pathetically grateful for the faintest response from a normal person,' wrote that perceptive journalist; and I can see now that all Griffin really wanted was sympathy and understanding – from me above all, who could somehow make it up to him with daughterly affection. At 16 I was too immature to understand all this; I only knew that to sympathise with his cause seemed disloyal to Dora. Griffin should have seen that, of course, but green inkers by definition are not clear-sighted. In fact Roddy's refusal to 'get involved' was the best ploy; but I was a dutiful child, and the burden of Family Problems lay heavily on my shoulders. *Rod just won't take it seriously*, I complained to myself, but *how do I answer this one? I'm so sick and tired of handling him gently – "With Care – Might Explode"*...

Roddy also happened to be a patient in the sickroom when Griffin's letter came, and while he was there we laughed it off together. Next day, however, after he'd returned to Foxhole, cured, I re-read the letter and fell to weeping into my pillow... Just then Curry came in to visit me, and I saw my escape route. Transferring my weeping to his shoulder, I showed him the letter and asked him to write to Griffin explaining how much it had upset me. Curry knew all the ins and outs of our family, of course; he had known John and Kate as pupils, and since those days had been a friend of Bertie, who used to stay at High Cross when visiting Conrad. We were not the only complicated family whose children he watched over *in loco parentis*.

I can see now that being reprimanded by Curry was a further humiliation to inflict on my poor old Dad; but it did the trick. It was not quite the end of green ink letters – green ink seeped into *all* Griffin's letters and his 'little talks' with me – but after this, he made a brave effort not to harp on about the past. Thereafter his assaults on me (for that's how I saw it) were all about Getting To Know You.

....

[6] *Simon Hoggart, in* The Guardian *of 7 November 1997. He was reporting a press conference called by the Tory ex-MP Neil Hamilton to protest his innocence, yet again, of corruption charges which a House of Commons Committee had just reported to be more or less proven. 'Mr Hamilton is now a member of what we hacks cruelly call the Green Ink brigade...'.*

*\ *\ *

At about this time I began to feel responsible for the world's problems as well as my family's. In keeping with my nearly-adult status I was a regular attender at the Sunday Evening Meeting, held at the Hall, at which some important issue would be aired, often by a visiting speaker. Two talks in particular – by Bertie Russell and Philip Noel-Baker, a Labour MP with a lifelong concern for international disarmament – alerted me to the dire state of international politics and a feeling that something must be done about it NOW! I was surprised to find myself not bored but quite interested in politics, and Curry's talk on *Am I a Liberal?* – which everyone knew he was – decided the general stamp of my allegiance (if Curry had suggested Hitler wasn't so bad after all, I'd have believed him). This awakening interest in international affairs influenced my later studies at university and, in due course, my working career.

Meantime, the spectre of Communism was haunting the corridors of the Senior School, sweeping up unwary young boys – including my beloved brother (not Lukas, however; he was far too canny). The evangelist was an older pupil, Julian Tudor Hart, who had returned to school to get further qualifications he needed for medical studies. There were one or two Communists on the staff – as there were in the House of Commons at that time – but it was Julian who got the lads into the Young Communist League (YCL) and rushing off to Plymouth to hear charismatic speakers. I already felt Communism was 'all wrong somehow', yet when Anthony H explained his recent conversion in our Philosophy class, I was ashamed to confess only ignoble reasons for opposing him: *I screwed up courage to say I felt myself superior to the working man... It's such a snobbish & really groundless thing to say, yet I can't help feeling I really <u>am</u> superior... At any rate the proletarian has no more right to govern than I have.* Later, in America, especially through courses in Political Science taught by a refugee from Hungary, I learned some better arguments.

The spectre of Communism haunted me at home too. In big sisterly fashion I had written to Dora my concerns about Roddy, and was reassured by her avowal that she herself was a socialist, and Roddy would probably grow out of Communism when he learned more about it. Yet in the Easter holidays I found myself *hemmed in by Communists* when I learned that Harold and Muriel – two older, married lodgers whom I liked and respected, were Party members, *and Mummy certainly talks like one*. Indeed she did; she was a fellow-traveller with the Party on many issues, and I was not yet able to detect the difference. On a later occasion I began to see the essence of political Dora when she embarrassed me in front of Curry with a tirade about Equal Pay (then becoming a vital feminist cause). *I sometimes wonder how she would get along without a grievance against someone or something to fight against.*

That was an eventful spring holiday. One evening we went *en famille* to a big rally at Central Hall, Westminster, addressed by all the famous lefties of the day, from Tom Driberg to J B Priestley. The main speaker was a prominent American lefty, Henry Wallace, whom I would later hear in America in a less friendly setting. I was very stirred, especially by Wallace, but forgot to tell my diary what they all said. The next day I took the American College Board exams, and felt I'd done very badly except in English composition. Later that week, in preparation for applying for my American visa, I signed a Deed Poll deleting 'Russell' from the name inscribed on my birth certificate. From the solicitor's office I went to meet my friend Akbar at Covent Garden. Having failed to get tickets in advance, we queued for 'the gods' at 2/6d each to see *The Magic Flute* (not a good production; we were very critical of the casting). I shall always be grateful to Akbar (whose real name was Aylwyn Lewis) for developing my taste for opera. He was older than me, having been at Dartington with John and Kate, but we had developed a strong friendship first through correspondence, while he was in the RAF, and later through outings in London and his visits to Dartington. From my diary of those years, I suspect a slight romantic interest on his side of which I was quite unaware.

To start the holiday, the family had spent a week in Paris, thanks to a generous friend who gave Dora the money to take us.[7] The city was grey in the aftermath of the war, and still greyer for me because Pat was with us (I prefer to remember France from later visits in the 1950s). Coming home, *It was so nice to see Lily again & to know we could get out of sight of Pat for some of the day.*

Time spent at home was increasingly fraught by my relations with the adults of the household. My unequivocal hatred of Pat, deserved or not, was easier to cope with than tension between Dora and Lily which sometimes showed itself. One day I was made very miserable by 'a sort of row' between them. *They weren't very serious but it upset me rather. I always want to cry when other people fight.* On another occasion I was listening to the radio in Lily's room when Dora came to ask, Why don't you listen in my room? I couldn't tell her the real reason – that I would feel impelled to leave when 'He' came in from the pub – but I realised that Dora was rather jealous of Lily, and felt guilty about it. *Poor old Mum, we hardly ever sit in her room...[and]...it's much easier to make a fuss of Lily somehow.* 'Making a fuss of Lily' meant giving her a bear-hug that she would fend off strenuously with cries of 'Gerroff, you daft bugger!' – the kind of hug any mother would love to get from her teenage children, who in England show no affection for their parents on principle.

---

[7] *The friend was Eric Estorick, Griffin's benefactor in advancing the money for his book on Ireland. Eric was given to sudden munificent gestures. Once he took me to Croydon airport in his limousine, just for the ride, and on another occasion treated me to dinner in his suite at the Dorchester Hotel.*

But Dora got no such hugs from me. Almost week by week I was withdrawing from her, by no means to the point of rejection but to a stance of cool appraisal. I'm surprised now to see how semi-detached I had become by the time I left for America. When she came to my room the night before I sailed – *She cried on my shoulder & was terribly unhappy. Oh God! I didn't cry much & I didn't know what to say to her, poor Mummy. Life is always too hard on her; some of it's her own fault but nevertheless one is sorry.* Sixty years later, one is even sorrier.

These diary entries are an important clue to my adolescent self (and the adult one too). I have never been able to cope with quarrels of any kind. If I am not involved myself, I simply want to run away, and if I do feel deeply concerned, I cannot argue a case rationally, only fume inwardly with rage and end up hating my opponent. I'm sure this disability derives from my childhood, especially those searing quarrels between Dora and Griffin, literally over my head, during the siege of Kingwell Hall. I have always remembered those moments of terror, looking up at two spitting, shouting giants who could not hear my pleas for them to stop.

If Griffin was a walking volcano, relations with Dora were a minefield too, and her relationship with Pat an endless series of rows over this and that. Growing up with such argumentative people, I should perhaps have become adept at quarrelling myself, but the opposite happened. I emerged from childhood unable to 'fight my corner' in the open, but full of hidden hatreds. Lily – calm, sensible, undemanding Lily – was always my refuge from all this.

As spring turned to summer at beautiful Dartington I reached the very peak of throbbing adolescence. My mood was always tied to the weather (it still is) and there can be few better places in the world to wake up on a fine May morning. Evenings were delicious too: *I can see the greenish light of the long-set sun from my window. It's magical.* One night I couldn't sleep for excitement at the prospect of a glorious Sunday ahead...and then it rained! There was man-made food for my emotions too – music above all. Curry's playing of a Bach chorale, not very proficient but always *con amore*, transported me to other realms. Along with every swooning experience of recorded Beethoven or Mozart, my diary registered some memorable concerts in the Great Hall. Britten's Ceremony of Carols, the singers and their flickering candles processing slowly to the stage in semi-darkness. The Griller string quartet playing wonderful Mozart, and '*a fantastic thing by Bloch which I didn't like but everyone else raved about*'. Earlier that week Carito and I had inspected the newly-installed Henry Moore sculpture in the Hall gardens, which I also didn't like (though I do now).

That last year at Dartington stretched my limited sensibility to the Arts about as far as it would go. I still loved big bands on the radio, and was

A MAN OF SMALL IMPORTANCE

Last months at Dartington, 1947 – photos from my album

Tea at High Cross: (from left) Andy Foss, Akbar, Bill, Marsie

Bill Curry

Me (on the right) with Pamela Deane

In the woods with the Nursery School

Roddy second left, Lukas far right

252

strangely moved by Bessie Smith on Lukas's wind-up gramophone, though I couldn't fathom why that gravelly voice had the effect it did. Trying so hard to be a highbrow, I felt rather ashamed of liking jazz and the blues (the music of such a bad boy as Lukas must be of no account, I assumed). Not until I heard Benny Goodman playing Mozart were these dilemmas resolved, to rescue me from a bad case of cultural snobbery.

Early in June I received the offer of a scholarship from Pembroke, the women's college of Brown University in Providence, Rhode Island. From then on all my thoughts and activities were suffused with excitement – I'M REALLY GOING! I went to London for a few days, where Griffin had recently moved, having finished the fieldwork for his book. I tried to involve him in my various missions, but his chronic unpunctuality irritated me, and my unresponsiveness, by now deliberate, irritated him. I was touched by his pathos, and felt guilty for my hidden thoughts – *I won't have to put up with this much longer* – but a heavier burden at that time was the realisation of Dora's sadness at my impending departure. I am still surprised, and have always been grateful, that she was ready to let me go so far, so young, to a place that represented everything she hated. It was an act of selfless parental devotion: she knew it was right *for me*, and bravely bore the wrench it meant for her.

Back at school, with little else to occupy my mind, I was preoccupied with thoughts of leaving. Curry absolved me from feeling guilty about Griffin – *that's a load off my mind* – and listened to my bossy-boots worries about Roddy's neglect of his studies (*damn cricket and Communism!*). My worship of the Curry household intensified – Bill, Marsie, their son Julian, so loving towards each other, so welcoming to me. How could I ever part from them? Dropping in so frequently at High Cross, conveniently en route between Aller Park and Foxhole, I agonised nightly about wearing out my welcome. Buckets of tears were shed, or choked back, when the days for parting inevitably came. The four years ahead, away from England, and Dartington, and all these marvellous people – including Akbar, who came for a weekend to say goodbye – seemed like a lifetime.

From Dartington I went to Cornwall for a brief family holiday. The beauty of the place provided more purple prose for my diary, alongside affection for old friends and nostalgia for our childhood there. Roddy and I went fishing with borrowed rods, but we didn't catch anything. We took a moonlit walk along the cliffs with John and Susan, also visiting from London. They were now living at Dartmouth Road with Susan's $2\frac{1}{2}$-year-old toddler Anne and their own daughter Sarah, aged 6 months. Susan's lack of interest and skill in mothering were already apparent, and Lily could foresee other troubles too, she told me when I got home. More family problems to be glad to get away from! (And how right Lily was.)

Pat and I left Cornwall ahead of the others, as I had things to do in London.

Mummy says I must be nice to Pat because he's so fond of me & is so sad that I'm going. I dare say he was, but I couldn't bring myself to care, and stolidly read a book on the train journey we shared. I needed all my emotional strength to fend off Griffin in the coming two weeks before I sailed. I knew I had to see as much of him as I could bear, while scurrying around on my vital errands.

Almost at once our relations reached rock-bottom. He was furious that Pat, rather than he, had been deputed to accompany me on a sensitive visit to the American consulate, and insisted I meet him afterwards. *He wanted to know all about the visa interview, especially about the parentage, & I had to be v. careful.*[8] Luckily he had an invitation from Mary Vorse for us to dine at her hotel that night. They talked about people I didn't know and I was rather bored, but mightily relieved not to be grilled by Griffin all evening. *Oh dear it's so difficult with Daddy – the moment he says "Why don't you <u>talk</u> about yourself, I don't <u>know</u> you at all", then I close up like an oyster.* But he kept on grilling, and I kept on squirming. Later that week:

> *The day as far as he was concerned was quite unsuccessful... I have no desire to talk to him, & that is what he wants most, & the more I see of him the more I want to be away from him. He gets madder & madder & I get sulkier & more bad-tempered... It'll be better next week with John & Sue around...*

It was better, on the night of our farewell dinner, but not before several other rancorous exchanges. One night when I had agreed to stay at his flat in Mecklenburgh Square, he asked me to join him first at a friend's place nearby. They were mourning the recent suicide of a mutual friend, Vera Meynell, and perhaps this tragedy diverted some of Griffin's attention from me. On our way back to his place, late, *I tried to explain myself to Dad – he seemed to understand...* But he didn't. Next day we spent a long, hot, miserable day together, on a boat trip from Westminster to Richmond and back. *My few words last night had no effect because today was just as difficult with Daddy. We will never be friends now... He <u>says</u> he's not going to see me all next week, he's going to work & not even see me off. OH YEAH.*

I suspect it was not just John and Susan's presence, but what they had to say, that helped to make our last evening a happier occasion. *We discussed lots of things but chiefly the family mess-up... Neither John nor Susie likes Pat & they want to get out [of Dartmouth Road] as soon as possible... For once I felt at ease with Dad in the room – John & Susan did that for us... We are on good terms now at last.*

---

[8] *I was applying for a visa as 'Barry', but my birth certificate still showed Bertrand Russell as my father. When I proffered it to the consulate clerk I feared this anomaly might be questioned, and had taken along the Deed Poll in case I needed to explain it, but he simply entered Bertie's name on the application form, so I said nothing. Perhaps Griffin had hoped I would make a point of saying that the birth certificate was incorrect, but I wasn't going to risk any delay in getting my visa.*

Such talk about the family, including open dislike of Pat, would have been music to Griffin's ears. John was still pursuing the campaign he had begun in Washington, to 'bring the family together' (a hopeless task), and it pleased Griffin to feel himself part of 'the family', in John's eyes at least. This was the rather spurious theme on which he and I reached a truce, which would be easier to keep now we no longer had to meet. I didn't see him at all the next day, my last – just a phone call to wish me Bon Voyage for the morrow: 23 August 1947.

Parting from everyone else was terrible. Saying goodbye to Lily was the worst – I had never before seen her cry. The years used to go by more slowly in those days, and 3,000 miles of ocean really was a barrier for people with no money. The miles and years stretching ahead seemed eternity to me, and I wept all the way to Southampton.

Not until that evening, having dinner on the ship, still alongside the quay, did I begin to cheer up. There were bread rolls on the table of a whiteness I had never seen before. My heart quickened to realise I was leaving Austerity England, with its grey 'national loaf' and 'Sorry, dear, no oranges today', and heading for the Land of Plenty.

CHAPTER 19

FLYING FREE AT LAST

Sixty years later, the 'eternity' of my four years in the United States seems like an unimportant slice of my life. They were very formative years, of course; when I came home in 1951, for the only time in my life I felt truly half-American. I had left Kate in Washington DC with her American husband and son; my new best friends were American; and I was half-minded to go back there myself in due course if the opportunity presented itself. But it never did. I started work, resumed old friendships and made new ones. Within a few years, apart from the novelty of American college friends stopping by in the tourist season, I felt as though I'd never been away.

Paradoxically, since he remained so incorrigibly American to the end of his days, my stay in Griffin's homeland had little to do with him. Awaiting me in the Purser's office on the *SS Aquitania*[1] at Southampton was a letter from Mary Vorse containing $5 for a bus ticket to visit her in Provincetown, and in due course I did so. It would be nice to be able to record a series of visits to all Griffin's famous friends in America, but in fact, apart from Mary Vorse, I met only one of them. As a rolling stone all his life Griffin tended to make friends in each new place, keeping up with old ones by occasional meetings rather than correspondence. In the post-war years several of them looked him up in London – I just missed meeting John Dos Passos there, the week before I sailed – but as he grew older, so far from his old haunts in America, his old friendships waned.

The relevance of these four years to my relationship with Griffin is therefore mainly in the maturing process they worked on me – the substance of this

---

[1] *I wrote to Dora on the ship's notepaper, bearing the heading* H.M. Hired Transport "Aquitania". *I made my booking through Cunard, presumably operating the service as a private company, but in fact the liner was still fitted out for its wartime role as a troopship, with two-tier metal bunks in every large space as well as in the cabins. It was packed with GI brides and their offspring en route to their new life in America. My return journey in 1951 on the* Queen Elizabeth *was much more comfortable.*

chapter. In America I felt wonderfully free of family pressures, just as Kate did by choosing to live so far away from England. We were the best of pals in those years, hugging ourselves with glee to be out of 'that family mess', feeling no obligation to any of our parents or step-parents beyond our duty letters home.

Boston and its suburb of Cambridge, where Kate was a graduate student at Radcliffe, was only an hour's bus ride from Providence. Her marriage in 1948 to a fellow student, Charlie Tait, gave both of us the first 'home of our own' we had ever felt comfortable in – even if my share was only their sitting-room sofa. Up to then Kate had had room-and-board jobs in other people's houses, and I vividly remember how proudly she showed me round their first, tiny apartment. How we gloated over domestic life, like a couple of street urchins housed at last! – quite absurd, really, since our home-life with Dora, though scruffy, never lacked the essentials, and Kate had spent years in the elegant homes of her stepmother Peter. Yet we had both grown up greedy for some indefinable *homeliness* missing from our partly-shared childhoods. Our obsession with it nearly drove Charlie mad, as he revealed to Kate (and she told me) only many years later.

While enjoying the freedom and excitement of my new life, I was also very homesick at times, missing Roddy especially 'like an amputated arm'. I soon gave up my diary, but my letters to Dora can supplement my memory. My correspondence with Griffin has not survived. I remember only two specific contacts with him during the whole period: the present he sent for my first

Kate and me – the best of pals

Christmas, the Concise Oxford Dictionary which still stands on my desk in daily use; and the letter he wrote for my lonely eighteenth birthday, spent in rural Connecticut, saying how much he wished he could send me a diamond ring, but unfortunately... *Yes*, I remember thinking, *I wish you could too...* (that ignoble cupboard love again). Probably by then he could no longer afford presents of any kind from his meagre earnings: once his advance for the undelivered book on Ireland was used up, he subsisted on occasional freelance journalism, and a tiny pension from the American government, for the rest of his life.

Freshman year: the dating game

My first year, 1947–48, was understandably a bit chaotic. Intellectually I was more mature than my classmates; socially I felt like a carthorse among all those well-groomed American fillies. With money left by John for that purpose, Kate and I had bought an entire wardrobe for me – described in minute detail, with sketches, to Dora – and spent hours turning up the hems. A few weeks later all this finery was cruelly outmoded when a sudden U-turn in the fashion world, the New Look, decreed calf-length skirts and bouffant petticoats. Another difficulty was my ineptitude at the dating game that came so naturally to other girls in the 'dorm', and here Kate was not much help. One evening she phoned at about 9 p.m. and was puzzled by my embarrassed shame to be discovered at home on a Saturday night (other girls would hide in their rooms and pretend not to hear the phone ringing). She 'had not realised it was Saturday', she said. (*Had not realised!*) Kate was 'a grind', you see – well, all Radcliffe girls were, to us Pembrokers – and could not appreciate the ignominy I was suffering.[2]

So preoccupied was I with 'having fun' that I was in danger of flunking my courses at the end of the first semester. This would have been disastrous as I had to maintain a good average to retain my scholarship. The pattern of an American degree course – at least in those days – was to spend the first two years (Freshman and Sophomore) acquiring a superficial general education, which would encourage sensible choices of what to 'major in' later on. The next two years (Junior and Senior) were largely given over to the chosen specialism and free-choice 'electives'; but opting to do Honours allowed more courses in the specialism. When the time came, I decided to major in History, with Honours, but I was nevertheless able to study almost as much Political Science, and also get a flavour of several other subjects. In later life, comparing this system with the more specialised English university education, I always argued that although ours may suit committed scholars better, the American Liberal Arts degree is well-designed for a larger swathe of intelligent but not seriously academic citizens – including people like me, who in 1947 would probably not

---

[2] *At that time Brown University, with about 3,000 students, plus 900 at Pembroke, its women's college, was a rung below the so-called 'Ivy League' colleges of the eastern seaboard. Since then, its academic reputation, and the size of the student body, has hugely increased. Pembroke is now fully integrated into one large co-educational institution.*

have gone on to any higher education had I stayed in Britain.

Once I got the knack of the system, I began to enjoy my studies greatly. In the first year my extra-curricular life centred round the Glee Club (the college choir), which travelled around giving concerts at other New England campuses. Then I gave it up because 'just enjoying singing' wasn't improving my mind, I wrote to Dora.

At Dartington I had thought myself too frivolous; here I complained of my classmates' ignorance and lack of interest in anything beyond their own immediate experience, until I discovered how little news of the outside world filtered through to the general public. At first I gasped at the food, the gadgets, the luxuries that everyone took for granted – and was shocked to find how soon *I* took them for granted. This was the period of the Marshall Plan, of determined government efforts to remind Americans of their continuing international responsibilities. Film shows of devastated Europe reduced me to tears and paroxysms of guilt, but were quickly shrugged off by young people who had had no direct experience of the recent war. I began to feel even more out of step with most Americans when the first signs of McCarthyism appeared.

Fear of internal subversion by 'reds' and other 'lefties' had begun before 1950, when Senator McCarthy started to exploit it for his own ends. The ground was well prepared by right-wing opposition to the New Deal before the war (see Chapter 12). I first became aware of the changing political atmosphere in the summer of 1948, when I was working as a mother's help for a Catholic family, called La Farge, at their summer home in Connecticut. I was dismayed by their reaction to the Hiss case and other trigger events,[3] but put it down to their ultra-conservative views that I'd already identified and disliked. Soon afterwards I found our old friend Una Corbett, a lifelong teacher in the American school system, castigating Communists in the ranks of her trade union. She may well have been justified, but the snakes in the grass she was describing seemed quite unlike the harmless Communists I knew at home. What on earth was going on?

That was the year when FDR's political heir President Truman was expected to lose to the Republican in the November election, partly because Henry Wallace, who had been a member of the sainted FDR's cabinet, was standing independently as a Progressive. I went to hear Wallace speak on the Brown campus, and as I came away from the meeting I met a large lady of the much-satirised 'clubwoman' type, puffing up the hill. Disappointed to hear from me

---

[3] *In 1948 Alger Hiss, a former State Department official, was accused of being a Communist spy, which he denied. After drawn out proceedings, he was convicted of perjury in 1950 (though he continued to protest his innocence for the rest of his life). American domestic politics was in a state of transition at this time. There was still widespread reverence for President Roosevelt, for 'saving us from the Depression' with his New Deal and then 'saving the world' by winning the war. Truman had inherited this goodwill when FDR died in office in 1945, and against all the odds he won the election of 1948. But the Cold War was now under way, and the tide of public opinion was beginning to turn...*

that she was too late to hear him, she slumped on a low wall, fanning herself, and explained that she'd just come to check out this guy Wallace. 'Is he for this country, or agin it?' As yet unused to American politics, I was shocked that a former cabinet minister, however unwelcomely liberal, could be seen as agin his own country.

In the summer of 1948 Kate had taken Charlie to England to meet the family. I was lonely and unhappy with the uncongenial La Farges. On my days off I used to bike several miles to sit alone on the beach, despising the brownish water of Long Island Sound. The only bright spot was a weekend visit to New York – knocked for six by my first sight of the skyscraper city (as who is not?), and delighting in the company of the first friend with whom I had common ground. Dinah Lauterbach had been born in England and had even attended a progressive school in London, King Alfred, before emigrating to the United States in 1940. She loved her new home city, and I could see its magic too. I hoped I'd get back there before I went home... (I did).[4]

Me with Mary Vorse

When Kate and Charlie came home, we went to Provincetown for two days to see Mary Vorse. How I loved that place, and Mary's house, and the *blue* sea, just like Cornwall. Did I have a subconscious memory of the holiday I'd spent on the Cape at the age of three? Mary wasn't at home that summer of 1933, and we had stayed at Truro, with Mary's friend Susan Glaspell. Now Susan had just died, in July 1948, leaving Mary the undisputed *grande dame* of the artistic

In front of Mary's house, on a later visit

---

[4] *I had missed the traditional first sight of New York from the deck of a ship because the* Aquitania *had docked at Halifax, Nova Scotia. From there I travelled by train to Boston, where Kate met me. Transatlantic passages were so scarce at that time, you didn't argue about where you landed.*

community graced by both of them since early in the twentieth century.[5] Provincetown had a fascinating earlier history too, as I learned from Mary's own book *Time and the Town*.[6] Bearing an inscription from Mary, 'with much love, Christmas 1950', that book is a cherished souvenir of Provincetown – of my visits, and the many times Griffin went there too.

Before returning to college I also had a week in Baltimore, Maryland, staying with Una Corbett and her daughter Joy, who had been a pupil at Beacon Hill until 1939, and was now a librarian. They showed me the sights of Washington DC, and urged me to come again. I did return later, when Kate and Charlie had moved their home, including my space in their sitting-room, to Washington. In 1949 they both gave up their PhD studies and Charlie got a job in the US State Department. This enabled them to start a family, and their first son, David, was born in 1951.

My visit to the Corbetts also had Griffin connections. They had known him in the old days, and Una now gave me a book from her shelf, inscribing it to Roddy and me: *Father And His Town*, by our uncle Richard Barry. In 1948 all I knew about Griffin's older brother Richard was that they had quarrelled a long time ago, and were no longer in touch. What a pity. I now know that he was probably still alive at this date, and thus I missed my only chance to meet another American Barry.[7]

* * *

My second year of dormitory life was more settled and satisfactory. I had a grip on the academic work, and a steady boyfriend, Wally Holbrook, made to measure for my requirements. He not only had some knowledge of the outside world but had been there – even to London – on overseas service. Many Brown students at that time were beneficiaries of the 'GI Bill of Rights' which gave free higher education to ex-servicemen, and we were a lucky generation of college girls who could choose these older, wiser boyfriends over spotty-faced youths of our own age. Wally and I went square-dancing every week, on outings with the International Society, and took each other home to be inspected. In

---

[5] *Frank Crotty's* Provincetown Profiles And Others on Cape Cod, *published in 1958 (Barre Gazette, Massachusetts), gives a whole reverential chapter to 'Mother Vorse' and her adventurous history.*

[6] *Mary Heaton Vorse,* Time and the Town: a Provincetown Chronicle *(The Dial Press, NY, 1942).*

[7] *I did not give Richard's book my full attention until I embarked on this project, when despite his fanciful style, it proved to be very useful for Chapter 3. A reference in a wartime letter from Griffin shows that he sent us a copy when it was published, in 1941, but this seems to have got lost. So this dedicated copy, 'with happy memories, from Una and Joy', is the only one in my possession. The* New York Times *of 24 May 1946 contains a brief obituary of Richard's wife Elizabeth, who had just died, aged 69. From the reference to 'her husband's latest work' (a historical biography), and no mention of any children, it is likely that Richard was still alive in 1948, and presumably died childless.*

Wally's honour, so to speak, Kate arranged for me to be fitted with a diaphragm, the preferred method of contraception in those days. In puritanical Massachusetts this was only legal for married women, but gynaecologists would make an exception for 'fiancées' about to tie the knot. 'And when is the happy day?' asked the white-robed figure, at my most undignified moment. 'December 15th', I replied without a blush.

I was dogged by financial problems. Earning pocket-money was easy enough: the college had a Placement Office matching up students with employers needing part-time help (including departments of the university), and for summer jobs too. But Dora was finding it increasingly difficult to pay my room and board fees, and the Bursar made my life a misery over unpaid dues. It was clear at the end of my Sophomore year that I'd have to take a room-and-board job for my last two years.

Sophomore year: with Wally Holbrook

Meanwhile, for the summer of 1949 I decided on the most popular summer job for college girls – waitressing at a resort, where off-duty hours could be spent on the beach. Ogunquit, Maine was a delightful small town with a white sandy beach and craggy rocks – physically quite like Cornwall, though without the special magic of the Cape. The weather was poor that year, and our earnings were disappointing, but the swimming was great. Wally came up to visit, and I pressurised him to stay on as company for me, though the only job he could get was ill-paid dishwashing.

During the following year – his last, as he was a year ahead of me – we drifted apart. Thereafter my male escorts were platonic companions, like the Englishman I came across in my final year, Bob Haythornthwaite, who had come for a year's graduate work in Brown's renowned Engineering Department. (He later emigrated back there with his English wife.)

Having no steady boyfriend was a distinct disadvantage during my Junior year. I was now living a longish bike-ride from the campus, working for the Whitaker family, and with other pocket-money jobs; no longer in the swim of campus life. The two dorms I had lived in were both old, clapboard houses on suburban streets near all the facilities of the Brown campus, where classes were held. Dorm life was socially restricted – we had to be in by 10 p.m. except for a ration of 'late nights' – but companionable. Now I was free of all that, but lonely.

I had chosen the Whitakers as a soft option because their children were school-age, but it was a mistake. To them I was a substitute maid, eating alone in the kitchen, with my own (palatial) quarters on the top floor of the house. For Christmas they gave me grander presents than anyone in my family could afford, and I hated them for it. 'Not that they were unkind to me', I wrote to Dora when that painful year was over, 'but because they were so bloody well-off and over-privileged and stuffy and ignorant and self-satisfied and unaware of anything important in life.' Eating in the kitchen rankled, as you can see. But Mrs Whitaker made wonderful brownies, and I was grateful to her husband for being well-insured. When my venerable bike was stolen that winter, he recovered the princely sum of $40 for me, which I badly needed. But I missed the bike. I'd brought it all the way from England, and it was probably the only adult bike in Providence. In America in those days, bikes were just toys for kids, who at 16 leapt straight into the family car, and soon acquired their own 'jalopy'.

There were academic pressures too, that year, and before it was over I was running to sympathetic adults for help. My tutor allowed me to take an 'Incomplete' in his course (completed with an essay written later in the Library of Congress, now Kate and Charlie's 'local'). Then the English-Speaking Union stumped up $300 to enable me to take up an eight-week 'internship' at the United Nations in the summer of 1950. What luck! There were about thirty of us, from all over the world. We lived at Columbia University in New York City, travelling out each day to the UN's temporary home at Lake Success for a mixed menu of instruction, discussion and 'work experience'. I worked in the NGO section (Non-Governmental Organisations) of the Department of Public Information. The other interns were mainly destined for government jobs in their home countries: Marjan Smole, for example, a handsome Serb, whose address in Belgrade translated as 25 Charlie Chaplin Street. As a trainee diplomat his second language had been Russian until 1948, when Tito's Jugoslavia broke with the Soviet Union (another key event of the Cold War). 'Now', he told me with a sly smile, 'we must all learn Engleesh.'

On the intern programme we had some free time to trail around New York unorganised. By this time I had two Pembroke friends who lived there: as well as Dinah, I had discovered a soul-mate in Lesley Davison, whose family

Lesley and me

A MAN OF SMALL IMPORTANCE

Intern programme at the United Nations, summer 1950

The whole group at Lake Success

We met Eleanor Roosevelt, a strong supporter of the UN…

…and were taught how to eat water-melon by our American hosts.

With Marjan, the handsome Serb…

…and other friends I made at the UN: one from Pakistan, two from Ethiopia.

background overlapped mine. Her father Edward (Teddie) was English, a poet and university teacher, and her mother Natalie a New Yorker. They didn't exactly know Dora but they knew *of* her; Lesley and her brother Peter had been to a mildly progressive school in America, and we all had a similar outlook on life.

The Davisons also knew a friend of Griffin's, the novelist Dawn Powell, whom Lesley and I visited once in Greenwich Village. Teddie and Natalie were my new Bill and Marsie – I fell for the whole family, and their home became my favourite place to be. Lesley was (is) a talented song-writer, and we were all mad about music. Having stood behind the stalls to see the original production of *Guys And Dolls* in 1951, we played the album over and over until I knew the words and every inflection of every song off by heart. For me it remains the best-ever American musical, *West Side Story* notwithstanding.

Teddie and Natalie Davison

By that time I also knew the United Nations Charter off by heart. The main studies of my final two years were far apart on the historical spectrum: American colonial history for my tutor Edmund S Morgan, then at the beginning of his distinguished career; and International Government with Leland M Goodrich, whose academic fame was already well-established. As an acknowledged expert on the UN's predecessor the League of Nations, he had helped to write the Charter which, it was hoped, would give the new peace-keeping body more 'teeth' than the ill-fated League. I hoped so too! It seems almost comical to recall it now, but in a brief moment of post-war optimism it really did seem possible 'to save succeeding generations from the scourge of war', as the UN Charter promised. At any rate I thought so, and resolved to do my bit to help the cause just as soon as I could...[8]

My final year at Brown was one of happy fulfilment in every sphere except romance. Better than a boyfriend, however, was the discovery of another soul-mate who has remained a best friend ever since. Judy Brown was also doing

---

[8] *In fact that moment when the UN might have 'worked' was already long past. By 1950, with the Korean War in progress and a nuclear arms race under way,* realpolitik *was ruling the world again. With the idealism of youth I did not realise what was obvious to me later when I came to teach and write about this period as History.*

History Honours, and we spent hours talking over shared courses, analysing the teaching of our professors, sizing up our chances with this or that fellow-student. Mostly we gossiped on street corners or in the campus coffee-bar, as Judy was living in a dorm and I with another family. In contrast to the previous year, my situation with the Barretts could not have been happier. John was a family paediatrician; Mary, apart from Quakerly good works in the city, was fully occupied with her three boys and baby Betsy, born during that year. The older boys sometimes gave me a hard time, but my special charge and delight was roly-poly Charlie, aged about two when I joined the household. His party piece was spinning round the living-room to *Goodnight Irene* on the record-player, until he collapsed in fits of giggles. I've long since lost track of all the Barrett descendants, but I felt a million years old when Mary's Christmas round-up of news in 1999 included the birth of *Charlie's first grandchild*.

In spite of the extra pressure of my Honours thesis, I enjoyed my academic work that year. Again in contrast to the English system, the American degree is an accumulation of 'credits', so that the last year is not a terrifying build-up to Finals but simply another set of courses, by this time all or mostly in the chosen specialism. In due course I graduated with the usual ceremonies, recorded fittingly for me with a photograph at the open-air dance on the Brown campus, which includes Barnaby and Mary Keeney alongside Judy, Lesley and me. The Keeneys were another family I came to know well. They lived near the Barretts, and the two Marys were friends. I used to baby-sit for them too, and once went away with them to some seaside place, I forget where. Barney was a History professor, who was appointed Dean of the Graduate School that year, and later became President of the University.

The degree I was awarded in June 1951 – *Magna (*not *Summa) cum Laude*, with High (not Highest) Honours in History – now seems to me an accurate assessment of my academic worth. Nothing to be ashamed of, nor to boast about either. Most parents would have been proud of this B+ daughter, triumphantly bringing home the prized BA in 1951. And I believe Dora *was*; she was my lifelong admirer, always exaggerating my talents because they were different from hers. But to my exacting father, I would discover, I was still a grave disappointment.

Before I went home to all that, however, I had a glorious last fling in America. With my passage home in September safely booked, I was footloose and fancy free in New York City. Once again fortune smiled, and bestowed on me a temporary job at the United Nations and a dinky little apartment all to myself – on Madison Avenue, no less! The job was in the NGO section where I'd worked as an intern, replacing an employee on home leave. The apartment was a sub-let of a sub-let: its official tenant had been recalled into the Army by the Korean War, and his replacement had fled the city for the summer, as many

New Yorkers do. But the heat didn't bother me; the new UN building on the East River was air-conditioned, and my little apartment had a big window opening onto a balcony, too high above the street to worry about burglars. It was a one-room flat with a miniscule bathroom, and a kitchen that folded away behind panelled wooden doors; more rent than I could really afford, but with my ticket home already paid for by Dora, how could I resist?

Romantic Judy Brown was my main companion that summer, cementing our friendship with magic moments like my 21st birthday on Jones Beach that she's been reminding me of ever since. Those days were especially poignant for Judy: she was in love with her handsome Brazilian boyfriend, whom she didn't marry but remembered ever afterwards with wistful regret. Like me she was in her first job, working for a tennis magazine – not that she had any interest in journalism; she just liked tennis. For both of us that time was an interlude of blissful irresponsibility. Looking ahead, we felt like those kids in the ad for Startrite shoes: two toddlers setting off hand in hand down a long winding road leading...where?

Judy Brown, 1953 – two years after graduating

Judy is a born and bred New Yorker, with a family history typical of that city – indeed so archetypal of 'the American experience' that it makes a neat conclusion to my American chapter. Her father had come from Russia in 1912, at the peak of the huge wave of immigration from eastern and southern Europe which upset the balance of the hitherto mainly WASP population. Though only 16 himself, he helped other members of his family over, including a younger brother who later died (the ones left behind he never saw again). Starting out as a delivery boy, he worked his way up to become a successful restaurateur, from which he had just retired when I came to know Judy. Her older sister was already a medical doctor, and Judy in her later career became the other kind, a PhD.

The American Dream fulfilled? So I always thought, but when I put that to Judy recently, she pointed out the flaws in the picture. In fact she wrote her History thesis at Brown on what she saw as the *myth* of the American Dream, partly with her own family in mind: 'I felt there was some fundamental lie about the pursuit of wealth and success, and my father was a victim of it.' He was a loving father, a kind and much-respected employer; but he was also the classic workaholic, so immersed in the business that as a child, Judy only saw him on Sunday mornings. Weekends were his busiest time – which meant no Friday evening *Shabbes* or Saturday synagogue to bind their daughters into their Jewish heritage, to which Judy paid little attention. Her father didn't mind that, having lost interest in religion himself over the years. When she later married a WASP, her parents were a little uneasy; but they were consoled by the fact that David was a doctor.

So there were losses as well as gains for the family in the achievement of worldly success. As a boy in Russia, her father had been a Talmudic scholar, a Cohen or 'holy man' perhaps destined for the rabbinate, which his own father no doubt hoped he would achieve in America. Instead he became converted to American materialism, and excelled in the practice of it.

Goodbye America!

From left: Lesley Davison, Mary Keeney, Judy Brown, Barnaby Keeney, me

Kate and Charlie with David Tait, born March 1951

The Barrett family

Graduation night, June 1951

If I'd known how long it would take me to get back to America, I might have shed more tears as I waved goodbye to everyone in 1951. When I arrived there in 1947 I knew I was going to enjoy myself but I didn't expect to *like* the place so much. For people like us, left-liberal in politics and priding ourselves on our cultural values, Hollywood and an often crass foreign policy project an unattractive image of America – the very last place you'd want to live. But as everyone who goes there discovers, America is not 'one nation' but the most diverse society in the world, where anyone can find soul-mates and a lifestyle to suit themselves. I tended to forget that in later years, constantly confronted by 'the image' and with only fading memories of my own experience to counteract it. Yet I'm glad I didn't follow Kate's path, pining for England through half a lifetime in America until at last she could come home to live.

I'd like to have re-visited more often, though. My visit in 1981, to attend the Thirtieth Reunion of our Class, was the first chance to see my college friends in their adult lives at home. They were still rooted there when I went again in 2001. Lesley lives in New York's theatreland, where she and her husband make their living, Dinah on the nineteenth floor of one of those slab apartment blocks. Her pretty little cat of 1981, like many New York felines, had been de-clawed to protect the furniture, and of course never went out to scratch the bark of the tiny trees I could see down by the main entrance. Twenty years later the trees had grown – quite a lush display, by metropolitan standards. But my thoughts were the same, comparing that concrete world with the trees and fields outside my window at home: '*I couldn't live here in a million years...*'

Judy had moved out to leafy Tenafly to bring up her children. This is the more typical homeground of affluent Americans: spacious houses screened from the road by flowering shrubs, the local supermarket with a display of variety and quality that in 1981 hadn't yet reached England (but soon would).

For the Reunion that year we drove up to Providence to be thrilled – dismayed – appalled in turn, by what had happened since we were last there. It was sad to find the old clapboard houses of colonial Providence, an area for cheap student lodgings in our day, now spruced up as Heritage sites, some with their interiors on view on payment of a fee at the door. Around the university the familiar topography had been altered by new buildings as Brown progressed up the academic status ladder (a process relentlessly continuing in the new millennium, I noted on my brief visit in 2001 to the Barretts, now both octogenarians). But what really saddened Judy and me in 1981 was the vandalised state of the common rooms and dorms, like any inner-city playground in England or America, and every open space bristling with brown-uniformed 'campus cops'. So different from the 'gracious living' Dean Nancy Duke Lewis had told us was part of our Pembroke education! Now that students were treated as adults, it seemed they could only behave like children. We preferred to remember the place as it looked when you had to be home by ten.

CHAPTER 20

STILL TRYING TO GROW UP

I remember my homecoming in September 1951 vividly. I was childishly pleased that both Dora and Griffin came to meet me at Waterloo Station, their joint effort seeming to make us the 'normal family' I still secretly yearned for. (Roddy was not there, however; at that time he was engrossed in left-wing student politics and was away in Poland or East Germany at one of the 'peace congresses' typical of the times.) We had an evening meal at Dora's new home in Hampstead, and then much excited chatter until Griffin returned to his modest bed-sit nearby, arranging to meet me again next day. During the night I awoke with the worst throbbing headache I've ever had in my life. Not knowing where to find an aspirin, I staggered into the bathroom for a wet cloth to hold over my eyes until I eventually fell back into slumber. How symbolic, I reflected later, of all the family headaches I had returned to.

Dora's and Roddy's circumstances had changed drastically in my absence. The Dartmouth Road household had broken up soon after I left, when the landlord reclaimed the house. John and Susan had gone to start their family life in Richmond; Lily and Walter to a place of their own in north London; Dora, Roddy and Pat to a family home I never knew, in the Baker Street area. There, Pat had died in 1949. At some date Roddy had abandoned the idea of making cricket his career, and Dora had coaxed him through a 'cramming school' in London to acquire the qualifications for higher education. He was now a student of Sociology and Economics at Regent Street Polytechnic (today the University of Central London), living with Dora in the old-fashioned walk-up flat at 18 Manor Mansions, Belsize Grove, to which they had moved after Pat's death. It had a small bedroom for me too.

True to form, Griffin had never finished the book on Ireland. The bylines on three articles about Ulster and the southern Republic tell their own story. In August 1949 he was 'gathering material for a forthcoming book'; by June 1951 he was 'an American newspaperman now living in London'. Occasional commisions from US journals like *The Nation*, where these articles appeared, were now his only source of income, supplemented by a tiny pension for his past work for the US government. He was always desperately poor. I'm sure every friend who came within hailing distance was touched for a loan. His never-paid debts may well have included arrears of rent as he moved (suspiciously often) from one bed-sit to another. A year before my return, Roddy had tried to negotiate a rented room for him in Dora's flat – a noble but doomed attempt at diplomacy, pitifully documented by a letter from Griffin that survives in Dora's correspondence. One remark among the usual 'green ink' passages strikes a chord with me. If she would agree to let him come, he begged, 'I think the children will benefit through all their future, in deep ways impossible to foresee, by seeing that their parents can behave like old friends who do not hate the sight of one another.' He was right. That's all I had really wanted since Griffin's re-appearance in my life in 1946, and was still hoping for when they welcomed me home together in 1951. If only they could forget that old quarrel and just be friends! I had thought, having no idea at that time how bitterly unforgettable 'that old quarrel' was. For Dora, at any rate, the burden of the past was too heavy – or perhaps she knew Griffin too well, fearing she would end up supporting him in his frail old age. She refused him a room in her flat; and who can blame her?

Of course Griffin wanted more than casual friendship from us, his children. Having failed to find a warm hearth with Dora, alone and almost friendless in a country he always disliked, we were his only source of emotional succour. I'm afraid I gave him very little. In the first few weeks, trying consciously to behave like an adult instead of the sulky schoolgirl of 1947, I visited him quite often in his room near Dora's flat. He still yearned to 'get to know me', and now that I was 21, with a university degree to my name, he expected to discuss *intellectual* matters, not the trivia of daily life. I felt like a butterfly under the microscope, aware that my feeble brain would yield only butterfly thoughts to his eager scrutiny. These tête-à-têtes with Griffin were always a painful reminder that I was not as clever as he wished me to be.

I felt burdened with guilt in other ways too. This pathetic old man was my father, my own flesh and blood – why could I not love him and care for him as any daughter *should*? One person who did show him the compassion he deserved was his friend Frederika, who from that time became a friend of all of us. She was a distant relation of Mary Vorse, but German, whose marriage to a minor aristocrat in her own country had made her Countess von Waldburg. Her husband had died during the war and she had fled from eastern Germany, ending up in England a penniless refugee. At this time she was working as a housekeeper for the family of a well-known psychoanalyst, Edward Glover, and used to bring left-overs of the delicious food she cooked for his household to sustain Griffin. One evening as I came away from visiting him, I met Frederika on her way there with a Kilner jar of creamed chicken in the basket of her bicycle. I made some complaint about Griffin's interrogations, and I've always remembered what she said: 'Remember, you and Roddy are his immortality.' I know she meant it kindly – she was trying to explain old age to callow youth – but I took the remark as a gentle rebuke for my undaughterly behaviour, and felt ashamed.

Griffin and Frederika visiting John and Dora in Cornwall, early 1950s

Ironically, since he must have envied me my niche in Dora's flat, I couldn't wait to get out of it. Within days of my arrival, I hated being there. The whole place seemed dark and gritty from the coal-fired boiler in the kitchen, crammed with books and possessions from the larger homes that had preceded it. Worse than the physical discomfort, however, was my resentful irritation to find myself sliding back into helpless dependency on Dora. But I couldn't leave until I had an income to pay rent elsewhere. As soon as I had, just as she had arranged my escape to America against the grain of her own wishes, it was Dora herself who found someone at her office looking for a flat-mate.[1] Early in 1952 I moved across town to 4 Redcliffe Square, Earl's Court: my first independent home, where I lived happily with a succession of flat-sharers for the next three and a half years. Situated on the other side of London, I could see less of Griffin – and felt much relieved.

The job which sustained my new life as a gal about town was tailor-made for me. For a weekly wage of £6.10 shillings – rising by three annual increments to £8 – I became the first Youth Officer of the United Nations Association of Great Britain and Northern Ireland. My task was to publicise the work of the UN and its agencies and to recruit young members for the organisation – badly needed by local branches whose members were mostly stalwarts of the pre-war League of Nations Union (as were several of the staff at our London headquarters). The natural recruiting ground for the Youth Sections of local branches that I began to form was UNA's vigorous semi-independent schools branch, the Council for Education in World Citizenship (CEWC), and part of my job was to help with its work. So as well as travelling

---

[1] *Dora's wartime civil service job had ended during my absence; I'm not sure exactly when. At this time she had an administrative job at the head office of Marks and Spencers, thanks to the good offices of Eric Estorick, whose other benefactions to our family I noted earlier (in Chapters 17 and 18).*

the country to attend committees and speak at meetings – seeing cities and hamlets of my native land completely new to me – I also found myself assisting CEWC's study tours abroad, and the annual four-day Christmas Holiday Lectures in London, which attracted big-name speakers and hundreds of schoolchildren from all over the country. I couldn't have written myself a better agenda for a first job – and that wage provided quite a gay life, at a time when tube fares were paid in pennies and theatre tickets in shillings. UNA's head office was in Charles Street, Mayfair, ideally placed to explore the West End after work, so far as funds would allow.

An international student conference in Holland, 1953

With my fellow leader Michael Stephens on a canal boat

Redcliffe Square, Earl's Court, was similar to neighbouring South Kensington, a world away from bohemian Hampstead. So was my life there, and most of my flat-mates. The rent of our cavernous furnished apartment was £1 or £1.10s each, depending on whether there were two or three of us, paid weekly to the ancient landlord who lived on the ground floor. He was notoriously mean, a sucker for the burglar who gained entry to the flat one afternoon on the pretence of 'assessing bomb-damage for compensation claims' (a widespread ruse at the time). The old boy politely led the thief through every flat, limping along one room behind while he grabbed everything of value in sight. A few weeks later the miscreant was caught, but unfortunately he'd disposed of his loot, including the partners of all the single earrings I'd been saving since he rifled my dressing-table.

We had two huge rooms and a small one, all used as bed-sits; a bright kitchen at the back; and a dingy bathroom overlooking the side alley, with an evil-smelling gas geyser that had to be adjusted 'just right' to trickle hot water into the rusty bath. If not 'just right', it would explode with a shower of verdigris fragments and flaking paint. American visitors were horrified by that contraption, but they loved the brass knocker on our flat-door, bearing a head of Abraham Lincoln and a stanza of the Gettysburg Address. In spite of its gloomy Edwardian furnishings and sagging bedsteads, I was sorry to leave that flat when the time came.

Not long after my appointment, Caroline Carter came to work for CEWC, and through her my working and personal lives became mingled. Her family moved in liberal-progressive circles overlapping mine; in fact Roddy and I had met her and her sister Jane on a sailing holiday with mutual friends, the Pritchards, in 1946. Now we all got to know each other better. One summer holiday I stayed with her parents, then living in Paris, where her father was working for UNESCO, and felt I had found another 'perfect couple' to admire as I had idolised the Currys at Dartington and the Davisons in New York.

Caroline became Roddy's girlfriend for a while and then, in 1957, she married our Dartington school-friend Lukas Heller. By then Lukas had embarked on his career as a Hollywood scriptwriter – a big leap for the lad about town I had known when I first returned to London, zooming around in an old black taxi-cab, the kind where the driver sat outside, all muffled up (and icy cold for the passengers too). But it was more secure than the extraordinary three-wheeler, nicknamed The Bug, that Roddy and Lukas's old Dartington mate Mickey Neville was running at that time. It was so close to the ground that I remember wondering, peering out at the hub-nuts of a bus as we waited at traffic lights, can the driver see us from way up there? My American friend Lesley had good reason to remember that car. She came to live in London for a year or so in 1953–54, staying part of the time with me, and was foolhardy enough to accept a lift to Paris with Mickey. When The Bug overturned on the road to Dover she came back, bedraggled but uninjured (though her guitar was), to make a new start in more reliable transport.

Apart from the Carter–Barry connections, I tried to maintain a certain distance between my life in Earl's Court and my Hampstead family. The gap was partly political. Though full of indignation about the social injustices all around me, I had already acquired the aloof scepticism that has kept me from joining any political party at any time in my life. The nearest I ever came to it was when my on/off boyfriend of this period took me to a Young Liberals coffee morning and I donated one shilling to their funds. In fact I worried about my inability to feel 'committed' to any distinct cause. I only knew what I was against, and one of these things was Communism (another was Conservatism, of course).

Roddy was still a Communist (he did not leave the Party until the great exodus of 1956), but that did not matter; our relationship was unconnected with politics. Griffin's views, also very left-wing, were moulded by his earlier life in America and his travels in the world, which I knew little about at that time. He liked to argue politics, as he liked to argue everything; but these discussions tended to bore rather than offend me – which of course offended *him*. It was really Dora's brand of didactic ranting and raving – the 'Communist front' politics of a fervent campaigner – that I could not stand. She was now deeply involved in opposing the Cold War and the arms race by every means available to her: speaking, writing and attending international conferences which, however laudable their declared aims, were always tainted by (usually hidden) Communist sponsorship. The East–West divide in world politics was much deplored in UNA circles too – it was undermining United Nations work and every other attempt at international cooperation – but our mantle of respectability and 'non-party political' stance allowed little more than hand-wringing on the sidelines. Such passivity was not enough for the likes of Dora!

At the time I might have 'explained' my antagonism to Dora in these terms; but in truth it was more personal than political. I was still trying to free myself from her domineering influence, which smothered her sons even more than her daughters. Roddy made his break too at about this time, staying briefly with me until he found a room with Tana Sayers, an American refugee from McCarthyism who became a lifelong friend. Roddy's 'defection' from the maternal home, following on from mine, caused a huge row with Dora. She rightly pointed out how uneconomic it was for three of us to live separately in one city. One of her ploys was to suggest that I should take over the Manor Mansions flat – an idea 'that makes me go hot under the collar even to <u>contemplate</u>', I wrote in a long, frantic letter, risking further wrath from her, and more guilt for me, though I larded it with protestations of love and admiration.

This letter, preserved by Dora, is revealing. 'The one thing I have over here in bourgeois Kensington', I wrote, 'is the thing I treasure above all else and which I guard with animal ferocity: independence of the family entanglements and freedom to live my stuffy conventional life which I know seems as meaningless to you & Roddy (and to Daddy) as your way of life seems to me.' Did any of them ever make such accusations? Surely not. No, this is *my* view of my life in Earl's Court, not theirs. Even then, I half-realised that these few years were an untypical interlude in the rest of my life, but at the time I badly needed that difference. 'Bourgeois Kensington' and all it stood for was my declaration of independence from the Russell–Barry family and all *it* stood for.

* * *

After three years I began to tire of my job at UNA, and had reached the ceiling of my salary. Although secretly I thought of Work only as an intermediate stage before marriage and a family (as I hardly dared admit to Dora), it seemed I should be looking for A Career. The civil service was the obvious choice. So I answered an advertisement, bought a hat for the interview, and in due course found myself accepted as a trainee Inspector of Factories for the then Ministry of Labour. When I was notified that my first posting would be Ashton under Lyne, I had to look it up on the map. In May 1955, with considerable apprehension, I moved 'up north'.

A UNA Youth Camp I organised at Hendon, NW London, August 1954; (right) me and my trusty assistant Gerry McGuigan.

My new work was a revelation in every way. Growing up in an arty-lefty sub-group of the middle class, I not only knew nothing of working-class Britain but had hardly met anyone connected with business life or the satanic mills which in those days still powered the British economy. It was high time to learn how the other half lived, and Ashton under Lyne, a red-brick mill town in eastern Greater Manchester, was a good place to start. Our District took in several contiguous towns spreading out into Lancashire and Cheshire, even to Glossop in Derbyshire. It had a wide spectrum of large and small industry, ideal for a trainee inspector. Some of my fellow probationers in more uniform industrial areas never saw a cotton mill or a dye works or a boiler factory. We used to meet to compare notes on training days and the occasional longer sessions where we learned the Factory Acts and trade regulations in which we had to pass examinations to become fully-fledged H M Inspectors. The rest of the time we were 'on the beat', and for most of us juniors that meant on foot. There were usually two or three inspectors to a district, of varying experience.

Then, and in later years, I was often quizzed by curious outsiders about my 'unusual' job. In fact, women factory inspectors were not a rarity; there had been many in the service, at all levels, since the first was appointed in 1893. When you think of the number of women employed in factories, then and ever afterwards, that is as it should be. Nor was it necessary to have a scientific or technical background: arts graduates could be taught as much as general inspectors needed to know. Like general practioners in the medical world, who refer special problems to specialists, so we called in Chemical or Engineering Inspectors when the need arose.

What I enjoyed most in that first posting was being shown the variety of local industrial processes. How else would I ever have learned how a felt hat is shaped, or a rubber tube extruded? And I was just in time to see every stage of the cotton industry, already dying from a flood of cheap imports (the beginnings of the global economy, though we didn't realise it then). What I remember most clearly are the solitary, trudging afternoons, ticking off a series of 'rabbits' for my end-of-week reports. That was our jargon for the various small workshops, often the back room or basement of a butcher's or baker's or coffin-maker's in the High Street – all legally 'factories' if they employed anyone a few hours a week. The summer of 1955, when I was learning my new trade, was unusually hot. Never shall I forget the little backstreet tripe factories with their heaps of steaming waste in the cobbled yard...

My five years in the Factory Inspectorate were an education for me. But I would never have made a good inspector. Just as in private life I could not bear quarrels or any 'unpleasantness', so I lacked the pugilistic instinct to take on factory owners, the abusers of workers' welfare, the sly avoiders of safety regulations. And the energetic inspectors who wanted to do

HM Inspector of Factories: writing up reports on Friday afternoon

so were shackled by our bureaucracy. The only effective technique I saw demonstrated, notably by the two women district inspectors I worked for, was the nuisance technique: coaxing, pestering, bullying and shaming recalcitrant employers until eventually they would improve conditions just to get the inspector off their back. Prosecutions were rare, red tape rampant, Higher Authority always over-cautious. My last boss retired early out of frustration when she couldn't take action against a notorious large firm over asbestos dust problems from which workers are dying today, and which were well known to be dangerous then. In some ways being a factory inspector was like working for UNA – much hand-wringing on the sidelines, but very difficult to make an impact.

Socially, Ashton under Lyne had little to offer me. Having started out in a spare room over the bar of a pub, shared with crates of lemonade and potato crisps, I was delighted when my boss found a little boarding house in his home village which had a vacancy. Marple, in Cheshire, had hills and woods and a marvellous aqueduct over a steep valley – one of those stretches of natural beauty you find within a stone's throw of satanic mills all over the North. It was connected by suburban railway to Manchester, stopping en route at Ashton and other places on my beat. At 'Aldersyde' there were two other lodgers, young bachelors, besides me. John was an engineer, engrossed in building himself a fibreglass car; Leslie was fixated on the Hallé Orchestra, which pleased our landlady, Ray, because her husband was a bit of a stay-at-home. We had little to talk about at mealtimes. I remember one heated discussion, when I defended reading a book as a valid form of recreation. John thought novels were 'not real life' and therefore a waste of time; when not building his car he went walking in the nearby hills. But I got on well with Ray, who was glad of some female company. The main discomfort was the cold in my top-floor room, which a small electric fire could not dispel. I wrote a lot of lonely letters in that room, and even tried my hand at a piece for the *Manchester Guardian*, rejected with a kindly letter. I believe it was that rejection that finally banished the idea, always lurking at the back of my mind, that I might one day be a writer.

In fact I did have a few contacts up there: the mother of a London friend, whom I stayed with at West Kirby, on the Wirral, and one or two friends of friends in Manchester. Vincent Crotty and his wife, from Dublin, were living close to a large mental hospital near Huddersfield, where Vincent was a consultant, and Mary also worked locally. I visited them several times, writing long letters to Dora relaying Vincent's advice about John. In 1953 John had begun his descent into schizophrenia, from which he never recovered. His marriage had fallen apart and Bertie and his fourth wife, Edith, had taken charge of the three little girls – Susan's daughter Anne and their own Sarah and Lucy. Dora was now battling on all fronts to get medical help for John, and access for him to his children, at the same time trying to keep herself afloat economically. It was a desperately worrying time for her. My letters show concern and occasional financial help; but I remember how glad I was *not* to be on call in London to help with this new set of family problems (later I was, and did).

I am rather surprised to find, from my letters that she kept, how warm and frank my relationship with Dora was at this time. In later years I became much more critical of her, and belatedly more sympathetic towards long-dead Griffin. At 25 there was no doubt where my loyalties lay, though I was determined to live my own life, as any 25-year-old should be. A letter of January 1956 apologises at length for being 'grumpy and often snappy' during the Christmas holiday, and goes on to explain how being at Manor Mansions gave me the feeling of 'slipping back into childhood and helplessness'. 'Ever since I went to America this business of being Independent has been supremely important, and I have to maintain it to keep happy.' Other letters full of adolescent soul-searching must have shown her I was not as grown up as I pretended; but I still valued her as an adviser and was ready to confide my innermost feelings, even my guilt about Griffin.

> I have never 'worked things out' with Daddy & I don't think I ever shall – my antipathy towards him continues & I think it is much deeper than any resentment I ever felt towards you. I suppose Freud would have something to say about that! Anyway I feel I shall never be 'reconciled' to Daddy and it is a source of bitterness to him, I know, and of guilt to me which I feel I shall carry with me all my life.

Before the end of 1955 my social life began to improve when Roddy joined me 'up north'. He had finally graduated – a little late, having had to repeat a year when he nearly got thrown out because he'd been putting all his energies into the NUS (National Union of Students). Dora had pleaded with the Poly high-ups to give him another chance, and they did. Now, after being automatically deferred while a student, he faced two years of National Service. He had decided to put forward a conscientious objection to military service. This allowed successful appellants – those whose plea was accepted as genuinely 'conscientious', not mere cowardice – to serve their country for the required two years in some other 'approved occupation'. Instead of the usual grounds of convinced pacifism, however, Roddy offered a different argument: he was not a total pacifist, and would not have been a Conscientious Objector in the war against Hitler, but he could not serve in an army prepared to use *nuclear* weapons. If his objection was allowed, he added, he proposed to spend his two years as a coal-miner – a kind of latter day 'Bevin Boy'.[2]

---

[2] *During the Second World War coal-miners were so badly needed that Minister of Labour Ernest Bevin organised a force of 'Bevin Boys' to help. Their names were chosen by lot from conscripts called up for military service. Most Conscientious Objectors worked in agriculture or teaching (we had several COs at Dartington), or in non-combatant roles such as ambulance-driving. But I'm sure no one who volunteered for mining would have been refused!*

I believe this was the first time – perhaps the only time – a Tribunal had had to consider an objection on these grounds, and we were all rather surprised when this one accepted it. Perhaps they concluded that anyone who chose coal-mining rather than the army in peacetime *must* be sincere (or crazy). Roddy's personal stand was in line with the future campaign of CND for the abolition of 'immoral' nuclear weapons, at that time held only by the United States, the USSR and Britain.[3]

In November 1955 Roddy duly became a coal-miner in West Yorkshire, just over the Pennines from me and conveniently connected by railway. At first he stayed with the Crottys, but soon found lodgings with a family close to the pit where he worked. He came to Marple for a weekend, and I went to stay with him. His landlady Mrs Haigh was rather churchy, but very nice. She used to turn up the Sunday morning service on the radio very loud so she could sing along with the hymns, and we did too. Roddy got on famously with her. I first tasted home-made lemon curd at her breakfast table, and she showed me how to make it.

For Roddy, his sojourn in the North was a conscious exercise in 'getting to know the working class' – making a virtue out of necessity, you might say, and in line with the interests of others of the New Left[4] who were re-discovering the working class at about this time. He intended to spend his free time writing, but he found this difficult at first as he was too exhausted after a day's work in the mine. Later he got transferred to the night shift, giving him the mornings free at home. This enabled him to make a start on his *Notes*, I reported to Dora – research which must have been useful for the TV play he wrote a few years later. Probably he also read a report published in 1956 of a two-year study of the (disguised) town of Featherstone: *Coal is our Life: an analysis of a Yorkshire mining community*.[5] Another investigator was the American Clancy Sigal, whose novel *Weekend in Dinlock*, published in 1960, also resulted from research in a Yorkshire mining village. He was a friend of Roddy's, although whether they met in Yorkshire or in London, I don't know. Two other friends of his were Canadians, Silvio and Bea Narizzano, then living in a suburb of Manchester. Silvio, a film director, had come to work for Sidney Bernstein at Granada TV. We visited them together, and they came out to Marple one Sunday. Roddy always knew far more interesting people than I did, and I was

---

[3] *The Campaign for Nuclear Disarmament (CND) was officially launched by Bertie Russell and Canon Collins in 1958. It grew out of protests in 1956 at the Atomic Weapons Research Establishment at Aldermaston, Berkshire, the target of later Aldermaston Marches, which became a regular feature thereafter.*

[4] *The term for a new grouping of the 'radical Left', consisting mainly of ex-Communists who left the Party in droves after events of 1956: first the revelations by Stalin's successor Khrushchev about what had been going on in Soviet Russia, and then the Soviet invasion of Hungary when it tried to break away from Moscow's control. The term only came into use later; I'm using it loosely here to include 'doubters' like Roddy who might not yet have left the Party, but soon would.*

[5] *By Norman Dennis, Fernando Henriques and Clifford Slaughter (Eyre and Spottiswoode, 1956).*

looking forward to sharing his social life from now on. Life 'up north' would not be so dull after all!

On 9 July 1956, I wrote to Dora from a temporary address – back at the pub in Ashton for two weeks, while my Marple landlady was away on holiday. It was a Monday, the day after my twenty-sixth birthday, which I'd spent with Roddy at the Narizzanos' flat in Didsbury. On the Saturday we'd been shopping (most of the letter was about the dress we'd bought her as a late birthday present), and on Sunday, our hosts having gone out for the day, 'we just sat around and read papers and played records & talked – nothing exciting but a very pleasant way of passing my birthday'. I had recently bought myself a second hand record-player, the first I'd ever owned since the wind-up gramophone I was given for my seventh birthday, and I was eagerly building up a record collection. In town I'd bought a single that was all the rage, Lonnie Donegan's *Rock Island Line*, which Roddy also used to sing. My friends Kit and Audrey Coppard had sent me from London a 12-inch 78 rpm, which arrived in pieces in its parcel. Roddy's birthday present was an LP of Dvorak's cello concerto, with Paul Tortelier as soloist. That night I played it over and over in the room over the bar of the pub...

These details of The Day Before are etched into my memory. Next morning at the office, I received a phone call to say Roddy had been badly injured in an accident underground and was in Pinderfields Hospital, Wakefield. My boss drove me to Stalybridge Station on the cross-Pennine railway, and two hours later I was at Roddy's bedside. I watched him silently, waiting for him to wake up after the operation on his back. The coal-dust was still visible round his eyes, and in the grooves of his cheeks.

Roddy's accident was my first encounter with tragedy – the first event of my life that *really hurt*. All I can remember of the first few awful hours is the grime on his face, reminding me of the way he'd been spending his days in between our spruced-up weekend meetings. Oh how we've all been admiring you, dear brave boy, I thought to myself as I watched him, but you were the only one who had to learn what it's really like down there in the bowels of the earth. Oh what a futile gesture, thumbing your nose at Authorities who didn't even notice! Why on earth did we let you do it?

CHAPTER 21

COPING WITH LIFE – AND DEATH

The roof-fall which broke Roddy's back was not a big accident injuring other miners; it crushed only him. His spinal injury left him a paraplegic, with both legs completely paralysed but his body above the waist unaffected. At first he had hopes of learning to 'walk' with the aid of calipers and crutches, but this proved to be impossible, as his doctor in Wakefield had kindly tried to warn him from the start. A paraplegic on arm crutches has to support his or her entire weight, and the problems of balance are insuperable. So from the age of 24 until his death at 51, Roddy lived in a wheelchair.

He spent the first six months at Pinderfields Hospital, well used to handling accident victims from the Yorkshire coal-fields. The excellent care he received there was only the first step in his recovery, of course: after his discharge there would be months of physical rehabilitation, and from the first day he had to work through the psychological adjustment faced by everyone struck down in this way. With great strength of character, in that clinical place, far from home and with only occasional visits from people he loved, Roddy somehow learned to be Roddy-in-a-wheelchair. I don't know if any of his friends helped him through the mental pain, but he did not burden me with it, nor Dora and Griffin. From the beginning he constantly reassured us that since *he* was optimistic about his future, we should be too.

Of course we all took it hard at first. Oh, the pity of it! And what a bitter irony, when he might have been safely in the army. But however distressed I felt, I knew it was worse for them. Dora always loved her sons best, and with John's breakdown Roddy had become even more precious to her. Of the four of us, he was closest to her thinking, carrying her baton into the future, so to speak. Yet she was hardened to tragedies, and still young enough to absorb the shock of this one. It was devastating for Griffin. I can still picture him and Dora arriving at the hospital on a bus from the railway station – Griffin gingerly dismounting, terrified of falling, his face drawn with anxiety and grief. For the first and only time since he had re-entered my life, I felt a rush of genuine love and pity for this poor old man, reeling from yet another blow of fate. In the time since I left London he had become very frail, dependent on a stick and pathetically thin. He needed tender loving care more than ever, just when no one had any time to spare for him.

For months after that, I was fully occupied with all the practical arrangements for Roddy's future. Of necessity I became the chief negotiator with hospital authorities, welfare officials of the National Coal Board (NCB), and, in due course, with estate agents and the landlord of the flat in London where we eventually set up a joint household. I believe I rather enjoyed the task: it brought out all my bossiness and self-importance in aid of a supremely worthy 'cause'. This officious little person jumps out of a letter to Dora full of information about what and where and when the NCB would provide for Roddy's welfare, in which I even offered to relieve her of bothersome Griffin. 'I am sorry he's been such a trial to you but I'll take chief responsibility for that when I get down.' Now I'm sure I didn't mean that, or do it. I was just trying to sound super-capable and big-hearted.

The NCB's welfare officer in Yorkshire, Mrs Bullock, was a tireless down-to-earth northerner, in sharp contrast to her counterpart at the head office in London whom I met later (so elegant and upper class I wondered if she'd ever visited a coal-mine – or were her welfare clients just the central office staff?) Mrs Bullock pulled every string and tugged every sleeve to ensure a smooth transition for Roddy from hospital to 'real life', and the best possible set-up when he got there. Apart from the NCB's standard provision for injured ex-miners, like the annual Christmas hamper and a TV set (still a novelty at that time), Mrs Bullock negotiated the perfect job for Roddy to take up 'whenever he's ready' at the NCB Film Unit in Covent Garden, London. When it seemed we might not have suitable accommodation ready in time, Mrs Bullock arranged a temporary berth for him at a hostel run by Stoke Mandeville Hospital, the other main centre for paraplegics. In the end it wasn't necessary: by Christmas 1956 the family was ready for Roddy's discharge from hospital.

Having got myself a new posting in London, I had luckily found a large ground-floor flat at 105 Broadhurst Gardens in red-brick West Hampstead. Roddy and I jointly signed a ten-year lease and somehow scraped together the large sum of 'key money' needed for unfurnished lettings in those days. Lily came to housekeep for us, knowing it would include semi-nursing tasks. She did not hesitate when I asked her to come; Roddy had been her favourite since babyhood, and she was as stricken as any of us by his plight. Walter, still in the same job Dora had found for him in 1945, was happy to live anywhere within reach of it. The Factory Department had obligingly transferred me from Ashton under Lyne to the Richmond District, accessible from West Hampstead by the delightful Broad Street Line railway. This oddly assorted household suited all of us very well, including Lily: she never minded domestic work and was glad to have lively company after ten years alone with Walter, who was a hermit except for going to work.

For me the years at Broadhurst Gardens were a happy re-kindling of my old camaraderie with Roddy, plus the adult independence I had established in the previous ten years. The architectural setting was faded Edwardian grandeur: my bed-sitting room at the front was huge, and Roddy's at the back even larger – a 30-foot ballroom in fact, opening onto a little balcony from which steps led down to the garden which itself opened into a vast space shared by all the houses that backed onto it. The space was 'gardened' only to the extent of occasional mowing – a private playground for kids and pets; and although we never found a way of providing a ramp from Roddy's room (the gradient was too steep), he could look out on all the goings-on and sniff the fresh air in fine weather.

The back garden at 105, with common ground beyond

I had organised a Roddy Fund among friends and family to provide some extra comforts for his new life: wall-to-wall haircord carpeting for his room, and a superior radiogram. Hi-fi had not yet been invented (for the likes of us, anyway), but he could turn up the volume without distortion on that contrivance to sing along from the adjacent bathroom. In 1956 these were *luxuries* for the genteel poor like us – not to mention the TV set, with a mere 14-inch screen and very poor definition, which nevertheless filled up the sofa and floor-space in our sitting/dining room for Saturday afternoon football. The TV, the music, the space indoors and out, Lily's ever-stretching meals, made '105' a mecca for Roddy's friends and mine, mostly still unmarried twenty-somethings at that time.

Above all, it was Roddy's magnetism that drew them. Looking back to the time before worsening health problems and stalled work-projects often dampened his spirits, I remember how ebullient and energetic he was in those early days. New arrivals in our circle would realise at once that no allowances were needed for the wheelchair. All the tiresome inconveniences of his condition – endless toilet routines, clumsy appliances, his 'fish' as he called it – a canvas bag concealed down the trouser leg, which collected his urine, and often had to be surreptitiously emptied down a street grating or into a bottle –

were laughed off to the edges of a busy life divided between the Rehabilitation Centre at Camden Town, his job as a trainee film editor with the NCB, and writing his first TV play.[1] Oh yes, and parties. In my memory he was almost inexhaustible, and nearly always cheerful. I often noticed how people with problems to resolve came to Roddy for amateur therapy – not that he invited their confidences, he just emanated the inner adjustment-to-life they were seeking.

'No allowances needed for the wheelchair' – Roddy in the early 1960s
(The children are two of Lukas and Caroline Heller's)

My own life alongside Roddy's glistened with new interests. My unfurnished room was more of a home than Redcliffe Square, because I could fix it up. Thus began a lifelong obsession with domestic *objets* – furniture and fabrics, ornaments and oddities, above all chinaware – at first mostly Victorian

---

[1] *This was* Pay Day, *transmitted in 1957. Directed by Stuart Burge, it launched the TV career of its lead actor, one Anthony Booth, who later found fame and fortune in the sitcom* Till Death Us Do Part; *and in 1997, as the father of Cherie Booth, achieved the dubious honour of becoming the Prime Minister's father-in-law. It is sad to record that this was the only play of Roddy's ever produced; and apart from a few articles in magazines, none of his writings thereafter got into print.*

pots and plates for daily use, later extending to eighteenth century porcelain which I could only ever afford when damaged or faulty. I discovered Portobello Road and went there every Saturday in my little car. Yes, my car! Mickey Neville – he of the notorious 3-wheeler 'Bug' – sold me my first Austin 7 for £20, but it was problematic because the passenger door flew open going round corners, so no 'instructor' wanted to ride with me. One day on my factory-inspecting beat I came across a 1931 model on sale for £27:10 shillings, including three months' tax. I painted it dark green, made seat covers in bright striped deck-chair material, and polished and lacquered the brass headlamps. Lukas taught me to drive it, and I was lucky to be able to practise on my own: petrol rationing after the Suez Crisis[2] had suspended driving tests for a period, and learners were allowed to drive unsupervised after one month. I used to rise early on Sundays and drive round and round the block to gain confidence. Oh how I loved that car! – though I nearly killed it driving up to Lincolnshire with my new boyfriend George Todd. No one had told me cars need oil from time to time, and when we got up there, the drive shaft seized up. No problem! A farmer friend of George's found someone to fit a second-hand one, and we were back in London in time for work on Monday.[3]

With George Todd (and his friends' baby) in Lincolnshire, spring 1957

I'm surprised to discover, checking up, for how short a time Griffin was a part of this convivial scene. In my memory of those days, the familiar burden of guilt looms large: 'We must have Dad over on Sunday' – or Monday, or Tuesday... He was eager for invitations of course, and Roddy did his best to fit him in. Among our friends he was an object of curiosity or mild ridicule, still seeming so out of place in England, where he hadn't yet learned that lodgings are 'digs', not 'diggings'. Lukas called him Mr McGoo, after the half-blind

---

[2] Anglo-French intervention in the Suez War of 1956 between Israel and Egypt provoked the Egyptians to block the Suez Canal, interrupting oil supplies to Britain. Petrol rationing was in force for some months until normal oil supplies were resumed.

[3] There's a lesson for today in that tale: the Austin 7 and other popular cars were so ubiquitous in the 1930s that spare parts could easily be found 25 years later. There was a little shop in Archway Road piled high with every conceivable second-hand part for pre-war Austin 7s and Ford 8s, where I used to go when a piece of mine needed replacing.

cartoon character who keeps bumping into things and misinterprets every encounter. Very apt. It was Lukas who would bring Griffin over from his room at the other end of Hampstead for an afternoon of cigarettes and whisky, Roddy's life-enhancing conversation and Lily's life-sustaining food. I wasn't yet a proficient driver, and in any case both Griffin and I would have hated to be squashed into the intimacy of my little car.

Our relations bumped along at rock-bottom in these last months of his life. He especially despised my petty-mindedness, and made careless – or maybe care*ful* – cutting remarks about me in company, sending me seething into the kitchen to make the tea. 'Oh, don't ask Harriet, she's only interested in *refrigerators*,' is one I've always remembered. Whether it was sparked off by some comment of mine (maybe that it would be nice to have one, which we didn't), or a summing-up of my incorrigible materialism, I don't know.

So far as I recall, he never asked about my job or any other aspect of my life – or perhaps he did, and I froze him off, as I was quite capable of doing. Roddy often chided me for sulks and ill temper during Griffin's visits: allowances must be made for age and infirmity, he would point out. Of course he was right. I do remember thinking, in the solitude of my room, *there must be something wrong with me, to feel so cold towards my own father...* I feared my adult character was permanently deformed by this emotional numbness.

The last known photo of Griffin (second left): at Audrey and Kit Coppard's wedding party, September 1955

One morning in May 1957 – I think it was a Saturday – we received a phone call from someone in the house of bed-sits where Griffin lived, to say he had been found dead in bed. Lukas took Roddy and me up to the morgue in Hampstead to see his body – the first dead person I'd ever seen, and I was chilled. There hadn't been a crisis of illness, so his death was a shock; but also, we both admitted, a relief. Though Roddy had always coped with him better than I could, for both of us Griffin was an awkward leftover from the family past at a time when we were only interested in our futures. There was not even a fund of shared family life to look back on, only those three weeks in Dublin in 1946. Dora was the one with a fund of memories of Griffin – how passionate and heart-rending, I would only discover years later – but if they brought any tears to her eyes in 1957, I didn't notice.

As next of kin, I went through the formalities – an inquest to ascertain the cause of death (a blood clot), registration of the death, arrangements for the funeral. Dora must have found the money for it, as Griffin's bank account yielded just £27. For the brief cremation ceremony, Roddy and I thought the largo from Dvorak's New World symphony would be fitting. But these were the days before you could take in your own tape-player, and on the crematorium organ it was almost indistinguishable from 'Jesu Joy of Man's Desiring'.

A month after the funeral, a letter arrived from the crematorium: Would we like the ashes scattered in the Garden of Remembrance? It would cost... (I forget the sum). If not, they would have to charge us so much a week for keeping the urn longer. So I collected the urn, and for some weeks we pondered what to do with the contents, ignoring predictable suggestions from irreverent friends. Should we scatter them in the rough grass of our garden? It hardly seemed appropriate, where our cat scratched about, and visiting children played. 'I know – what about putting it up there?' – or words to that effect – and the deed was done.

So that's how Griffin's ashes came to be stowed away in a cupboard. In fact it was not a real cupboard, but a space under the stairs that had been covered with plasterboard, then wallpapered over, in the crude conversion of the house into flats before we lived there. Over time the wallpaper had come unstuck, revealing the 'cupboard' high up near the ceiling.

Through all the comings and goings of the next nine years we gave the hidden urn scarcely a thought. When I returned in 1966 to help Lily clear the flat at the end of our lease, we conveniently forgot the contents of that cupboard and left it undisturbed.

Reflections

Working through my long-ago relationship with Griffin has yielded no dramatic answer to the question I started with: Why did I dislike him so much? My teenage diaries, unread since I wrote them, and letters to Dora I didn't know she had kept, have shown me little more than the usual tangle of emotions and faults on both sides to be found in any complicated family. Thankfully there was no hidden trauma to spoil the rest of my life. After his death Griffin slipped away into memory very easily, taking with him the guilt that had weighed me down for ten years. No longer feeling *there must be something wrong with me* because I could not love him, I have lived my own adult life with scarcely a backward glance at this fractured relationship.

Now, however, now that I've trudged by his side through all those years of loneliness and humiliation, I feel I must work out the moral reckoning. Whose fault was it, that everything went so drastically wrong between us?

By the time he reached England in 1946, Griffin had pretty well given up on Dora. All hopes were now focused on me – such high hopes, and on my side too, that perhaps we were both bound to be disappointed. My disillusion was the puncturing of a childish dream which I felt deeply at 16, but soon got over in the process of growing up. In 1951, when I returned from America, I was eager to get to know Griffin as an adult, and if at that stage he had been able to be the indulgent, helpful, worldly-wise adviser I needed, I might have fallen on his neck and become a grateful daughter. Instead I found him poor and needy, semi-dependent on me – at least on my visits – and still determined to unload his grievances on me. In the usual pattern of family relationships, our lives were 'out of sync': what he needed in his mid-sixties was a settled, mature daughter able to care for an ageing parent, not an uncertain, unconfident girl still looking for help to get launched in the adult world.

Not that he *wanted* me to be a homely, domestic sort of daughter. Far from it. Griffin's disappointment in me was simply that I wasn't another Dora: first, that I wasn't willing, or fit, to fill the space in his life he had always hoped she would occupy; and secondly, that I didn't have her blue stocking intellect. Griffin was an intellectual snob of the first order. His youth and the best years of his working life had been spent among the American literary *avant garde*, and later, in England, the radical-progressive world of Bertie Russell and other intellectual stars. He felt at home in a rarified intellectual climate.

Before the Second World War even the 'poor' among these artistic people, on both sides of the Atlantic, had servants to cook and clean, leaving them free to write their books all day and talk all night if they chose to. That's just what Griffin liked to do (though in his case the daytime activity tended to get neglected). The women of this world were emancipated 'new women', not homebodies who spent their lives in the kitchen; that was left to others. Griffin courteously appreciated the domestics in the background, but from on high, seeing them almost as a different species from cultured people. This attitude was not uncommon among the intelligentsia in those days,[4] but most of

---

[4] *'You're not still frightened of the servants?'* asks Virginia Woolf's sister Vanessa Bell *in a recent film,* The Hours, *set in Bloomsbury society of 1925. That Virginia might be, is seen as a weakness by Vanessa.*

Griffin's friends (and certainly Dora) nevertheless had to function in the humdrum world of mortgages and gas bills. Griffin was never a husband or a householder, and took no interest in 'homes' except as a polite guest. His own current bed-sit or apartment was equally unimportant, so long as it was cheap and convenient.

'Intellectual snob meets middle-brow housewife' – well, not quite, but to become a housewife was certainly one of my ambitions, and in Griffin's eyes it was a betrayal of my feminist inheritance to aim so low. Nor was I specially interested in the latest works of literature, or current political developments, and certainly could not discuss them at his high-flown level. Having waited so long for me to grow up, and assuming my parental genes would have given me a 'first class mind' like Dora's, he was dismayed to meet the shallow person that in his eyes I had turned out to be.[5] My feelings were hurt too: despite a sneaking suspicion he might be right – I really *was* stupid, as I had often felt among cleverer friends – I considered myself to be a fully-formed adult, and if he didn't like me even now, he never would! My mood turned from conciliation to defiance.

I was not fully-formed, of course, but groping through that uncertain fledgling phase of life when young people need constant reassurance and encouragement. Aware of the high intellectual standards of my own family, slightly ashamed of my lowly domestic yearnings, I was also desperately keen to be nice enough for someone to want to marry me. Dora, John and Kate all had academic minds beyond my reach, and although Roddy was closer to my level, he was far more imaginative, kinder and less selfish than I knew myself to be. These were the self-doubts that Griffin's attitude seemed to confirm. In fact his crime was not so heinous: only the common parental mistake of wanting his favourite child to fit his desires, instead of accepting the person I actually was. As a parent myself, also not blameless in that respect, I can now forgive that error as I couldn't then.

At Broadhurst Gardens, had Griffin lived longer we might eventually have reached a reasonable accommodation – with Roddy's mediating influence. But it would have been difficult, when I was so hostile and Griffin so old and cantankerous. Both he and I had – as I still have – a capacity for unreasonable anger. Whereas he was all-forgiving, and in typical American fashion would have liked to 'have it out' and then be friends again, one of my unlovely traits is to be *un*forgiving, and in typical English fashion to prefer to suppress my anger rather than make a scene. Left alone in a room together, we would sit in

---

[5] A 'first class mind' is not Griffin's phrase, but Dora's, for she too instinctively admired intellect above all else, despite her declared reverence for 'proletarian values' and her genuine love and respect for individual proletarians like Mrs Ainger and Pat Grace. In my eyes that puts her a step up from Griffin, who once complained to Dora, begging her to write, that his only news of me and Roddy came from Lily's 'illiterate' letters. Lily's letters illiterate? Just because she didn't get her commas and capitals in the right place? Anyone who ever received one will remember how much she conveyed with her unselfconscious scrawl – much more than any grammar school prose could impart.

simmering silence, all communication lost. Having seen myself in later years behave in the same curmudgeonly way towards other people I have cast into outer darkness, I freely admit now that the failed relationship with my father was not all his fault.

There were other sins of omission in those last months of his life. (Roddy shares the blame here, but he had more excuse than I did.) I don't mean our casual treatment of the ashes – of course we should have scattered them somewhere, anywhere, but none of our family thinks of bodily remains as sacred in any way, so that episode has always seemed to me the joke it was at the time. But why did we treat the *living* Griffin so casually? For some time before he died, he was obviously weak and unwell. Why didn't I behave in decent daughterly fashion – albeit with gritted teeth – and make sure he was getting proper medical attention? Why didn't we feed him regularly, with Kilner jars of creamed chicken if we couldn't have him round? And when he died, did I try to inform his old friends in America? I must have written to Mary Vorse, the only one of them I knew, and presumably left it to her to pass the word on. It did not occur to me to send a notice of his death to the *New York Times*, where he might even have rated a brief obituary. Instead we let him fade into nothingness in a foreign land, unremarked and uncelebrated. It's a fine time to be offering apologies, and no earthly use to Griffin, I know, but – *mea culpa* for all that.

Much sadder thoughts arise from contemplating the wasted life that preceded his death. It was partly his own fault, of course. The 'wild oats' phase of youth that most young men get over by the age of 25, Griffin prolonged until he was past 40. Striving to be a writer, he never seriously tried to overcome the bad work habits he blamed on his upbringing (which didn't handicap brother Richard, we note). Meeting Dora led to a fateful downward slide, and she too must be called to account for that. No matter how distressing her own situation, it was shameful to string Griffin along so selfishly until the arrival of Pat made him dispensable. (Did she ever consider *the reader* of all her anguished letters?) By declining to make up their quarrel later – at least with friendship and warmth in his lonely exile – she left Griffin with his stored-up recriminations unacknowledged and unassuaged. So the Ancient Mariner fastened on me to hear him out.

The 64-dollar question that remains to be considered is, could he have built a successful career, a happier life for himself, if he had never met Dora? On balance, I think the answer has to be No. It's tempting to surmise that some other kind of woman could have given him the 'faith in himself' he seemed to need – as Dora too may have hoped, after 1935, to salve her conscience. And the good woman's home could then have become his home too. (Griffin's lifelong rootlessness still saddens me, having taken such delight in all the places I've lived in. Human beings are not meant to be tumbleweed, blowing aimlessly across the surface of the earth: we derive strength from being rooted in it.) The problem here is that the kind of woman content to play merely a back-up role to her man did not attract Griffin. Had he not met Dora, it's more likely he would have continued bed-hopping through his acquaintance until the pastime ceased to appeal – or until *he* ceased to appeal.

The key to Griffin's success or failure, as with everyone, lay within himself. Analysing my own slow emancipation from childhood has shown me the crucial importance for a contented later life of the self-confidence and self-knowledge I acquired in that fledgling phase. 'Know thyself', said the Greeks, and by the time I was 30, I more or less did. Dora's unstinting support of my ego more than outweighed Griffin's disapproval. With a fair share of luck, and aware of my own limitations (especially the lack of a first class mind), I've been content with the fortune and coped with the misfortunes doled out to me.

By contrast, the Griffin I've come to know seems always to have been striving for the unattainable – in his youth, to be the Great Novelist so many of his friends became; in his love affair, to be the macho protector of a woman whose needs were quite different. From scrappy evidence, I can only guess at the youthful influences that made him the way he was. Events of his 'fledgling phase' that I know so little about, from when he was 17 until his migration from California to New York, must have set him off down this crooked path – quarrels, rebuffs, jealousy of his superstar older brother; even the very ethic of can-do America that has led so many others to disappointment. Unluckier than me, Griffin lacked the support of his dominant parent, his father, to give him confidence, and learned his own limitations the hard way, by failing to achieve his aims.

In work, he foolishly despised the branch of his craft in which he excelled. As a skilful factual writer in the era of serious magazine journalism, before radio and television had become rival forums for political and cultural debate, he had marketable talents suited to his time. He was finely attuned to the Arts, and a sympathetic critic. Mary Vorse and Anna Wickham would attest to his sensibility in that sphere. Like most writers he was a natural freelancer; in Griffin's case more than most, for in every employment his irascibility and a low boredom threshold – of fools, and of tedious work – were his undoing.

A freelancer in any field, however talented, must also have ingrained in their character the discipline to *keep going* until a job is done. This is what Griffin patently lacked, and failed to learn from several outstanding role models. Mary Vorse's recipe for writing – 'Apply the seat of your pants to the seat of your chair' – she claimed had been passed around their literary circle by Sinclair Lewis, so Griffin must have heard it too; and then over many years he watched Mary demonstrate the advice. Later he had Dora's 'little lectures' on the same theme, and another shining example to follow. Yet he seemed unable to benefit from all this wise counsel, and throughout his working life could only manage brief or incomplete displays of his undoubted talent. What a pity.

AFTERWORD

I left the Broadhurst Gardens household when I married my cousin Harold (Chris) Unwin in 1960 and moved to Sheffield. Chris was a sales representative for the English Steel Corporation (ESC), making long trips to Latin America (where he had lived from 1950 to 1958, working for another Sheffield steel firm). Barney was born in Sheffield in 1961 and Tom in London in 1962, just after Chris had moved to ESC's London office and we had taken a flat in Aberdare Gardens, West Hampstead, a few streets away from Broadhurst Gardens. Chris died suddenly in January 1963.

In 1962 Roddy married Susie Kaneti, an Israeli of Turkish origin. They bought a flat in Elsworthy Road, Hampstead, leaving Lily and Walter at '105' to live out the ten-year lease we had signed in 1956. When I began a teacher-training course in 1964 it was Lily to the rescue again, minding Barney and Tom every weekday while I attended Garnett College in Roehampton, on the other side of London. At Garnett I met Colin Ward, both of us preparing to teach in Further Education. When we married in 1966 and bought a house, Lily and Walter came to live on the top floor, where Lily's Room became Barney and Tom's football parlour and games room. Lily's help enabled me to continue teaching part time after Ben Ward was born in 1968.

19 Schubert Road, Putney, was our home until we moved to Suffolk in 1980. Walter had died in 1972. After a severe stroke, Lily chose to go home to Southport in 1977 to be near her brother's family, after nearly 40 years helping out the Russell–Barry–Unwin–Ward family in one role or another. She died in 1981, aged 84.

Roddy inherited all the Barry charm, and a large degree of Barry restlessness. As with Griffin, it's hard to know whether to blame weakness of character or the blows of fate for many unrealised work-projects, after his early success described in Chapter 21. (Certainly it was not lack of talent.) In 1965 his marriage to Susie ended when he took up with Claire Wullschleger, a

German-Swiss. Their marriage too did not last. From 1964 onwards Roddy lived mostly abroad, in Israel, Italy, Italian-speaking Switzerland, and then in Formentera, a Balearic island, where he settled with his last partner Pilar Ruiz, a Basque, until his increasing health problems forced them to stay within reach of London hospitals. He and Pilar were married in 1981. In May 1982 Pilar gave birth to Roddy's son Mao Barry, conceived by Artificial Insemination Donor (AID). Roddy was just 51 when he died, in April 1983.

For the last 30 years of Dora's life she was burdened with problems arising from John's chronic schizophrenia, and the same illness afflicting his daughters Sarah and Lucy. In the 1950s, with the help of others, she maintained some personal freedom for her own ceaseless campaigning and writing; but from 1966, when she gave up her London flat and moved with John to live in Cornwall full time, inevitably her life became more circumscribed by his needs. Nevertheless she battled on, bombarding newspapers, attending committees and conferences to promote this or that cause, from abortion law reform to environmental conservation to rationalist education – and, above all, the campaign for nuclear disarmament. In the last few years of her life journalists and television film crews trooped down to Carn Voel to record her eventful life, her current concerns, and her enduring spirit. She died at the age of 92, in May 1986.

John's unexpected death in December 1987, and Kate's return from America to live at Carn Voel, brings my story round full circle to where it began.

ACKNOWLEDGEMENTS AND BIBLIOGRAPHICAL NOTES

How I came to know what I now know about my father is a story in itself. At first, my chief interest lay in Griffin's relationship with Dora and with their children – the tale that began in 1928. Much of what I later learned about him and his background came indirectly through other people's researches, starting with my husband Colin. Before I had begun the project, on a visit to the International Institute of Social History (IISH) in Amsterdam, where my mother's papers are housed, Colin was browsing through its archive of the London *Daily Herald* and came across a front-page article, datelined Moscow, February 26 1920, 'From Our Special Correspondent GRIFFIN BARRY'. This confirmed one of the few facts I then knew about my father's pre-Dora life: that he had once been a reporter for the *Daily Herald*.

Later, engaged on his own researches in libraries far afield, Colin would routinely scan the pages of likely books for me and photocopy relevant passages by or about the famous people Griffin knew. These scraps of information would make a useful introduction, I thought, to the story of misguided love and unhappy parenthood that I would draw out of the sheaves of letters bequeathed by Dora. That Griffin had once been someone of account made the story of his later tribulations all the more poignant.

Coincidentally, while I was following my own trail through the Russell–Barry saga, Ray Monk's two-volume biography of Bertrand Russell was being written and published. Monk's work usefully clarified the Russell dimension of my story as it began to take shape – particularly his account of the divorce, in writing and in our conversations, which helped me to make sense of Dora's letters to Griffin during that turbulent time. Similarly, Bertie's letters to Dora at key moments in their relationship, published in 2001 under Nicholas Griffin's editorship, showed Bertie's feelings about events I'd previously seen only through Dora's eyes. Talking to Kate about Russell affairs was always helpful.

The Russell connection also led me to information about Griffin's own life unconnected with Russells. Bill McGuire, an American who had known him in the 1940s and was well acquainted with their liberal-lefty world, was assisting an English friend, Charlotte Kurzke, to identify the cast of characters, including Griffin Barry, in a fascinating memoir of the Spanish civil war left to Charlotte by her parents. Knowing of Griffin's role in the Russell family, Bill approached Alan Ryan, a Russell scholar, for Kate's address, a letter she passed on to me, and thence came my fruitful liaison with Bill and his friend Charlotte Kurzke. Her mother's recollections of Valencia in 1937 showed in real life one of my childhood legends – Griffin as a reporter in the Spanish civil war. I am very grateful to Charlotte for allowing me (and other interested friends) to see the remarkable document bequeathed by her parents. I only hope it will one day get into print so that others can read it too.

Another fortunate contact arose from Denys Blakeway's TV biography of Bertrand Russell, broadcast in the BBC2 Reputations series in May–June 1997. A publicity piece in *The Guardian* of 26 May 1997 about Kate and me ('A Tale of Two Sisters', by Libby Brooks) found its way to Jennifer Vaughan Jones in Madison, Wisconsin. As a biographer of the English poet Anna Wickham, Jennifer had been trying for some time to find out more about her poet's influential friend Griffin Barry. A photograph he had given to Anna in 1922 (see page 30) had led Jennifer to the Hoover Institution on War, Revolution and Peace at Stanford University. Their archives confirmed Griffin's service during the First World War with Herbert Hoover's Commission for Relief in Belgium (CRB), and then with the American Red Cross. The Hoover Institution's archivist, Ms Cissie Dore Hill, later provided me with copies of the CRB's Bulletin, and even correspondence with Griffin, which enabled me to track him through Europe and Russia for a few years after the war.

Until my contact with Jennifer Jones I knew nothing of the poet Anna Wickham, whose poem celebrating my arrival in July 1930 was inscribed by Dora into my Baby Book. The original poem, in Anna's own hand, was almost the only offering I had to exchange with Jennifer, not only for glimpses of my father in the 1920s, before he met Dora, but for details of his brother Richard that her researches in pursuit of Griffin had turned up. I could now identify Monrovia, California, as the fictional town in Richard's book about my grandfather, *Father and his Town*. The City of Monrovia's chief librarian, Monica Greening, took immense trouble to research the Barry family's California background portrayed in Chapter 3, even including in the package she sent me the front page of my grandfather's newspaper on the day he said farewell to his readers. It was Jennifer Jones, once again, who later helped me to document the Barrys' earlier years in her own home state of Wisconsin.

These lucky finds aroused my curiosity about other aspects of Griffin's life hitherto unknown to me. In 1997 my friend Jenny Gould went to Cape Cod for a holiday, and offered to try to locate and photograph Susan Glaspell's house near Truro – the house I dimly remembered staying in with my father in 1933. Along with a wallet of photographs (I took my pick for Chapter 9), Jenny brought back a wealth of written material from local sources, sufficient for several chapters about Provincetown People and their world. Most intriguing for me was a book she had bought in the town, *Provincetown as a Stage*, by Leona Rust Egan, which included a page or two about the early years of Griffin's friendship with Mary Vorse. I eagerly wrote to the author and received by return a wad of letters from Griffin to Mary in 1916, with a promise from Egan to write soon from her winter home in New York 'with questions of my own'. But she never did write; nor did anyone reply to my follow-up enquiries. Some calamity must have befallen my new friend. I owe her an important contribution to Chapter 1, but I shall never know what lay behind certain enigmatic (unsourced) remarks about Griffin in her book.

This was not the only disappointment I met, as an amateur and largely desk-bound researcher. There must be more letters in Mary Vorse's voluminous archive at Wayne State University, but as Griffin was not one of her 'more noted correspondents' individually indexed in the inventory sent by the archivist, to locate them would have meant a trip to Detroit to trawl through 31 boxes of correspondence. Doubtless Griffin popped in and out of all his friends' correspondence – as I know he did in Dawn Powell's (another cache I failed to obtain). Most of all I'd like to have found the item suggested by Powell's diary entry on 5 January 1943: 'Wrote story of Griffin. First short story in years. Coby pointed out spots for clarification.' Imagine Griffin immortalised by Dawn Powell's acerbic pen! But her biographer, Tim Page, could not identify this story among the 'hundreds' she wrote; nor could Jenny Gould, when she located in the States a rare library copy of *Sunday, Monday and Always*, the only published collection of Powell's short stories.

Another friend, Taylor Stoehr, deserves special thanks here for his dogged efforts on my behalf in Boston Public Library. To him I owe samples of Griffin's writing in *Newsweek*, *Travel*, *The Nation*, and an English magazine called *Everyman* which I hadn't even heard of, after my feeble efforts from this side of the pond had yielded nothing. These articles from the 1920s and 1930s, on a wide variety of literary, political and environmental topics, confirmed what I had perceived in his remarkable letters – my father was a very competent writer.

Several friends have suggested researching Griffin Barry on the internet. Two attempts turned up only Barry Griffin, a policeman in Georgia, USA. Then, by a fluke, my friend Roman Krznaric located a letter buried in the papers of one Sophie Treadwell in the archives of the University of Arizona, which slotted neatly into Griffin's adventure with the CRB in 1915. His friendship with Sophie Treadwell, an actress and author who died in 1970, evidently did not last, for I came across no other references to her. How many other acquaintances of Griffin's may have left a trace of him somewhere? The researcher's disease is infectious... (luckily, I am immune).

Notably absent from my sources for this memoir are the personal and family records that usually launch biographers on their quest. There must have been some papers in the meagre room where Griffin died, apart from the folder of Dora's letters that found its way into her archive. Address book – writing in progress – pension records? Did I once have such items, and lose them? Possibly. I believe I mislaid a box of odds and ends in my transition from itinerant lodger to settled householder in the 1960s. Regrettably I did not share my mother's careful concern for posterity.

This youthful lack of concern returned to haunt me in the midst of my work. In the summer of 1940 Griffin wrote several letters from Bear Island, 'ten miles off the Maine coast', owned by a friend of his whom he only named as 'Rosy', aged 33, who was the secretary of the Dalton School in New York, 'a progressive day school'. That summer she was taking paying guests 'in the old house her dead parents lived in and in one or two cottages...'. She gave Griffin a map of the bay, which he sent to me. It shows part of Penobscot Bay, including Bear Island and, among many others, Swan's Island, where he had apparently spent another summer before the First World War. At the end of a letter to Dora, dated 8 August 1940, he wrote:

> I have had a family trunk sent here from California to store, as being a secure and friendly place. All that is left of my family are in it – the history of its ups and downs through 60 or 70 years in photographs and letters and household objects. I would like Harry to see how beautiful her grandmother was in the seventies when she was a young teacher in Wisconsin, and from some scribbled notes how her grandmother was planning to buy clothes for her grandchildren in 1936 just before she died.

In a letter to me the previous day, he had sent some foreign stamps for my collection:

> I found a real treasure trove in an old family trunk that arrived this week from California – all that is left of my own family. My older brother Richard went round the world when he was young and my mother had saved all his letters and there were some beautiful stamps on them for you – some Egyptian and some Japanese and some Indian.

There's no other reference to Rosy, or Bear Island, in Griffin's correspondence. It seems likely that trunk was later transferred to Mary Vorse's house in Provincetown, the nearest to a permanent base in America Griffin ever had. In a letter to me of 18 March 1959, two years after Griffin's death and seven years before her own, Mary wrote: 'I have never gotten around to looking over his papers but hope to this spring when I go to the Cape in early May. I'll write you about the contents then.' Whether she ever did, I don't know. This letter seems to have been my last contact with Mary. In 1959 I had little interest in Griffin or his belongings, and the next few years were very eventful ones in my own life. Did Mary's death in 1966 even register with me, far away in London? That's when I should have written to her son Joel O'Brien to enquire about those 'papers' – but I didn't.

In April 2001, planning a visit to America, belatedly I wrote to Mary's biographer, Dee Garrison, hoping to trace the O'Briens. She telephoned to say that Joel and his wife were now both dead, but that their daughter Sally O'Brien worked for an independent radio station, WBAI, in New York City. Unfortunately my efforts to contact her there, by phone in America and later by letter, met no response.

It's probably too much to hope that this cache of Barry memorabilia still exists somewhere. But you never know...

* * *

Many other friends have helped in the writing of this book. Tony Gould's comments on early chapters made me feel it was worth carrying on; and several years later, that the final result was worth getting into print. Along the way, valuable source material and information trickled in – sometimes unexpectedly, such as David Goodway's identification of the mysterious 'Lady Hastings' whose photograph appears on page 174. From America, Lesley Perrin and Peter Davison sent me books and press cuttings about the friends of my father's youth. Judy Macdonald had to research her own family among older relatives to give me the potted version of it in Chapter 19. Other Americans who earned my deep gratitude are the librarians and archivists I never met, who patiently answered my enquiries; and one I did meet, Ed Belka, librarian of Eau Claire High School, who manned the photocopier one hot June afternoon in 2001 while Jennifer Jones and I rummaged through dusty school records from the 1890s.

It was easier to research my own school life than Griffin's. As well as the Beacon Hill pupils whose words I have used to portray the school – Sue Murray, Ati Gropius Johansen, Susan Downes and David Correa-Hunt – the reminiscences of two other former pupils helped: Jonathan Pritchard and Jennifer Heseltine. Jenny's birthday party photo and those of Barbara Wright (on pages 195–7) gave me close-ups of childhood friends through the mist. But what chiefly brought to life the days at Kingwell Hall were my conversations with Barbara, whose memory of her time there is still razor sharp. She is almost the only person still alive who witnessed the Dora–Griffin conflict at first hand,

and can remember Griffin, even the angry man she knew, as a charmer. It was good to have her recollection of him to set alongside the sad old man of the 1950s that is my own clearest memory – a picture confirmed by Roddy's first wife, Susie Barry, and by Audrey Coppard, whose wedding in 1955 occasioned the last known photograph of Griffin, reproduced on page 287. To all these friends, my warmest thanks.

Tributes are also due closer to home: to Colin Ward, my resident encyclopedia, for support and assistance beyond enumeration; to Barney Unwin, for contacts and books via the internet; to Anne McLean and Alan Balfour, for computer services and advice obligingly scaled down to my level.

My sister Kate has always been a source of reassurance, not only in the writing of this book but through many of the childhood traumas it relates. I'd like to record here, alongside the evidence, my lifelong gratitude to her for helping me to survive them more or less unscathed.

BIBLIOGRAPHY

Alberti, Johanna *Eleanor Rathbone*, Sage Publications, London, 1996

Atholl, Katharine (Duchess of Atholl), *Searchlight on Spain*, Penguin, London, 1938

Baker, Carlos (ed.) *Ernest Hemingway Selected Letters 1917–1961* Granada, London, 1981

Barry, Richard *Father and his Town*, Houghton Mifflin, Boston, 1941

Bell, Adrian *Only For Three Months: The Basque Children in Exile*, Mousehold Press, Norwich, 1996

Berlin, Isaiah *Personal Impressions*, Hogarth Press, London, 1980

Bennett, David H *The Party of Fear: From Nativist Movements to the New Right in American History*, University of North Carolina Press, Chapel Hill & London, 1988

Bigsby, C W E A *Critical Introduction to Twentieth Century American Drama, 1900–1940*, Cambridge University Press, 1982

Cowley, Malcolm *Exiles Return: A Literary Odyssey of the 1920s* Viking Press, NY, 1951

Crotty, Frank *Provincetown Profiles and Others on Cape Cod*, Barre Gazette, Massachusetts, 1958

Davis, Charles F (ed.) *Monrovia-Duarte Community Book*, Arthur Cawston, Monrovia, California, 1957

Dos Passos, John *The Best Times: An Informal Memoir*, Andre Deutsch, London, 1970

Egan, Leona Rust *Provincetown as a Stage*, Parnassus Imprints, Orleans, Massachusetts, 1994

Fishbein, Leslie *Rebels in Bohemia: The Radicals of* The Masses, *1911–1917*, University of North Carolina Press, Chapel Hill, 1982

Garrison, Dee *Mary Heaton Vorse: The Life of an American Insurgent*, Temple University Press, Philadelphia, 1989

Glaspell, Susan *The Road to the Temple*, Frederick A Stokes Co., NY, 1927

Griffin, Nicholas (ed.) with Alison Roberts Miculan *The Selected Letters of Bertrand Russell: The Public Years, 1914–1970*, Routledge, London and NY, 2001

Goldman, Emma *My Disillusionment in Russia*, C W Daniel, London, 1925

Gould, Jean *The Poet and Her Book: A Biography of Edna St Vincent Millay*, Dodd, Mead and Co., NY, 1969

Herzberg, M J *Readers' Encyclopedia of American Literature*, Methuen, London, 1962

Hetherington, S J *Katharine Atholl: Against the Tide*, Aberdeen University Press, 1989

Historical and Biographical Album of the Chippewa Valley, Wisconsin, 1891–1892

Jones, Howard Mumford and Rideout, Walter B (eds) *Letters of Sherwood Anderson*, Little, Brown, Boston, 1953

Jones, Jennifer Vaughan *Anna Wickham: A Poet's Daring Life*, Madison Books, Lanham, New York and Oxford, 2003

Kennedy, Richard S *Dreams in the Mirror: A Biography of E E Cummings*, Liveright, NY, 1980

Langer, Elinor *Josephine Herbst*, Little, Brown, Boston/Toronto, 1984

Lansbury, George *My Life*, Constable, London, 1928 and 1931

Ludington, Townsend *John Dos Passos: A Twentieth Century Odyssey*, E P Dutton, NY, 1980

Ludington, Townsend (ed.) *The Fourteenth Chronicle: Letters and Diaries of John Dos Passos*, Andre Deutsch, London, 1974

Mainiero, Lina (ed.) *American Women Writers From Colonial Times to the Present: A Critical Reference Guide*, New York, Vol. 2 (1980), Vol. 4 (1982)

Mellow, James R *Inverted Life: F Scott and Zelda Fitzgerald*, Souvenir Press, London, 1985

Mellow, James R *Hemingway: A Life Without Consequences*, Hodder and Stoughton, 1993

Meyers, Jeffrey *Edmund Wilson: A Biography*, Houghton Mifflin, Boston and NY, 1995

Meynell, Francis *My Lives*, Bodley Head, London, 1971

Modlin, Charles E (ed.) *Sherwood Anderson Selected Letters*, University of Tennessee Press, Knoxville, 1984

Monk, Ray *Bertrand Russell: The Spirit of Solitude*, Jonathan Cape, London, 1996

Monk, Ray *Bertrand Russell: The Ghost of Madness*, Jonathan Cape, London, 2000

Page, Tim (ed.) *The Diaries of Dawn Powell, 1931–1965*, Steerforth Press, South Royalton, Vermont, 1995

Pfaff, Tim *Settlement and Survival: Building Towns in the Chippewa Valley, 1850–1925*, Chippewa Valley Museum Press, Eau Claire, Wisconsin, 1994

Pierce, Bob *Pierce's Piano Atlas*, 1990 edition, Long Beach, California, 1990

Postgate, Raymond *The Life of George Lansbury*, Longman, London, 1951

Russell, Dora *The Tamarisk Tree: My Quest for Liberty and Love*, Elek/Pemberton, London, 1975

Russell, Dora *The Tamarisk Tree 2: My School and the Years of War*, Virago, London, 1980

Russell, Dora *The Tamarisk Tree Vol. 3: Challenge to the Cold War*, Virago, London, 1985

Slocombe, George *The Tumult and the Shouting*, Heinemann, London, 1936

Tait, Katharine, *My Father Bertrand Russell*, Harcourt Brace Jovanovich, NY/London, 1975

Thomas, Lately *When Even Angels Wept: The Senator Joseph McCarthy Affair*, William Morrow & Co. Inc., NY, 1973

Vernon, Betty D *Ellen Wilkinson 1891–1947*, Croom Helm, London, 1982

Vorse, Mary Heaton *Time and the Town: A Provincetown Chronicle*, The Dial Press, NY, 1942

Who's Who in America, Vol. 12, 1922–23